Soviet and Communist initiatives. He also asks such provocative questions as: Are political assassinations morally—or practically—justifiable? Should we intervene secretly in foreign countries? What is the place of secret operations in an open society? This book is bound to spark political debate on the role of CIA and American intelligence for years to come. It is must reading for everyone concerned about the future of America in a competitive world.

Photo by Brock Rositzke

HARRY ROSITZKE was born in Brooklyn, graduated from Union College, received his Ph.D. in Germanic philology from Harvard University, and, from 1936 to 1942, taught English at Harvard, the University of Omaha, and the University of Rochester. After four years in the army—the last two with the Office of Strategic Services in London, Paris, and Germany—he went to work for the CIA, where he remained for the next twenty-five years. In Munich in the early fifties he conducted intelligence operations into the Soviet Union and Eastern Europe. From 1957-62 he was station chief in New Delhi, where his principal responsibility was working against Soviet and Chinese intelligence targets. In Washington, from 1962 until his retirement in 1970, he worked on domestic intelligence operations against Soviet and East European officials in the United States and coordinated operations against Communist parties abroad. He is the author of *The USSR Today* and *Left On!*, a political satire on American society. Currently he writes and lectures on secret operations and intelligence, and raises beef calves on his farm near Middleburg, Virginia.

THE CIA'S SECRET OPERATIONS

THE CIA'S

SECRET OPERATIONS

ESPIONAGE, COUNTERESPIONAGE, AND COVERT ACTION

Harry Rositzke

READER'S DIGEST PRESS

Distributed by Thomas Y. Crowell Company, New York, 1977

Library of Congress Cataloging in Publication Data
Rositzke, Harry August.
    The CIA's secret operations.
    Includes index.
    1. United States.   Central Intelligence Agency.
I.   Title.
JK468.I6R67   327'.12'06173   76-50629

ISBN 0-88349-116-8

10 9 8 7 6 5 4 3 2 1

To the memory of

LOWRIE CAMPBELL
CHARLES KATEK
RICHARD WELCH

BOOKS BY HARRY ROSITZKE

The CIA's Secret Operations
The Peterborough Chronicle
The USSR Today
Left On! *The Glorious Bourgeois Cultural Revolution*

ACKNOWLEDGMENTS

I am grateful to those of my colleagues in this first generation of American "spymasters" who were willing to share their experiences with me even after I retired to my unclassified farm. I am indebted to Howard Roman, who worked with Allen Dulles on his intelligence writings, for his assistance in the preparation of the early chapters, and to Nancy Kelly, my editor at Reader's Digest Press, for the sharp edge of her pruning shears.

Many hitherto classified facts have now been made public in the various reports of the official Washington investigations. I have found it useful to cite some of these now open facts and to quote some official conclusions on matters beyond my competence:

Report to the President by the Commission on CIA Activities within the United States, June 1975 (the Rockefeller Report).

Alleged Assassination Plots Involving Foreign Leaders, an interim report of the Senate Select Committee on Intelligence Activities, November 1975.

Covert Action in Chile 1963–73, a staff report by the Senate Select Committee on Intelligence Activities, 1975.

Foreign and Military Intelligence, Book I, part of the Final Report of the Senate Select Committee on Intelligence Activities, April 1976.

CONTENTS

"I wish to be useful, and every kind of service necessary to the public good becomes honorable by being necessary."

NATHAN HALE

INTRODUCTION

In the late spring of 1944 I went from the Office of Strategic Services in Washington, where I had been editor of a weekly intelligence bulletin in the Research and Analysis Branch, to a similar job at OSS/London. There I encountered an old friend from Harvard, Philip Horton, author of an excellent biography of Hart Crane and in the late 1930s curator of the poetry room in the Widener Library. Horton was improbably installed at a desk in Secret Intelligence. Soon after I arrived, the intelligence demands generated by the Normandy invasion led to the coordination of SI and R&A intelligence dissemination in a joint Reports Board.

Horton was put in charge; I was assigned to the new board as the R&A representative and eventually as Horton's deputy for political intelligence. In this capacity I worked closely with Horton's deputy for military intelligence, a bright, breezy and sardonic former instructor in linguistics from the University of Rochester. This was Harry Rositzke.

In the autumn we all went on to Paris. Rosizke's job was far more important than mine. I was greatly impressed by the efficiency and aplomb with which he managed the intricate problems involved in getting intelligence from agents behind the lines to armies fighting in the field. The pressure was unrelenting. Lives, even battles, depended on the accuracy of reports on order-of-battle, troop movements, weaponry and on the speed with which information was transmitted to the appropriate commands. The cool and resourceful Rositzke was plainly a brilliant intelligence officer. When the pressure was occasionally off, we wandered around Paris, discussing the diversity of subjects, sacred and profane, meditated by men in their twenties in hectic times when war was the reality and peace only a faint hope.

Harry Rositzke thought then of resuming his academic career. We moved on to Germany in the spring of 1945, making our headquarters in a champagne factory outside Wiesbaden. The Soviet Union was growing as an intelligence problem; no surprise to those whose sympathies lay with the democratic left in Europe. I was demobilized in the autumn and returned to literary pursuits. I was not much surprised to hear in due course that Rositzke had decided to stay on in intelligence. War had made him a professional. Peace evidently offered him scope for analysis and action on questions more urgent than Anglo-Saxon grammar, his previous specialty.

I saw him from time to time in the next years. When in the United States, he came to New York for occasional reunions with Horton, William Casey, Jay Gold, Walter Lord and other wartime comrades. In 1961 I learned that he was CIA station chief in New Delhi, where Kenneth Galbraith was about to go as ambassador. Galbraith was healthily suspicious of the CIA. I assured him he would have no trouble with Rositzke; their senses of humor were too much akin; also their senses of reality. Galbraith told me later they had gotten along fine.

In time Rositzke retired from the Agency. Soon the CIA became the subject of public concern and then of congressional inquiry. Controversy centered less on CIA's primary purpose, which is the collection and analysis of intelligence, than on its secret operations: espionage, counterespionage and most especially "covert action,"—that is, clandestine undertakings designed to influence events in other nations. From his farm in Middleburg, Virginia, Rositzke volleyed barrages into the debate. His contributions were independent and informed, sometimes critical of the Agency, sometimes of the critics. The debate itself showed the need for more information as to what the CIA has actually been up to in its secret operations over the last thirty years. Rositzke has now tried to meet this need in this fascinating book.

The CIA's Secret Operations is not, nor is it represented as being, nor in the nature of things can it be, the complete story. But it is much more complete than any account available to the public. No other nation would have permitted so candid and sustained a disclosure in so sensitive a field. E. H. Cookridge, in the preface to the American edition of his story of the British Special Operations Executive (called *Set Europe Ablaze* in the United States; *Inside S.O.E.* in England), describes the problems he met in telling the story, a quarter-century later, of British covert action during the Second World War. Rositzke's work carries aspects of the American story up to the 1970s. One doubts whether the CIA would have cleared such a book a decade ago. Its publication now is a salutary by-product of the belated surge of public concern.

All students of *Ashenden,* Eric Ambler, Le Carré and Deighton will find this work absorbing. Rositzke, however, is less interested in romantic effects than in the larger and grimmer context. Some may be surprised by his skeptical portrait of "the Cold War mentality," his conviction that Moscow's postwar strategy was basically defensive, his observations about "the myth of a Communist monolith" and his unsparing critique of the "military mindedness" of the containment policy. Some too may be surprised by his belief that the CIA took on many tasks in the Cold War years it should never have accepted. But the CIA contained more heresy than its critics have supposed. This was doubtless part of the legacy of General Donovan. No intelligence operation in modern history was more free-wheeling and heterodox than Donovan's OSS.

Still Rositzke remains a professional. Those who find the very idea of espionage distasteful will be put off by his matter-of-fact acceptance of spies and spying as a part of international life (and even some who agree on the inevitability of espionage will wonder at the matter-of-fact exploitation of professors, graduate students and journalists). But Rositzke cannot imagine—no more can I—a world of competitive nation-states without espionage, nor does he see much sense in giving the other side an unimpeded monopoly of the clandestine arts. His book makes a powerful case for the necessity of a national intelligence service.

At the same time, as a professional, he resents what he considers the misuse and abuse of CIA by higher authority. He argues in particular that the CIA has become, despite itself, a pillar of the Imperial Presidency. Presidents, he writes, have systematically employed it as a mechanism through which they can conduct foreign policy without diplomats, carry out military actions without the armed forces, intervene at will around the world without congressional authorization and scrutiny.

While there is some truth in this, I think that he pushes the idea of an innocent and obedient CIA, acting only on "express" presidential instruction and authorization, a good deal too far. The record, as I read it, indicates that the Agency acted on its own in a diversity of ways, some of very considerable importance. The Senate Select Committee on Intelligence Activities (the Church Committee) could uncover no specific evidence, for example, that any President ordered the assassination of Castro or even knew about it. John McCone, as head of CIA, was never told about the Castro assassination projects until, two years after he took the post, he read in a newspaper article that his agency had a relationship with a

Chicago gangster. Even then he was given to understand that the projects had been terminated, though in fact they were continuing. The manifestly illegal CIA program of mail intercepts ran from 1953 to 1973 during the terms of four Presidents; but "no evidence could be found," according to the Rockefeller Commission, "that any briefing of any President occurred." Even the CIA Inspector General, the Rockefeller Commission reported, "was sometimes refused access to particularly sensitive CIA activities."

The recent disclosures about the CIA and the FBI suggest to me an inherent danger in intelligence agencies. They form a society of their own, with purposes and standards distinct from those of the nation. Prolonged immersion in the segregated, self-contained, self-justifying world of deception and secrecy tends to erode links to reality. Intelligence operatives begin to see themselves as the appointed custodians of the national security, so much more knowledgeable on these matters than elected officials who merely come and go. They begin to feel themselves morally authorized to do things on their own that they deem in the interests of the republic. The misuse and abuse of the CIA may have been as much the result of the inner momentum of an isolated and hallucinatory bureaucracy as of the interference of Presidents. The idea of appointing politicians as heads of intelligence agencies is conventionally denounced. I wonder. It seems to me that what these agencies need most of all is leadership schooled in the principles and procedures of accountability to the democratic process.

Still the understandable disgust provoked by recent revelations can go too far. The CIA, ironically, is almost taking the place in American demonology once occupied by the Communist Party. Conspiracy nuts smell out CIA connections as their predecessors a generation ago smelled out CP connections. In some quarters anyone who ever worked for the CIA is assumed to be its faithful agent in perpetuity unless he can prove he has really "broken" with his master. The proof required seems to be, as it was when J. Edgar Hoover and Joe McCarthy were riding high, the willingness to "name names."

Actually, intelligence operations in America are as old as the republic. Long ago the 64th Federalist commended the new Constitution for providing means by which the President could "manage the business of intelligence in such a manner as prudence may suggest." Early Congresses routinely equipped Presidents with secret service funds—a practice regularized by a law of 1810 providing for "contingent expenses of intercourse between the United States and foreign nations." "The experience of every nation on earth," said James K. Polk, "has demonstrated that emergencies may arise in which it becomes absolutely necessary for the public safety or the public good to make expenditures the very object of which would be defeated by publicity." What the Cold War did was to give intelligence operations a magnitude and an immunity that transformed the character of the problem. But the excesses of recent years illustrate a danger; they do not eliminate a need.

The future of the intelligence community remains a vital issue for Congress and the people. The problem is to insure restraint and accountability without abandoning necessary secrecy. Rositzke makes a number of useful recommendations. He believes that the CIA has grown too big, too bloated, too bureaucratized. He wants to contract its size, to alter its priorities and to restrict its mission to consequential objectives. Surely nothing would do more in a short time to improve our intelligence effort than to cut the intelligence budget. With less money available to indulge operational fantasies, the CIA would be compelled to concentrate on primary and serious tasks. There seems to me particular value in Rositzke's proposal of a counterintelligence ombudsman, appointed by and responsible to a joint congressional committee on intelligence, to whom any federal employee with reason to suppose that his agency is carrying out unauthorized activities can blow his whistle.

The CIA's Secret Operations furnishes essential material for a missing chapter in the history of the Cold War. It will also, I believe, contribute significantly to the struggle for a national intelligence service that will be at once effective, prudent, controlled, responsible and accountable.

Arthur M. Schlesinger, Jr.

AUTHOR'S PREFACE

The secret operations of the Central Intelligence Agency in the last thirty years have been part of America's effort to cope with the reality of the Soviet Union. During these years—the Cold War, the more temperate sixties, the uneven détente of today—Soviet power and Soviet intentions have transfixed Washington's view of the world.

When this country emerged from its isolationist past after World War II, the Soviet Union became our major adversary. Since then, the steadily expanding base of the Soviet Union at home, its mammoth investment in political action abroad, its rapid buildup of a nuclear strike force, and the increasing strength of Communist parties in Europe and Asia, all have combined to form the most enterprising revolutionary movement society has yet produced.

Today, as in 1946, even though Europe and Japan now are industrially strong and China is becoming more powerful, the world remains essentially bipolar. It is a world of two social systems in conflict. For Moscow it is the reality of America that counts, for Washington the Soviet Union. America has responded to the Soviet challenge by a policy of containment, an attempt to curb the expansion of Soviet power and influence. This policy has been, with a few exceptions, anti-Soviet, anti-Communist, anti-Marxist and, until recently, anti-Left. From the Truman Doctrine of 1947 until the recent efforts to repel or retard the extension of Communist influence in Chile, Portugal, Italy, and Angola, the strategy of containment has monopolized our diplomacy, our military and economic aid, our armed forces, and our propaganda.

The secret operations of the CIA have played a threefold role in this strategy:

Our espionage operations have been aimed at penetrating the terrain, the top bureaucracy, and the foreign connections of a tightly closed society whose secrets are of vital concern to American security. For almost fifteen years after World War II the CIA's intelligence targets were dictated almost exclusively by the Department of Defense.

Our counterespionage operations have been directed mainly at controlling or exposing agents working in the West for Soviet intelligence—the most competent and aggressive secret service in the world today.

Our covert action operations have played the most direct role in our overall policy of containment. Designed to influence the course of events in other societies, they have ranged from the secret support of radios, newspapers, political parties, and labor unions to the conduct of guerrilla operations, armed invasions, and secret wars.

It is these covert actions that have been systematically publicized and have tarred the CIA with the image of ineptness and immorality.

The successes of containment, both open and covert, came early, the failures later. Until Stalin's death in 1953, American actions stabilized a democratic Western Europe, repelled an armed Communist threat in Greece, forced the Russians out of Iran, stopped the aggression in Korea, and overthrew a Communist-run regime in Guatemala.

From 1955 on, however, when Moscow began its drive for influence in the Third World, containment has met with failure after failure. In a mere twenty years the reach of Soviet power and influence has extended into Indochina, India, the Middle East, the horn of Africa, black Africa, and Cuba. Even at the height of its military and diplomatic power in the late fifties and early sixties, America proved an inferior adversary to the Soviet Union in the competition for global influence. Covert actions shared in our failure: the support of Indonesian rebels against a leftist regime, the abortive invasion of Cuba, the support of anti-Communist parties in Italy, the supply of arms to the Angolan rebels.

The reasons for the failure of containment are not hard to find.

To start with, containment is not a positive policy designed to advance our national interest, but a defensive policy designed to react to Soviet initiatives. We have followed this defensive strategy against a cautious but persistent forward strategy carried out by a young and powerful nation-state devoted to changing the status quo in the interests of its own security and prosperity. We have followed a policy of military containment against what is essentially a political, economic, and ideological crusade. We have relied on military hardware and regional alliances to counter an adversary that has never employed its own troops outside its defense perimeter. We have throughout been deprived of a clear-headed view of reality by a military-mindedness blind to the powerful nationalist, racial, religious, and economic forces at work in the world that have little to do with the Soviet-American confrontation.

The White House bears direct responsibility for the failures (and the few successes) of open containment, as it does for the failures (and few successes) of covert action. An extension of diplomacy and war by secret means, covert action has formed the third arm of American foreign policy. Six American presidents have employed their covert arm to supplement, sometimes to substitute for, their open diplomatic-military efforts to contain the Soviet Union. I know of no major covert action operation initiated by the CIA without the express approval of the White House or the National Security Council. Until a hardheaded look is taken at our failed strategy, the discussion of a new American foreign policy can only be clouded by placing blame on its instruments: the State Department, the Pentagon, and the Central Intelligence Agency.

The high priority placed upon secret operations by successive American presidents has enlarged the small postwar American intelligence service into the large-scale CIA bureaucracy it is today. In 1946, when many of the first generation of American operations officers joined the new peacetime intelligence service, the Cold War and containment had not yet jelled. We were a small espionage and counterespionage outfit devoted to finding out what was going on behind the scenes in Stalin's Russia and in a devastated Europe threatened by communism.

In my own case the draft and wartime accident led me from the job of English instructor at the University of Rochester to the role of Army drill instructor and military censor, thence to an assignment with the Office of Strategic Services in the European theater. Two experiences in OSS diverted me from my academic career into a twenty-five-year stint as a professional intelligence officer.

During my first OSS assignment in London I handled the reports being radioed in from our agents in German-occupied France on the location and movement of German divisions before D-day. Our military commanders were particularly concerned about the movements of the armored divisions. Among the reports coming in was a series from the OSS agent in Chartres. In early May he began transmitting detailed observations on a hitherto unidentified armored division in his area, and in short order it became clear that here was the "missing" Panzer Lehr division that had been brought back from Hungary to prepare for the Allied invasion. As D-day neared, the Chartres agent began reporting the assembling of flatcars in the railroad yards and other signs of impending movement. His almost daily reports on Panzer Lehr up to and after D-day permitted the Allied commanders to forecast the time and place of its arrival at the beachhead.

Later, in an intelligence review at Supreme Allied Head-quarters the Deputy G–2 singled out the Chartres reports and commented that they may have saved ten or twelve thousand Allied lives. "You can be satisfied," he said, "that the OSS has already paid for its budget in this theater."

That convinced me secret intelligence was not a game.

My awareness of the new Soviet reality was less abrupt. Even before the war ended, I read the daily digests of the East European radio broadcasts that described in detail the steps being taken by the Russians to integrate both the Allied and enemy states of Eastern Europe into their new western buffer. OSS reports from the Allied Control Commission in Rumania gave a closer view. Rumanian communists were brought along from Moscow to staff the new government. Soviet security officials with automatic arrest lists of "enemies of the people" set up and ran the Rumanian security and intelligence services. Rumania was russified at a stroke.

In Berlin, Vienna, and along the frontiers of the occupation zones, we saw firsthand the brutal handling of repatriated Soviet citizens and the wholesale arrests and deportation of countless Germans.

A kind of emotional cement was added to these scattered observations by an unofficial mission to Soviet-occupied Berlin a few weeks after VE-day. No one knew what the Russians were doing in Berlin, and three of us, one a Russian-speaking ethnic Rumanian, volunteered to sneak into the Soviet zone and find out. Tense and somewhat apprehensive, we spent five hours getting across the zonal border and six hours in Berlin.

Several visual impressions remain as clear in my mind now as they were then. The straggling column of German boys and old men being herded east along Berlin's Ring Road. The stream of Russian soldiers carrying paintings and rugs out of Hermann Goering's villa to a long line of sedans at the curb. The Studebaker flat-bed trucks in front of the Siemens-Halske factory loaded with large drill presses and lathes whose shiny steel surfaces reflected the broken sunlight like modernistic sculptures in a burned-out slum. I recalled the stories of East European refugees, details of the sacrifice of families, social classes, intellectuals, and journalists on the altar of the new proletarian state.

Russia moves west, went through my mind. *Europe will never be the same again.*

Our man in Chartres proved to me the value of secret-agent operations. My trip to Berlin cemented the reality of the Russians in my awareness. When the time came, in the spring of 1946, to decide whether or not to return to the University of Rochester for the fall term, I opted for Washington. What forced my final decision was a strong gut reaction. I could not see spending the rest of my life on the humane nurture of the younger generation when my own generation faced what was clearly a political and humanist threat to its values and institutions.

I have never regretted the decision. For the next twenty-five years I had a series of assignments as varied and stimulating as any man could want from any profession. For the first eight years my major concern was the Soviet Union and Soviet intelligence, both in Washington and in Munich. Five years as station chief in New Delhi gave me not only an Asian perspective on world events, but a rare close-up look at the Soviet-Chinese relationship. A staff assignment to review our covert action programs, a three-year stint recruiting Soviet and East European diplomats stationed in the United States, and a final two years coordinating operations against the Communist parties and the New Left in Europe each had its own challenge and flavor.

There was constant refreshment: training young case officers, recruiting and handling agents, face-to-face dealings with Soviet intelligence officers. I worked closely with some of the best and brightest men in Washington, men who could match the talents of our best teachers, lawyers, journalists, and diplomats. Above all, living out front during some of the most dynamic decades in man's history could not fail to stimulate the imagination and discourage the ruts more bounded professions can nourish.

Why, at this late date, write about my old profession?

In 1970, when I retired from CIA, I wrote happily about unclassified matters: a short handbook on the Soviet Union, a political satire on American society, a "political Nixon" along Maoist lines, brief essays on rural diplomacy and natural pollution. For three years I had each day to myself, and I did what I wanted.

In the summer of 1973 my old agency became contaminated by Watergate, and during the next three years the CIA was the repeated target of the Congress and the press for abuses of power and violations of morality. From Watergate on, "CIA" was criticized, vilified, lampooned, and investigated. It became a lucrative whipping boy for the media, a favorite target for righteous congressmen, an object of suspicion for many Americans.

When they were not ludicrous, the charges were grave: the CIA was an "invisible government" out of presidential control, a "Gestapo" spying on American citizens, an "immoral instrument" for masterminding coups and assassinations abroad, a "sinister force" in the clean air of American diplomacy.

Serious questions of morality and legality were raised. Is it right to use secret means for achieving diplomatic ends? Is it proper to spy? Is it a violation of American principles to intervene in the domestic affairs of other nations? Can a secret service operate in an open society?

The debate, in and out of Congress, was one-sided from the start. It focused on "abuses," and was featured by truths, half-truths, and untruths, by ignorance and prejudice, by vehement charges and lame responses. Few heads remained cool. The Year of Intelligence in Washington created a strange spectacle that dismayed our friends abroad and delighted our enemies. Only history can place it in perspective.

The public record, as it now stands, is unbalanced. No institution, private or public, can be fairly measured by its mistakes or stupidities alone. It is also unbalanced for the simple reason that CIA's espionage and counterespionage operations were barely mentioned throughout the public examination—and these have formed at least eighty percent of the work of all CIA's operations officers from the mid-fifties on. Covert actions have occupied only a small proportion of our man-hours, but they have commanded more than their share of money and White House attention, and they have inevitably had more than their share of publicity in shaping the image of CIA.

This narrative attempts to balance part of that record. It is not a history, official or unofficial, of CIA's secret operations. It is an account based mainly on my own twenty-five years of experience in planning and executing overseas operations, and naturally focuses on what has been my major professional interest from 1946 on: operations against the Soviet Union, the Soviet intelligence services, and key Communist parties.

In writing this open book about a closed profession, I am mainly concerned to replace ignorance and distortion with fact, to place these facts in the perspective of their time, and to pass one man's judgment on their usefulness or lack of it to the nation's welfare. It will give the curious citizen a candid view of what his secret intelligence service has been doing since World War II. For the historian it will supply some footnotes to the Cold War, for the student of America's foreign policy a record of the interplay between open and covert diplomacy. To the dyed-in-the-wool anti-CIA critic it will, of course, give more ammunition.

I have imposed severe restrictions on myself in writing this open account. There are no true names of agents or American operations officers, nor is there enough data on any agent to identify him. There are no diplomatically sensitive exposés—there have been far too many that have hurt our national interest. There is no treatment of our extensive relations with friendly foreign intelligence services—our secrets are half theirs. The hundreds of operations that are discussed are, for the most part, placed in areas rather than specific countries. Not only where they happened, but when, is often left vague. I have used whatever professional acumen I possess to see that no unfriendly intelligence service learns anything from these cases that it does not know now.

When I submitted my original manuscript to the Central Intelligence Agency for security review, only six cases were brought to my attention that might endanger someone. Two affected men still presumably alive in the Soviet Union, one involved a man now in Eastern Europe who might still be recruited. These I have omitted or disguised further.

My secrecy oath concerns only the disclosure of operational facts. My judgments and opinions in these pages are my own and are not subject to review by anyone but the reader. They are often critical. The CIA was given many tasks, particularly in the Cold War years, that we should not have accepted. We were forced by military pressures into tactical wartime operations beyond the capacity of a peacetime service. We did work that should have been done by the Department of State or by Defense, if at all. We were overused and misused.

We also made our own mistakes, for we had to learn our business the hard way: by experience. I have tried to strike an honest balance in assessing our performance, for no record, even a secret record, can be set straight by a whitewash.

Secret operations, it must be stressed, are not the primary function of the Central Intelligence Agency. Without them CIA would continue to play an indispensable role in our

national security structure. The central function of CIA is to
collate and evaluate all information from all sources and to
provide the White House with complete and objective situation reports and national estimates on global events. It is this
"finished intelligence" that can help the policy makers form
intelligent policy decisions. Secret agent reports play only a
minor, if sometimes crucial, role. In 1947 Congress placed
intelligence analysis and secret operations in the same
agency. In my judgment this was a mistake, but the virtues or
defects of the one should not affect public judgment of the
other.

Though espionage is one of its major themes, this is not a
handbook for spies. I do not deal with the elaborate tradecraft
of secret operations, the techniques for keeping secret connections secret. Though essential to the profession, they can
be learned by a high-school graduate and require nothing but
care and patience in their application. Concealing a microfilm in a Hershey bar, using a hollow tree for a dead drop,
splitting a Jello box or a dollar bill as a recognition signal,
putting a warning chalk sign on a subway entrance—these
tricks are common to all intelligence services, crime syndicates, and underground Communist parties. The jargon and
adventures of spy stories rest on these mechanics, for they
create the climate for hairbreadth escapes, murderous mistakes, and technical ingenuity. To intrude them here would
only romanticize the record.

The guts of most secret operations are two men—the agent
and his handler, or case officer—meeting in private to trans-
act their business. Each has his foibles and strengths, and it
is this human element that has attracted me throughout my
career. At its best, espionage, like politics, is a humanist
profession.

THE CIA'S SECRET OPERATIONS

1

WAR, HOT AND COLD

In the spring of 1948 the White House saw war with the Soviet Union as imminent.

Soviet-American tensions had been mounting steadily since the Yalta conference in 1945. Even before the war with Hitler ended, the Russians had moved rapidly to integrate both the Allied and enemy states of Eastern Europe into their bloc. One by one, most brutally in Poland, these states were russified, then communized. By the end of 1947 all but one were ruled by one-party governments under Soviet control. An independent but cautious democratic government survived in Czechoslovakia in a coalition with the Communist Party.

Western Europe was in shambles and appeared ripe for revolution. The Italian and French Communist parties led a wave of strikes in 1946, and the Italian Communists were threatening to achieve power by the ballot box. In May 1947 a large-scale Communist insurrection broke out in Greece. Moscow was putting pressure on Turkey to "return" the provinces of Kars and Ardahan to the Soviet Union, and laid claim to the province of Azerbaijan in Iran.

Washington was becoming increasingly uneasy.

On March 12, 1947, President Truman went before a special joint session of Congress to deliver the message that marked the turning point from protest to action against Soviet initiatives. In his long and complex message he asked for military aid to Greece to fight the Communist guerrillas and to Turkey to help resist Moscow's territorial demands. Tucked in the text was a single sentence that was to become known as the Truman Doctrine: "I believe that it must be the policy of the United States to support free peoples who are resisting attempted subjugation by armed minorities or by outside pressures." Containment from the beginning addressed itself both to domestic Communist subversion and to the exercise of Soviet national power.

Aid to Greece and Turkey was a direct response to Soviet pressures, the Marshall Plan a few months later an indirect response. The Marshall Plan's offer of goods, grants, and loans was designed to stabilize the weakened nations of Europe and permit their orderly development. The offer was accepted by the nations of Western Europe, but turned down by Stalin for both the Soviet Union and its satellites. Europe became the divided Europe Stalin wanted. He speeded up the consolidation of Eastern Europe (Hungary was brought under party control in June) as the United States quickly became the dominant political and economic force in Western Europe. In Berlin and Vienna the two protagonists were face to face.

Then came the war scare, triggered mainly by two events.

In February of 1948 the Communist Party took over the government of Czechoslovakia through a Soviet-inspired internal coup and destroyed the last independent nation in Eastern Europe. The Prague coup sent shock waves through Washington. American bombers were assigned to British airfields, and military preparations in occupied Germany were speeded up.

In early March of the same year General Lucius Clay sent

an alarming telegram from Berlin reporting "a subtle change" (which he could not define) in the attitude of the Soviet command and warning that war might come "with dramatic suddenness." The Clay telegram brought the threat of war to a point of near hysteria in the minds of Washington's policy and intelligence bureaucracy. The CIA, then just six months old, predicted that a war was not probable within the next sixty days, but could look no further ahead.

The subtle change noted by General Clay in the Soviet attitude was created by Soviet preparations to force the Allies out of Berlin, the sole Western island in the heart of Soviet Europe. In May the Russians began to block communications and movement of supplies between Allied-occupied West Berlin and the Western zones of Germany. Rejecting a proposal to break through the blockade with American ground troops, President Truman authorized the creation of the Berlin airlift. Throughout that fall and winter American transport planes kept the West Berliners from starvation. Scores of Allied airmen lost their lives, but their determination forced the Russians to lift the blockade in May 1949.

The Berlin blockade brought the first face-to-face military confrontation of the Cold War—a term that came into popular use that same year.

The immediate military threat was an armed Soviet attack on Europe. By late 1947 it had become clear that the Soviet troops stationed in East Germany and Poland far exceeded the strength required to occupy the two countries. The Czech coup solidified Soviet control over another section of the invasion corridor. The March crisis forced the Pentagon to a realistic estimate of what these troops could do: They could, in purely military terms, reach the English Channel. The Berlin blockade intensified White House concern that they might.

What the White House and the Pentagon wanted to know were the precise capabilities and actual intentions of the Soviet military forces in northeastern Europe. With the target areas effectively sealed off from normal Western observation, the only recourse was to send in agents. The first charge placed upon the CIA in the spring and summer of 1948 was a straightforward espionage mission—a peacetime mission under wartime conditions.

The intelligence requirements were passed to the operators mostly by word of mouth. I recall our first briefing on the situation in the small crowded conference room of the ramshackle "tempos," a group of temporary World War I buildings in Foggy Bottom that were part of CIA headquarters.

The briefing by the colonel from the Joint Chiefs of Staff was precise, earnest, and urgent. Fully equipped with maps, overlays, and markers, he sketched a persuasive scenario of a two-pronged assault on Western Europe by Soviet divisions advancing through the northern plain. He named the divisions in East Germany and Poland that would move. He placed arrows along their line of advance. He pointed to the Czech airfields in western Bohemia that would provide air support for the ground troops. He ended with a strong plea for agent coverage in all three areas.

It was an abrupt demand to make upon a handful of amateur operators in a new and untried intelligence service.

Like most of my colleagues in that room I had begun working in the postwar intelligence service two years earlier. Most of us had been with the wartime Office of Strategic Services. When its chief, "Wild Bill" Donovan, said farewell to the men and women of OSS at the nearby Riverside Skating Rink in September 1945, he announced the end of "an unusual experiment": "This experiment was to determine whether a group of Americans constituting a cross section of racial origins, of abilities, temperaments and talents, could risk an encounter with the long-established and well-trained enemy organizations."

A slice of that cross section survived in the tempos. The

men were a heterogeneous assortment of origins and temperaments. WASPS rubbed shoulders with first-generation ethnics and an occasional naturalized Russian, Czech, or German. New Deal liberals and the sons of European Social Democrats leavened the middle-of-the-road Americans without political complications. There were a few high-school graduates, but most had finished college, some had graduate degrees. Some had worked behind enemy lines with French, Italian, Greek, and Yugoslav partisans. Others had parachuted into France after D-day, sent agents across the lines as Allied forces moved into Germany, handled agent reports in Bern and Stockholm, worked with the British in counterespionage operations against the German Abwehr, composed and broadcast anti-Nazi propaganda. Almost all spoke some language in addition to English. Some were trilingual.

Among the men I came to know best were two prewar journalists, a state trooper from the Midwest, several sons of missionaries, a lawyer of Arab descent, a former postal clerk, several high-school and college teachers.

The women, many with European backgrounds, had been deskbound during the war: reports officers, counterintelligence analysts, and operational assistants of one sort or another.

We were almost all quite young. Some men, in their early thirties, became the first heads of area divisions in Washington and our first station chiefs abroad. Most, in their twenties, became the first case officers to recruit overseas agents. We were all amateurs in peacetime operations.

I recall a day in early 1947 when a colleague and I went to lunch in the cafeteria in one of the tempos. As we entered, he stopped by the door and looked at the scene—almost a hundred people of every size, shape, and color. Some were nattily dressed, some sloppily. A dozen accents, regional and foreign, cut the air.

"Do you think," he said, "that anyone walking in here could possibly imagine what brings all these people together?"

Why were we there?

I suspect that the main reason most of us stayed on in the government after the war was the appeal of a secret profession or the attractions of a life abroad. Some, of course, stayed on out of inertia, those with no other experience except the OSS, those whose home towns had nothing to offer them but a dull job. Others were stimulated not so much by their wartime experience as by their awareness of what was going on in the turbulent world outside the United States. Many were clearly motivated by a desire to continue serving their country.

None of us was there for job security. We were, for all we knew, temporary employees of a temporary organization unauthorized by Congress. After the dissolution of OSS in September 1945, its secret intelligence and counterintelligence branches were placed under the Secretary of the Army as the Strategic Services Unit and then, in the spring of 1946, in another stopgap agency, the Central Intelligence Group. We all felt that eventually there would be a permanent American intelligence service, but there was none then.

Up to the March 1948 crisis we lived in a state of benign neglect. Very few officials in the Department of State or the Army or the White House even knew of the existence of the SSU or the CIG. We had no legal authority, and no one gave us any guidance. No one sent over any intelligence requirements. The Department of State was reluctant to give any of its foreign service slots or titles to these undiplomatic strangers, and most of our officers abroad were housed by the Army in Germany, Austria, Italy, and Japan. The Federal Bureau of Investigation looked upon us with distrust, if not hostility.

It was a curious state of limbo, but we were busy— cleaning out the old OSS records, setting up files and routing systems, processing personnel returning from the field, editing and disseminating the paltry agent reports coming in, checking names against our primitive central registry, screening captured German and Japanese documents, writing up training manuals, report procedures, and agent questionnaires.

My own focus during those confused and unexciting months was on Soviet and Communist matters, the interest that had brought me into the service. Within six months my name, my job, and my affiliation were on file in Moscow.

On reporting for duty in March 1946 I was given a security briefing by an earnest young man who enjoined me against divulging to anyone (including my wife) where I worked and what I did.

In April I sent a routine request to the administrative unit asking them to arrange for subscriptions to several periodicals put out by the Soviet Communist Party. One day in September I found in my in-basket a magazine in a brown wrapper postmarked Moscow. Its address label read:

Harry Rositzke
Chief SPD/S
SSU
2430 E Street
Washington, D.C.

The man who wrote for the subscriptions had obviously not been briefed by the security people in the devious ways of setting up cover addresses for a secret service.

SSU stood for the Strategic Services Unit, our designation at the time, and SPD/S for Special Projects Division/Soviet, a staff section that had been set up for me after I discovered on my return from Germany that no one at headquarters had any special responsibility for Soviet matters. Our major operating units were regional divisions such as the Far East and European divisions. There was no division for the Soviet Union that early in the game.

There were, on paper, three sections of SPD/S: for Soviet intelligence, for "international communism," and for the

Soviet Union itself. The first two were staffed by one man and one woman in each. The third was without anyone; our Russian speakers were then all on overseas assignments. It was this section, however, that became the nucleus of the Soviet operating division. Its mission was solely to establish intelligence agents *within* the Soviet Union.

In my first six months on the job, I spent most of my time recruiting suitable people for my three sections—and reading. I combed through our wartime registry to unearth whatever it held on the Soviet Union, on the Soviet intelligence services, and on the normal functioning of legal and underground Communist parties.

Most of the captured German and Japanese documents on the Soviet Union were only mildly informative, dull, or out-of-date. Two counterintelligence writeups of Soviet espionage cases, however, I found both fascinating and instructive. The first was the Japanese version of the career of Richard Sorge, the brilliant German journalist who became the confidant of the German ambassador to Tokyo and ran a network of highly placed agents on the side. A single piece of his reporting—that the Japanese would not attack the Soviet Union in the east—permitted Stalin to transfer to his western front a number of divisions that may have been crucial to his successful resistance against the Germans. The German intelligence writeup of the now famous "Red Orchestra" spy network in Western Europe featured the life of its chief, Leopold Trepper, a brilliant and brash Galician Jew who worked under the nose of the Gestapo to supply Moscow with remarkably detailed military and logistic information from Nazi-occupied Europe.

There were few other solid reports: a detailed academic analysis of the secret Berlin headquarters of the Third Communist International that ran espionage and covert action operations throughout Europe until Hitler wiped it out; the interrogations of Communist Party officials who had worked underground before and during the war; some organizational analyses of the various Soviet security and intelligence services.

At night, and on weekends, when I was not hoeing a half-acre garden to strengthen a weak sacroiliac joint, I read Marx and Engels, most of Lenin, some of Stalin, a dull writer indeed. Out of my academic urge to understand what might make a bright young man become a Communist I tried to put into simple English the main propositions of Marxist-Leninist thought. I came up with nineteen—from the materialist view of history to the "guaranteed" final achievement of a Communist society. I began to lecture on Communist theory and Soviet intelligence to our own trainees and to classes in the State Department and the Pentagon. We were all breaking new ground.

Meanwhile, the President's advisers were busy working out the unification of the armed services and a new command structure for our national security apparatus. On September 18, 1947, two years almost to the day after General Donovan's farewell speech to the OSS, the Central Intelligence Agency was established by act of Congress.

CIA came into being as part of the overall restructuring of the American military establishment. The National Security Act of 1947 created the U.S. Air Force, the Department of Defense, and the National Security Council. It was the most far-reaching and controversial legislation ever passed by Congress affecting the nation's ability to conduct its foreign affairs. A minor part of the controversy centered on what to do about a national intelligence authority. Some wanted it lodged in the Department of State, others in the new Department of Defense. Others wanted an independent agency reporting directly to the President through the new National Security Council. The last group won out.

We were no longer plagued by uncertainty. We were now an official American intelligence service, a directorate (the Office of Special Operations) within the Central Intelligence Agency. The CIA itself was set up for the primary purpose of collating and evaluating the information coming into Washington from *all* the various intelligence sources—the Department of Defense, the State Department, the National Security Council, and the intelligence arms of the Army, Navy, and Air Force. Its main job was, and is, to prepare research and analysis reports on crucial situations abroad for the President and his policy advisers.

The inclusion of secret intelligence operations within the new agency was a matter of some debate before the National Security Act was passed. There were strong objections to having a single agency with the authority both to collect secret intelligence and to process and evaluate it for the President. The objections were overruled, and CIA became a unique organization among Western intelligence services, which uniformly keep their secret operations separate from their overall intelligence activities.

No direct allusions to espionage or counterespionage appeared in the National Security Act, but a minor subsection of the act authorized CIA "to perform such other functions and duties related to intelligence affecting the national security as the National Security Council may from time to time direct." That meant secret intelligence operations. Our service was born in secret.

Within a year the National Security Council even more secretly assigned another function to CIA: to carry out covert action operations in addition to its intelligence gathering.

In the brief two years between the dissolution of OSS and the founding of the CIA the world was changing as rapidly and dramatically as it had during the war. Scores of nations were going through political transformations—by civil wars, coups d'etat, forced occupations, rigged elections, mob action, troop mutinies. Some were inspired by the competition of civilian and military elites, some by mass protest against misery, some by religious fervor, some by Moscow.

During these two years of convulsion abroad and demobilization at home, the Washington-Moscow axis was, on the surface, relatively quiet. Publicly, the White House attitude toward Russia was friendly, or at worst ambivalent, and the wartime sense of camaraderie with the Soviets lingered on. As late as the 1948 presidential campaign President Truman could say, "Old Joe is not such a bad guy."

The public lull did not extend into our embassy in Moscow. In February 1946 George Kennan, our chargé d'affaires there, sent the Department of State a reflective eight-thousand-word telegram assessing the Soviet postwar outlook and the probable shape of Soviet foreign policy. The gist of his analysis, made public the next year in the famous Mr. X article in *Foreign Affairs,* was that America must develop a policy of containment to counter Soviet expansionism. How Kennan saw the world came out most graphically in his final lecture to the National War College on June 18, 1947: America was "a lonely, threatened power on the field of world history. . . . A part of the world is subjugated and bent to the service of a great political force intent on our destruction."

There were three elements in the "Communist threat": the war scare, the spy scare, and the Red scare.

Triggered by the Berlin blockade, the war scare reached its peak with the Soviet explosion of an atomic bomb in September 1949 and the invasion of Korea less than a year later. Korea convinced President Truman and most Americans that "Communism has passed beyond the use of subversion to conquer independent nations and will now use armed invasion and war."

As early as 1945 it was discovered that Soviet military espionage operations had reached deep into America's atomic secrets. Public hearings in 1948 made it clear that Soviet spy rings had been operating in Washington before, during, and after the war. Judith Coplon, an FBI employee, was arrested for espionage in 1949 and Alger Hiss tried for perjury the same year. The headiest melodramas were to come out of the "Red A-spy net," the British and American spies who were delivering the secrets of the atomic bomb to Moscow. Klaus Fuchs, a brilliant atomic scientist, was arrested in England on his return from the United States, and in March 1951 the trial of Julius and Ethel Rosenberg for passing atomic secrets to the Russians began in New York in a highly charged public atmosphere. A simple equation led to the spy hysteria of 1951–52: The A-spies were responsible for the invasion of Korea, for without the atomic bomb the Russians would not have dared provoke the United States.

The "Red menace" was first uncovered by a committee of the Republican Congress in the summer of 1948. It intensified with the success of the Communist revolution in China in October 1949, for the "loss" of China was ascribed to the "Reds" in the Department of State. During the next four years a series of sensational disclosures and emotional debates culminated in the Red witch hunt of Senator Joseph McCarthy.

The loyalty investigations of these early years left the CIA relatively unscathed. Many of the Communists who had worked in the OSS were well-known and left government service of their own accord, or were quickly screened out in the intensive postwar investigation of all CIA employees. We lost a handful of headquarters and field personnel on security grounds, most of them practicing homosexuals or committed alcoholics who were judged easy targets for Soviet blackmail. Some non-Communist leftists were asked to resign.

Still there was an atmosphere of caution in the front office. I recall two conversations with my chief, an Army colonel.

In the fall of 1948, after finishing the summary of Marxism-Leninism I had worked up in my spare time, I proposed to send copies of "The Gospel According to Marx" to our field stations for the enlightenment of our case officers, especially those working on Communist parties. The colonel was adamant. If a congressman got his hands on a copy, he would accuse the CIA of indoctrinating its personnel with Communist propaganda. I argued the "know your enemy" line, but he was not persuaded. Finally he agreed to send out the study on one condition: that it be classified.

Although it was based solely on open sources, it was sent to the field under the protection of a cover sheet marked "Confidential."

That same winter I wanted to hire a naturalized American, the talented son of an Austrian Socialist, to set up and manage some specialized files on the Soviet Union. The colonel called me in and we reviewed the man's personal history statement. The answer was no. "I won't have a Socialist in my organization. So far as I'm concerned, there's no difference between Socialists and Communists."

By now there was no longer any uncertainty in the minds of the colonel's men in the CIA's Office of Special Operations. The Soviet Union was the enemy, and the "Soviet target" our intelligence mission. We were professionally and emotionally committed to a single purpose. We felt ourselves as much a part of the American crusade against Stalin as we had against Hitler. We worked hard and long hours, at night and on weekends, in an atmosphere of impatient tension. The Cold War was a hot war for the operators: Our agents' lives were at stake.

Even now, as the emotions of the time can be recollected in relative tranquillity, it is hard to define the precise quality of the public mood in which we began our work. Words like *hysteria* and *paranoia* come quickly to mind, and if the main element in the first is "emotional excitability" and in the second "systematized delusions of persecution," both are relevant. They are, however, heavily loaded words, and perhaps a less analytic and more neutral term, the Cold War mentality, is safer.

In its extreme form, the Cold War mentality saw the world as a dangerous place in which a nation must be constantly on guard or face destruction. It has ruled the minds of the Soviet leadership since the 1917 Revolution. For more than a decade, starting in 1948, it ruled the thinking of the leadership in America.

The Cold War prism saw the main threat to America in

the halls of the Kremlin. The bogey was Stalin, a despot and
a devil, a devious plotter with a Blueprint for World Con-
quest. Each move fit: the take-over of Eastern Europe, the
threats to Greece, Turkey, and Iran, the Berlin blockade, the
invasion of South Korea. An invincible Stalin was shaping
history by his clear purposes and inflexible determination. In
George Kennan's words, the Russians "had always to be de-
monic, monstrous, incalculable, and inscrutable."

The world was divided into two parts: "Communist" and
"free." All countries were either good or bad. Those who did
not take sides were bad (neutrals like Nehru were not trusted
by either side until the mid-fifties). The Cold War became a
holy war against the infidels, a defense of free God-fearing
men against the atheistic "Communistic system."

There was no serious dissent from this view for a decade.
The White House, the secretaries of state, both parties in
Congress, the press, and the reading public all viewed the
Communist threat through the same prism. It was the last
great consensus in America on our foreign purposes, as solid
and pervasive as the anti-Hitler crusade of the war.

The image underlying the Cold War mentality was that of
a powerful and aggressive Soviet Union. No one questioned
the capacity of the Russians to carry out their Grand Design
to rule the world. Few questioned the corollary: Either the
United States or the Soviet Union would win, for the conflict
was a fight to the finish.

As it turned out, the image was an illusion. The specter of
a powerful Russia was remote from the reality of a country
weakened by war, with a shattered economy, an overtaxed
civilian and military bureaucracy, and large areas of civil
unrest.

That illusory image was at least partly due to a failure of
intelligence.

Nineteen forty-six was a fatefully late beginning for the
secret service of a major industrial power in the twentieth-
century world—almost thirty years after the Soviet services

were born. By 1946 Soviet intelligence had agents operating in Washington, New York, London, Paris, and Rome. No Western agent operated in Moscow.

Had there been even the rudiments of an American intelligence effort in the Soviet Union during the war, or had we concentrated on intelligence operations against Russia and Eastern Europe in the postwar lull, the course of the Cold War might have been different. It was our almost total ignorance of what was going on in the "denied area" behind the Iron Curtain that helped create the false image of a super-powerful Soviet Union. A few well-placed sources in the civilian or military hierarchies in Moscow, East Berlin, or Warsaw might have dispelled that notion.

Even if the Soviet Union had had the capacity to move west, there was no objective evidence of a Soviet intention to pursue a policy of military aggression. Stalin, however irrational, was above all cautious—in Berlin itself, in Greece, Turkey, and Iran—and was careful not to provoke the United States to a counterblow. Though himself weak, he was ready to capitalize on American weakness—within limits. The facts available even at the time suggested the far greater likelihood that Moscow's postwar strategy, including the conversion of Eastern Europe into a western buffer, was basically defensive. I argued this thesis with some of the CIA analysts working on Soviet estimates and with some Pentagon audiences, but it was not a popular view at the time. It is nonetheless a simple fact that no scenario was written then, nor has it been written since, to explain *why* the Russians would want to conquer Western Europe by force or to bomb the United States. Neither action would have contributed in any tangible way to the Soviet national interest and would have hazarded the destruction of the Soviet state. This basic question was never raised, for the Cold War prism created in the minds of the diplomatic and military strategists a clear-cut world of black and white; there were no grays.

During these early years I saw this mentality at close range in some of my own case officers, in foreign service colleagues, and perhaps most often among senior military officers. This state of mind is very satisfying to those who hold it, for it combines simplicity with a sense of superior virtue. Unfortunately, it can also make a man nearsighted. Since he cannot see the reality beyond his own fixed images, he misinterprets the real world and is therefore unable to deal with it effectively. I have always felt it more important to understand the Russians than to dislike them.

The worst effect of this closed-circuit thinking within the intelligence community was naturally on the analysts who were asked to predict Soviet intentions. They had only a modicum of fact to go on: fragmentary and for the most part exaggerated readings of Soviet military capabilities. Translating those capabilities into intentions and cautiously predicting "no war within the next six months," then again "no war within the next six months," they rarely gave heed to the vast array of political, social, and economic facts that would have made it ridiculous for Moscow to incorporate another dozen satellites into its shaky empire.

In some of the recent discussion of "Who started the Cold War?" the question has been raised: Did CIA's secret operations play a role?

Hardly.

For almost three years after World War II the Office of Special Operations was a headquarters outfit of fewer than two hundred officers managing seven overseas stations with sizable rosters only in Army-occupied areas. By 1948 it was only beginning to reconnoiter the other side of the Iron Curtain from Berlin and Vienna, where the movement of agents was mainly a steady flow of Soviet spies to the west. The first airdrop of American intelligence agents on Soviet terrain took place in late 1949. The CIA had no mission or component to carry out covert propaganda or paramilitary operations until 1948–49, and only after the start of the Korean war did it engage in offensive operations against the Sino-Soviet orbit. By then the Cold War was already hot.

It was during the eighteen months after the March crisis that CIA's secret operations were assigned their initial missions against the Soviet target:

1. To collect secret intelligence on the Soviet Union itself, its military intentions, atomic weapons, and advanced missiles; on Soviet actions in Eastern Europe, North Korea, and North Vietnam; on Moscow's connections with foreign Communist parties and groups fighting for national liberation; and on the Communist parties themselves—their sources of funding, their secret or illegal activities, their fronts and interconnections.

2. To place American agents within the Soviet intelligence services, and to counter Soviet efforts to neutralize anti-Soviet émigré groups and to penetrate the American and European military and political establishments.

3. To carry out covert actions designed to weaken Soviet control over its own population and the peoples of Eastern Europe; to weaken pro-Soviet regimes and Communist parties throughout Eurasia; and to advance the interests of friendly governments and pro-Western parties and leaders against Communist encroachment.

None of us took these tasks lightly. Our immediate major missions called for operating within an area from Eastern Europe to the Pacific tightly closed to Western access, controlled by large and efficient security services, and populated by a scared, informant-riddled citizenry. Our service faced the exact converse of the operating area enjoyed by Soviet intelligence: the open and easily accessible societies of the West, laced with men who out of greed, anxiety, or other complex motivations, were willing to work, often in high places, against their own countries.

It was a tall order, but the mood in the White House and the Pentagon was uptight and urgent: do *something*, whatever the cost. The cost proved to be high.

2

TO RUSSIA BY AIR

On the night of September 5, 1949, in the dark of the moon an unmarked C-47 rose from the runway of an airfield in the American zone of Germany and headed east. It was piloted by two Czech airmen who had flown for the Royal Air Force during the Battle of Britain. Behind them two young Ukrainians crouched in the fuselage with heavily loaded parachute packs. Each had a small suitcase strapped to his waist.

Rising to five thousand feet, the plane crossed the East German and Polish borders on a course to the Western Ukraine. American radar tracked the plane, and American monitors intercepted the urgent radio messages that Soviet radar stations were sending to their command center reporting the unidentified plane overhead. There was no reaction from the ground.

As the plane neared the drop zone, the Czech copilot moved back from the cockpit to alert his passengers. They were singing at the top of their voices the refrain of the Ukrainian partisans:

> Belt after belt, on into battle,
> Ukrainian insurgents never retreat.

The plane gradually lowered its altitude to six hundred feet. At a signal from the copilot the two men jumped, one right after the other.

The plane rose and circled west following a more southerly route back to its base.

The two Ukrainians had exfiltrated overland to the west from their hideout in the Carpathian mountains almost a year earlier. They had been sent by the leadership of the Ukrainian resistance movement that was fighting to prevent the Soviet reoccupation of their territory. Their mission was to promote the cause of Ukrainian independence in the West and to get American support for the resistance fighters. After ten months of intensive training as radio operators and intelligence reporters, the two men were now returning to their comrades. Four days after the airdrop they announced their safe arrival over their radio. CIA now had a two-way link with the strongest nationalist movement within the Soviet Union.

The Ukrainian nationalists, even four years after the war, were still a powerful force against the Soviet regime. Khrushchev, who was transferred from the Ukraine to Moscow about this time, is an eloquent witness:

> The Carpathian Mountains were literally out of bounds for us because from behind every bush, from behind every tree, at every turn of the road, a government official was in danger of a terrorist attack.*

The Ukrainian drop was the first deep penetration of the Soviet Union in a CIA program designed to give the White House early warning of a Soviet military attack.

During the next five years, until well after Stalin's death and the gradual opening up of Soviet terrain to foreigners, CIA agents were dispatched into Russia by land, sea, and air

---

*Khrushchev Remembers, translated and edited by Strobe Talbott, Little, Brown, Boston, 1974, p. 95.

from Scandinavia, West Germany, Greece, Turkey, Iran, and Japan. They covered intelligence targets from the Murmansk area to Sakhalin, mostly on the margins of the Soviet land mass, some deep within. Their task was to satisfy priority intelligence requirements from the Pentagon that could not be satisfied by any less expensive or dangerous means.

During those five years the CIA operated almost solely as an instrument of the Department of Defense and its theater commanders. Their need was great.

The Soviet Union had become a "denied area" at the end of the war. It was denied to Western diplomats, journalists, and tourists, to visual observation, photography, and talk with its citizens. It was denied even to foreign Communists, who were carefully shepherded on their brief visits, for to Stalin they were, first and foremost, foreigners.

In 1946 intelligence files on the Soviet Union were virtually empty. Even the most elementary facts were unavailable—on roads and bridges, on the location and production of factories, on city plans and airfields. Scores of Air Force researchers were compiling Soviet bombing target dossiers from out-of-date materials in the Library of Congress.

Nor did the information coming in from Europe or the Far East in the next three years do much to fill the gap. It came mostly from Soviet and East European refugees, Soviet prisoners of war who had not been repatriated, German prisoners in Russia who had, and deserters from the Soviet forces in East Germany, Austria, and Korea. Most of it was trivial, much of it spotty, garbled, or out-of-date. Perhaps the most useful piece of information was a series of fragmentary reports on the location of German technicians and equipment evacuated to the Soviet Union that provided the first hard information on Soviet guided-missile production and testing.

Nothing of value came out of Russia itself. The American Embassy in Moscow was isolated. Its reporting personnel, from the ambassador on down, and the handful of Western journalists as well, lived on official handouts and private speculation. A few official visitors from the West now and then broke the seal around the capital, but most could supply detailed information only on their hotels and on the Moscow subway.

There were, as always in times of intelligence famine, many volunteers to supply "reliable" information on Soviet military matters. Dozens of intelligence mills operated throughout Europe ready to sell their secondhand or fabricated hot items to anyone with a little money. It became a time-consuming task for the CIA to run down and expose these mills.

Even poor sources on the Soviet Union were drying up by 1948 when the March crisis and the Berlin blockade created the war scare in Washington. "Early warning" became an almost panicky requirement. It was officially estimated that Soviet forces were capable of reaching the English Channel in a matter of weeks. By the fall of 1949 it was estimated that Soviet bombers were capable of dropping bombs on American terrain. It was an axiom in Washington that Stalin was plotting war. When would it come?

The heat was on the CIA to answer that question. The Pentagon sent over detailed requests for essential information: the location of Soviet military units and aircraft, the condition of Soviet airfields, above all Soviet military plans. In session after session with Army and Air Force colonels, we hammered out what we judged were realistic requirements that we had some hope of satisfying with our slender resources.

I recall vividly one heated session in a Pentagon conference room. It started with an Army colonel banging his fist on the table and shouting, "I want an agent with a radio on every goddamn airfield between Berlin and the Urals." We looked at the maps and came up with a more modest plan.

In another session the Air Force representative expressed a strong interest in having CIA supply him with a specimen of the Soviet TU-4 strategic bomber, preferably complete with pilot. I told him we would keep his request in mind.

It became clear early in these talks that radio-equipped

agents at strategic locations within the Soviet Union were the only hope of reporting quickly on Soviet preparations for an attack on Europe or the United States. They had to be dispatched by air for they could not carry their radio equipment overland across the Soviet border. Once in, they would have to survive on their own, to become "legal residents" able to live in their target areas as ordinary Soviet citizens.

We were ill-equipped for the task.

In the Soviet Union in 1949, there were no carefully prepared drop zones, no friendly reception groups outside the western Ukraine and the Baltic states, no help to be expected from the spy-inoculated population, no safe house or barn to hide in, no end to an agent's mission except to go a thousand miles by train or on foot and exfiltrate across the well-guarded southern borders into Turkey or Iran. Once inside, an agent faced each day the most efficient internal security service and the densest informant network of the twentieth century.

We were confronted with two major technical problems in these operations. The first, to get the agents in, was solved very simply. Once the decision had been made by the director to return the two Ukrainian couriers to the Carpathians, we sought the required support. CIA already owned several C-47's and had recruited Czech and Hungarian crews to man them on occasional short-term missions into Eastern Europe. What was needed for the longer flights into the Soviet Union was more expert ground maintenance, a highly secure take-off and landing field, and the preparation of competent flight plans.

The Ninth Air Force in Germany had what we wanted.

One morning I visited the Air Force chief of intelligence (A-2) in his impressive Pentagon office and posed the problem. I told him of our facilities, the target areas we would be concerned with, and what we needed in the way of ground support. He agreed without hesitation to send appropriate instructions to the Ninth Air Force in an eyes-only cable, and we wrote out a draft together.

The Air Force, of course, had a priority interest in the early warning mission of our agents, but the A-2 also pointed out that the Soviet ground reaction to our overflights would provide him with the first hard intelligence on the state of Soviet ground defenses against air attack.

Our arrangement was the least bureaucratic and most quickly coordinated project of any serious CIA operation I know of. It was never cleared with the Department of State, though presumably it was with the President, and only in the early fifties was the secretary of state informed.

As it turned out, four years of these illegal overflights caused no diplomatic embarrassment. Soviet ground crews monitored every flight—from the Baltic down to the Balkans, from the Balkans out over central Europe, from West Germany east into the Ukraine and back again to the American zone. They shot at some (their reaction time was carefully measured), but the lumbering C-47's survived every flight. Yet Moscow did not protest. Apparently Stalin accepted these hostile flights as a normal element of the Cold War both before and after Korea.

Our second major problem, the preparation of adequate documents for the agents sent in, was the most difficult technical challenge we faced. Once in, an agent had to fit smoothly into the rigid Soviet control system. That system was, and is, the most effective of any modern state.

Soviet control of its citizens is exercised by all elements of the party and the government, but the professional task of detecting and rooting out dissidents, saboteurs, and spies belongs to the Internal Directorate of the KGB,* whose security and counterintelligence units operate from the federal

---

*The civilian arm of Soviet intelligence is the Committee of State Security, or KGB (from its Russian initials), so named in 1954. Its predecessors have been known under a variety of names since the Russian Revolution: the Cheka (the Extraordinary Commission for Combating Counterrevolution and Sabotage) from 1917 to 1922, the GPU (State Political Directorate) and the OGPU, the NKVD (People's Commissariat of Internal Affairs) from 1934, the NKGB and the MGB from 1941 to 1954. To avoid confusion I have used the designation KGB even for

down to the rayon, or county, level. The ordinary police make frequent document checks throughout the country, especially at railroad stations, but the KGB's secret police carry out the more systematic job of investigating suspicious characters or following up tips from informers.

In some respects a greater threat to a man living illegally in a town or city is posed by his neighbors, for the strongest element of the Soviet control system lies within the mind of the Soviet citizen himself. Surrounded by informants, warned by the evidence of others whose sons or husbands have vanished, propagandized by the party and press in recurrent spy-scare campaigns, he is cowed and cautious. He knows enough about provocation to suspect that anyone seeking his help is sent by the KGB to test his loyalty. Stalin convinced his people that their country was riddled with Western spies, and many were eager to report strangers, denounce fellow workers, and spy on neighbors as suspect "Western agents." An agent was as likely to be turned in by a traveling companion he talked to as caught by a police spot check at a railroad station.

Personal documents are the nub of Soviet control over its citizens. Each man and woman is required to carry a basic identity document, or internal passport, valid for five years and different for each Soviet republic. Other required papers include a labor book, which records past and current employment (with all entries signed by factory personnel managers), a military status book, and, when appropriate, a party book or an officer's identity book.

The preparation of forged documents for the agents being sent in required not only samples of legitimate documents, but a vast amount of precise information to fill them in prop-

---

the earlier periods. Its internal directorate (Second Chief Directorate) is comparable to the Federal Bureau of Investigation, its foreign directorate (First Chief Directorate) to CIA's Office of Operations.

Soviet military intelligence, a part of the Soviet General Staff, is the Chief Intelligence Directorate, or GRU.

erly. This so-called operational intelligence had been haphazardly collected since 1946, and some of it was usable for documenting the agents sent in three to five years later. Knowledge of the personnel and history of Soviet military units destroyed with their records during the war, of bombed-out factories and houses, of city and town birth records that had burned came in especially handy. These and other facts of wartime history helped guarantee that false birth dates and addresses as well as nonexistent landlords and employers could not be checked out in a police investigation.

The exacting job of producing valid internal passports was enormously complicated by the Soviet passport reregistration campaign from 1949 to 1953, aimed at catching up with the large number of Soviet citizens carrying false or altered documents. Each citizen required a live witness to identify him before he could be reregistered—an imposing task for a recently dispatched solo agent.

The main stock of internal passports for various Soviet republics came from captured German archives, all of them fabricated by the Germans. Not until 1951 did CIA learn the process (*Sammelpress*) by which Soviet documents were printed.

Each agent's legend, or fictional life history, both supported and was supported by his documents. Once he landed and became another Soviet citizen on his way from one place to another, he had to be ready to talk about himself, his past, his present, and his plans. Into his story were woven all the facts and experiences of his real life history that could safely fit his new identity, but learning his legend nonetheless made great demands on his memory and his imagination.

These legends were designed to stand up against casual questions by other Soviet citizens or in a routine KGB check. None could stand up against a professional KGB interrogation. Each agent realized that once his words or acts prompted police suspicion, he was through.

The crucial elements in these, as in any other secret operations, were not the mechanics but the men: the agent who went in and the case officer who trained and nurtured him before he went.

Fortunately, the CIA had a group of experienced and highly talented Americans who spoke fluent Russian, Ukrainian, Lithuanian, and other regional languages to act as case officers. They included naturalized Americans born in the Soviet Union and brought up in Europe or the United States by Russian or Ukrainian parents. Some had learned their Russian in college or at the Army language schools during the war. Some had served as interpreters in Berlin, Vienna, and Korea.

They were joined, after the Korean war broke out, by a mostly younger breed of Russian speakers who came into CIA operations eager to take part in what many of them saw as the first battle of World War III. They were men of energy and talent, men with good career prospects in civilian America who chose to fight what they saw as a threat to their ideals.

I knew them all—I had recruited many of them during my headquarters tour—but I began working with them only after I arrived at our base in Munich in May 1952 as chief of Soviet operations. My responsibilities included not only the dispatch of agents into the Soviet Union and the recruitment of agents for dispatch by our other bases in the Middle East and Japan, but counterespionage work against Soviet intelligence operations in our area—and, a year later, agent operations from Munich into Eastern Europe.

The base headquarters in Munich was on the fourth floor of an old German barracks cut off from the military offices below by a barred gate, and my own office was a bare attic room with slanted ceilings even shabbier and darker than my old room in the Tempos. It was there, and in our Saturday night parties at out-of-the-way restaurants in the country, that I got to know these case officers.

I have never worked before or since with a group so highly motivated and totally committed to doing a job. They knew the hazards their agents faced, and each man was devoted to one end: to get his agent into the Soviet Union, and to do everything humanly and technically possible to reduce to a minimum the hazards the agent would face once he was in. They worked with a zeal and a sense of camaraderie I have never seen in peacetime. I am still grateful to them.

The agents themselves could come from only two sources: former Soviet citizens who were then living in Western Europe or the refugees and defectors who were still coming out. Each was a traitor to the regime and automatically subject to the death penalty. Their courage and competence, and their willingness to take on a long-term, probably fatal mission, were the sine qua non of any possible success.

Agent candidates were recruited from displaced persons camps in Germany, from among recent Soviet military defectors in Europe, Turkey, Iran, and South Korea, and through the auspices of various émigré groups. Military defectors and men sponsored by an émigré group were carefully interrogated and assessed by their prospective case officers. Our spotters in the DP camps helped interview recent refugees and brought likely candidates to our notice. These men were quietly approached to determine if they were willing to undertake a mission into the Soviet Union. Those who agreed to this vague proposal were taken out of the camp, lodged in a nearby safe house for further interrogation and assessment, and accepted or rejected for a mission.

A few of the successful candidates were ethnic Russians, but most belonged to minority groups: Balts, Ukrainians, Armenians, and Georgians with direct links in their native areas. All were single, young, bright, and highly motivated.

Their reasons for volunteering were mixed. The Lithuanians and Latvians saw the Russians as occupiers of their homelands. The Ukrainians, among the strongest nationalists in the Soviet Union, wanted to fight the Russians (as Russians, not as Communists) for the independence of the Ukraine. Other ethnic Russians opposed the Communist dictatorship for personal reasons (the fate of their parents or their village) or out of a more general hatred of the "oppressors."

The earliest missions those men were assigned were one- or two-man intelligence operations designed to establish "legal residents" who would cover assigned early warning targets and report any signs of impending Soviet military moves. When the Soviet A-bomb became a reality, intelligence coverage of suspect atomic energy installations joined early warning as a top priority.

The varying fates of these missions were reflected in scenes of elation and frustration in my attic office.

On one wet day in late May two case officers burst through the door with good news. They had returned the day before from the airfield from which their agent had been dispatched. They announced that he had just reported "all is well" in his first brief radio message. We celebrated that night at a Gasthaus in a Munich suburb.

The following September my deputy came in with a long piece of ticker tape. The Moscow radio had just announced the capture of two "imperialist" agents who had confessed to their nefarious "sabotage" mission. The broadcast gave details of their interrogation, including the cover names of their case officers and a garbled location of their training site. We spent hours speculating on when and how they had been picked up: at the drop zone? at the railroad station? in their target area? The Moscow radio gave no details on what was to us the vital question: Had we gone wrong? If so, where?

That broadcast depressed and frustrated us all, both the Americans and the agents in training. No agent dropped out. They knew from the beginning that the cards were stacked against them.

Our only steady source of satisfaction came from the intelligence reports we received from the agents who had safely reached their target areas. Measured against the extraordinary effort devoted to getting them there, the results were meager. In terms of early warning, they were a total failure for one simple reason: There were no early warnings to be reported. No Soviet divisions moved west for an offensive into Western Europe. No strategic bombers took off for the United States. Had there been radio-equipped agents sitting near every TU-4 runway and major rail hub, none would have had occasion to transmit a warning message.

The story of Ivan Petrovich (neither his true nor his cover name), twenty-four years old, a Russian from the northern Ukraine, will serve to illustrate what launching an operation into the Soviet Union demanded.

High on the Pentagon's list of priority early warning targets during those crucial years of 1949–53 was the strategic bomber base at Orsha in the western region of the Soviet Union on the main railway between Minsk and Moscow. It was one of the three key bases to be placed under observation by a radio-equipped agent.

Our Russian and Ukrainian spotters in the displaced persons camps had been instructed to look for a man from the area who was willing to go on a dangerous mission—they knew nothing about the mission itself. After screening a dozen potential recruits, one of the spotters sent back a note strongly recommending a young Russian who had lived in the area during his earlier years and had fled to the American zone of Germany some eighteen months before. The son of a mechanic on a machine tractor station near Vitebsk, he was tough, bright, self-assured. He was fed up with camp life and eager for an adventure.

Once singled out, Ivan was brought to a safe house near his DP camp, a house used only for the preliminary assessment of agent candidates. Here he was put through a series of exacting tests—a full-dress medical examination, measurements of muscular coordination and psychological stability, learning aptitude both verbal and mechanical. Our doctors and psychologists had him for three days.

A Russian consultant on our staff then retraced with him

his life history in painstaking detail: every place he had lived, everything he had done, every person he knew or who could recognize him inside. He was asked trick questions, put through a long session of hostile interrogation, and given several lie-detector tests—all designed not only to test his honesty, but to measure his responses to stress and to strengthen the cover story he might use on his mission. Ivan passed his preliminary screening with high marks, and only then did he meet the two case officers who would make the final decision.

Sam was a thirty-year-old naturalized American with one team mission to his credit. His partner, Fred, learned Russian during the war, and could pass as a Russian from the Moscow area. The three men spent the day in casual conversation. Impressed with Ivan's energy and enthusiasm, Sam and Fred accepted him for the Orsha mission, and took him to an isolated chalet on the shore of a lake in southern Bavaria.

For almost a year the three men slept, ate, drank, and worked together with a single purpose.

Here is one day in the life of Ivan Petrovich in the seventh month of his training.

Sam calls him at 6:30 A.M., and the two in army fatigues jog through the woods behind the house down to the lake and back again. They eat a heavy breakfast of bacon, scrambled eggs, and fried potatoes prepared by Fred—there is no housekeeper—and then the two-hour "tradecraft" session begins. They are still on "observation and reporting," and the subject for the third day in a row is Soviet aircraft recognition. Pictures and silhouettes of Soviet planes are flashed before Ivan, and he calls out the identifying data—by now he is almost perfect. The second hour is devoted to a critique of the report Ivan has made after watching a nearby American airfield for three hours from half a mile away. His estimates of the length of runways, the location of terminal buildings, and the frequency of takeoffs and landings are carefully corrected.

The professor arrives at ten for his weekly session. A former Red Army captain and secondary-school history teacher, he is a specialist in contemporary life within the Soviet Union. Ivan has been outside for two years, and the professor's job is to bring him up-to-date—on trolley fares, the cost of bread, the latest regulations on getting or changing jobs, etc. They talk about items on the black market in the larger towns, especially documents and radio parts. The two go over some recent newspaper clippings from *Pravda*—a regulation on intercity train travel, restrictions on the use of photo supplies by amateurs. They exchange some current Russian slang.

The two hours after lunch are reserved for radio communications. After a month of indoctrination and daily practice at the nearby air base, Ivan has been practicing at home. He lugs the big RS-1 transceiver onto the living-room table and raises his base. He has encrypted his report on the American airfield and sends it to the base. The base replies, but Ivan constantly interrupts: "Too fast, too fast." He is good at sending, slower in receiving.

Finally he turns off his set and deciphers the message from the base. For the next half hour he listens to a taped message on his cylinder recorder to sharpen his ear and speed up his reception.

Before he finishes his instruction, he will be able to take apart his RS-1 and make minor repairs. He is a natural mechanic; he tinkered with radios as a kid when the only radios available were made from cannibalized sets, discarded parts, and chicken-wire aerials.

The photography session with Fred is next. The two have worked for several days on taking outdoor shots with a Minox camera disguised as a cigarette lighter. Today they walk down to the lake and take some distant shots—a sailing boat, a lakeside cottage, a parked Mercedes-Benz. Ivan will develop them that evening.

The evening session is relaxed but crucial. Art, the document man, arrives after dinner. He knows Soviet documents better than a KGB officer—the paper and inks used, the signatures of scores of legitimate issuing officials, variations in work and transit permits in various rayons.

Art concentrates on working out the details of Ivan's life in Russia during the two years he will have spent in Germany. The three men talk about possible jobs and addresses that fit Ivan's age and ability and that can be documented. They tentatively come up with two years at a dam construction project in the northern Ukraine.

The workday ends at 10:30 P.M. The following day Ivan will make his third live parachute drop on a nearby Army artillery range.

After ten months of intensive training, Ivan was ready for his mission in time for the fall drop schedule. He was equipped from shirt to shoes with items of Soviet or East German manufacture, and carried for barter and bribery several wristwatches and some five-dollar bills available to Soviet troops in Germany. Once in, he would be "clean" except for the radio in his suitcase.

On a dark night in September the C-47 dropped him on an open field three miles from a village with a railroad station. He had been instructed to bury his parachute on landing and get to the station before dawn. The train was due at 7:20 A.M. Within thirty-six hours of the drop Ivan came up on the air to announce his safe arrival. There had been no air alert in the drop area, and he had reached the outskirts of Vitebsk without incident. His message contained no danger signal.

During the next thirteen months Ivan sent five radio messages and three letters with secret writing messages to addresses in West Germany. After working part-time on a street-repair gang (foremen of hard labor teams are notoriously casual about passports and labor books), he got a job as an electrician in a canning factory named "Stalin's Road." He cached his radio in a woods about two miles from the airfield, and made a point of walking by the airfield once or twice a week. He reported his observations in four of his messages, but during the entire year there was no unusual traffic on the airfield.

In his last secret-writing message Ivan reported that he had legalized himself with a set of documents he had bought on the black market. Using the radio, he felt, was becoming dangerous, and since the airfield was still quiet, he had decided to sign off.

Ivan had carried out his primary mission: to report any activity at the Orsha airbase that might indicate preparations for a strategic air strike against the West. That was the major contribution Ivan and other of our early warning agents were able to make to the analysts in Washington. There were, of course, other items of military information (aircraft identifications, airfield and army installations, etc.) and of security and living conditions, but early warning was the main task. That there were no warnings to report would not become clear until several years and many airdrops later.

These early airdrop operations faced three major security hazards from Soviet intelligence—in the Munich area, in the Soviet Union itself, and, unknown to us at the time, in London.

Operating out of its headquarters in the Karlshorst compound in East Berlin, the KGB displayed an extraordinary interest in the anti-Soviet émigrés resident in Allied-occupied Germany. These émigrés from the Ukraine and Byelorussia, from Azerbaijan, Georgia, and Armenia not only posed a political threat as potential claimants for power within the Soviet state, but they were obviously the main reservoir of potential agents for Western espionage. Even before the first American airdrops, the KGB was working hard to monitor and neutralize them. Its main task in the Munich area was to find out whom we had recruited, where they were being trained, how and when they were dispatched, and where in the Soviet Union they were operating.

The KGB Karlshorst center worked two tracks: sending in bogus émigrés from East Germany and recruiting émigrés already in the Munich area. The second was the easier to counter.

The Karlshorst procedure was routine. A Ukrainian or a Georgian working for Radio Liberation in Munich was approached by a German or a Russian "from East Berlin" who delivered a letter or photograph of his relatives in the Soviet Union. The visitor urged the prospect to rehabilitate himself by working for the Soviet service. Often the letter contained an open or implied threat of reprisal to his family back home, sometimes it offered money. Once recruited, the new agent was given the means to communicate in secret writing with East Germany and urged to buy a radio receiver for a one-way voice link with the KGB headquarters. When an agent had proved himself, he was frequently invited to visit East Berlin (with Soviet-supplied documentation) for face-to-face talks with his KGB case officer and, for outstanding performance, a free trip to his homeland.

Some of the émigrés who were approached in this fashion came voluntarily to an American official, often in terror. Others were nosed out by our spotters in the émigré communities, and the threat of arrest or exposure usually brought out the full story. Those who were willing and able were encouraged to accept their Soviet assignment and report back to a CIA case officer.

Running these double agents back into the Karlshorst headquarters not only told us what the KGB wanted to know about our operations but what they did not know.

A typical case was that of a well-known émigré journalist with wide contacts in the emigration. He received a telephone call from a professed member of a Soviet athletic team in West Germany who brought him greetings from his brother in the Soviet Union. Under CIA control he visited Karlshorst where he was "recruited" and trained in microdots and photography and given the tasks of reporting on his émigré acquaintances, spotting and cultivating likely agent candidates for the KGB, and of penetrating the CIA to uncover its operations into the Soviet Union. His double mission lasted for several years, with personal meetings in Karlshorst three times a year. During that time he was able to identify more than a dozen KGB case officers in Karlshorst, to give the location of some of their safe houses, to recommend to the KGB several agent candidates who worked for the CIA, and to provide a misleading picture of CIA relations with various émigré groups.

Once we had a number of KGB agents working for us, we were able to feed agents of our own choice into the KGB net.

One carefully tailored case involved a Georgian working in Radio Liberty. He had been approached by the KGB a year earlier (Radio Liberty was a key Soviet target) and at our instruction had agreed to work for the Russians, maintaining contact through an East German courier from Karlshorst. The courier on one of his trips asked our man to recommend another politically active Georgian who might be useful to the KGB. After several consultations with his CIA case officer, he recommended B as a likely candidate. A few days later B received a visit from an American who told him he might be approached by a Soviet emissary in the next few weeks—and would he be good enough to accept any offer made to him. Puzzled but willing, he agreed. Three weeks later—to his great surprise—he was approached by a Soviet courier.

These double-agent operations uncovered scores of Soviet couriers, contact points, and agents in the American zone and gave us a detailed picture of KGB personnel and facilities in East Berlin. Their immediate value, however, was to provide continuing reassurance that the Karlshorst KGB had not penetrated our training bases or our air dispatches. On the basis of the hard evidence we had, our operations in the American zone itself were secure.

A greater and more subtle security hazard faced us when the Internal Directorate of the KGB decided to play back airdropped agents caught on or near the drop zone. Their purpose was mainly to ferret out the names or locations of other American agents in the Soviet Union. It was clear at the time that the Soviet security services were genuinely convinced that their country was riddled with large numbers of Allied spies. Their concern was unjustified, perhaps even more so than the spy mania in Washington during the same years.

In almost all cases of KGB playback the captured agent transmitted his control signal to inform the base in Germany of his arrest.* We played along as long as the KGB was willing, for our only purpose was to keep our agent safe for as long as possible. In one radio playback the KGB spent over a year and a half trying to inveigle us into making contact with the captured agent through another American agent on Soviet territory. The KGB handlers were frequently clumsy in running their end of the operation. In one of their more careless efforts, a playback via secret-writing correspondence to addresses in Europe, analysis of the handwriting in the agent's letters showed that they had been written for him by seven different persons.

The gravest security threat to our airdrop operations, as it turned out, lay in London and Washington in the person of a senior British intelligence officer.

H. A. R. (Kim) Philby joined the British Communist Party during his undergraduate days at Cambridge in the early thirties and was recruited by Soviet intelligence before World War II. After a stint as journalist (and secret Soviet agent) in Spain during the civil war, he was recruited into the British Secret Intelligence Service and rose rapidly to become the head of its counterespionage section in London. There, in the late forties, and in his subsequent assignment to Washington as the British liaison officer with CIA, he sat astride British

---

*In his final communications briefing each agent was briefed with great care on the indicator, or danger signal, he was to use in a message to warn his case officer that he was transmitting under Soviet control. During World War II confusion about the danger signal often left both German and Allied services the victim of turned radio agents who thought they had alerted their base.

operations into the Soviet Union, an ideal spot for Soviet counterespionage.

I sat around the conference table with Philby in London, and across from him at lunch in Martin's restaurant in Washington. I found him highly intelligent and a competent professional, precise and careful. Both qualities ran deeper than I suspected, for only a rare talent for living a split life and absolute self-control in or out of his cups could have kept him in place in the British service for over ten years.

It was during these years that Philby learned a great deal about our own air operations into the Soviet Union. He did not, as has been asserted, know "what the CIA knew about Soviet operations," for the British were informed about our own operations only when it was absolutely essential to avoid confusion or duplication. Even so, Philby knew far too much, but since he was never broken before his defection to Moscow in 1963 (he was suspect from 1951 on), it is impossible to determine precisely what information he gave to the Russians and which of our operations he helped destroy.

It is easy in retrospect to sum up this crash program: The results were not worth the effort. At the time, however, when a Soviet military offensive was considered imminent, it was a wartime investment whose cost was not measured by the Pentagon. In my own view there was some profit. The mere existence of radio-equipped agents on Soviet terrain with no early warnings to report had some cautionary value in tempering the war scare among the military estimaters at the height of the Cold War.

Another possible value of these operations fortunately proved to be an illusion.

On a trip back to Washington from Munich in 1953, when the air-dispatch program was becoming a controversial issue, I had a talk with the CIA director. During a review of the results since that first drop in 1949, he sat back and made a reflective comment: "At least we're getting the kind of experience we need for the next war." And that war, for him and for many others in Washington, was not very far away.

Air dispatch of radio-equipped agents virtually ceased in 1954. Not only were the losses too high and the expenditure of effort too great for the results achieved, but the Soviet orbit was beginning to open up after Stalin's death and the war scare in Washington had toned down somewhat. Finally, too, illegal overflights violating Soviet terrain were being assessed for what they had always been: a direct provocation of the new Soviet leadership. As the wartime atmosphere dissipated, diplomatic concerns overrode the frantic Pentagon requirement "do something, do anything" to detect the enemy's intentions.

In the spring of 1949, when I had made the arrangements with the A-2 for Air Force support of our air dispatches, our conversation ranged over other possible ways for satisfying the early warning requirement. We both agreed that the solution would ultimately lie in the air. A high-flying airplane with a precision camera could produce in a few hours more visual data than a hundred agents could in a year of observing and reporting. But neither the plane nor the camera for high-altitude overflight was yet within the competence of American technology, and the men on the ground paid the price.

Two years after the last agent was dropped into the Soviet Union, the U(tility)-2 spy plane made its first peripheral flights along the Soviet borders.

3

THE SECOND CIRCLE

Some of our operational planners saw the approach to the Soviet target as a series of concentric circles. The inner circle was, of course, the Soviet Union itself, and airdropping agents close to military targets was the most direct approach. The second circle was the array of states around the Soviet Union, both its satellites in Europe and its Communist neighbors in Asia, that provided opportunities for a less direct, two-step approach to the Soviet target. These were more accessible and less tightly controlled than Soviet terrain in the late forties and early fifties. In the third circle were the major nonruling Communist parties in Europe and Asia whose leaders were in frequent contact with the Soviet party leaders.

In the second circle—East Berlin, Warsaw, Prague in the west, and North Korea and China on the east—there were two groups of possible sources who were in a position to report on what was happening inside Russia. The first, of greater interest, included senior Soviet military officers and civilian "advisers" who were shaping the internal structure of the new Communist nations. Next came the senior native Communist Party officials in the puppet governments who were in direct contact with the Soviet party. These were men who, through contacts with the local Soviet ambassador or through visits to Moscow, had at least a parochial vision of Stalin and his Politburo colleagues.

Our agent operations into the second circle, however, rarely reached the Soviet target itself. The same pressures for military intelligence from within the Soviet Union acted to force CIA to cover military targets within the second circle, and the strategic approach to Moscow via the satellites became secondary.

With the March crisis of 1948, Soviet military capabilities in Eastern Europe joined early warning from the Soviet Union at the top of the list of intelligence priorities. An interagency intelligence committee in Washington listed indicators around the Eurasian landmass and drew up "essential elements of information" that concentrated heavily on Soviet installations and activities in the northern tier of satellites: East Germany, Poland, Czechoslovakia.

Indications of a Soviet ground advance into Western Europe were growing. Soviet troop strength in East Germany and Poland was expanding steadily. The satellite air forces were being supplied with Soviet MIG fighters, and runways on Czech and Polish airfields were being extended to accommodate Soviet bombers. Scare reports on an impending attack came by the dozen from East European refugees.

Fortunately, Soviet-occupied territory was not the terra incognita the Soviet Union had become.

Within weeks of the end of World War II American and Soviet authorities met, mingled, and quibbled along the occupation lines in Berlin and Vienna. A sketchy picture of Soviet order of battle information began to emerge. Once the American authorities ceased the automatic return of Soviet military deserters, Soviet defectors began to fill in the gaps. In the first six years after the war well over five hundred

Soviet military and civilian defectors fled to the West. Most of them ran out of fear: fear of punishment for fraternization, for criminal offenses, drunkenness, jeep accidents. Many of the enlisted men wanted to marry German girls, a few wanted simply to have a better life.

An occasional defector was run back into East Germany to pose as a soldier in good standing, circulate, and come back with any information he could pick up. A Soviet major in Dresden, working through his German girl friend in West Berlin, reported regularly on Soviet troop units and movements from the fall of 1947 to December 1949, providing highly useful insights into Soviet intentions during the height of the Berlin blockade.

Operations of this sort, infrequent and unplanned "targets of opportunity," injected some hard facts into the mass of "intelligence" from the thousands of East European refugees flooding the military intelligence desks in Washington and the American zone.

As up-to-date information on Poland, Czechoslovakia, and Hungary began to give out with the declining number of escapees, the Army commanders in Europe clamored for news of what was going on behind the borders. Everyone got into the act: not only the half dozen American military agencies, but British, French, and German outfits as well. Everyone competed for the émigré "know-how," their linguistic ability, their friends outside, their possible contacts inside. Professional intelligence fabricators flourished. In the American zone alone dozens of intelligence units, hundreds of interrogators and military intelligence officers, thousands of "agents" were working across the borders of East Germany, Poland, Czechoslovakia, and Hungary.

The CIA, designed as a strategic intelligence service, quickly became caught up in these cross-border operations. From Berlin, from the American zones of Germany and Austria, from Vienna, Greece, and Turkey, CIA units began to concentrate almost exclusively on the satellite target.

By 1948 the dividing line between the two armed camps that ran from Lübeck on the Baltic to the head of the Adriatic had become a fortified barrier with only Berlin an easy transit point.

THROUGH THE BERLIN GATE

The dispatch of agents into East Germany via Berlin was an easy task before the building of the Berlin Wall in 1961. Only good documents and a railway ticket were needed. These operations were also eased by the readiness of many educated East Germans to work for the West and of many West Germans to recruit relatives and other contacts in the East. The CIA had a rich supply of German-speaking case officers to handle them.

Various simple mechanisms were devised to attract persons of special interest. For example, an advertisement was placed in West Berlin newspapers inviting persons with certain technical qualifications to apply for a job as a teacher. East German applicants were screened and replies sent to those in jobs of particular intelligence interest inviting them for an interview in West Berlin. Many of the candidates, almost all anti-Soviet, accepted assignments to report on their current work in return for eventual resettlement in West Germany.

A more routine approach to recruiting East German officials in sensitive areas was simply to ask an educated refugee: Whom do you know who might be helpful to the Americans? If he came up with someone of interest, he was asked to invite him to come to West Berlin for a visit (the refugee was paid ten marks a day while he waited). When his friend arrived, he was introduced to a CIA officer in a safe hotel room. After listening to the CIA proposal, he was free to accept or reject the offer. Scores accepted.

One of the most ingenious Berlin recruitments was carried out via the rectum of a goose. A CIA officer, who had met a senior East German official on several social occasions, sent him a goose for Christmas with a persuasive letter enclosed in a small metal cylinder thrust up its rear end. When the official's cook found the cylinder, he brought it to his employer, who, impressed either with the letter or with its method of delivery, agreed to a secret meeting and became a useful agent.

Activities within both the party and the administration were covered to the hilt for years by our Berlin base. Scores of couriers rode the Berlin S-bahn, the main traffic artery between East and West Berlin, in both directions each week. They serviced agents who had penetrated high circles of the ruling party, the government's economic ministries, the railway and postal administrations, the police and the militia. Thousands of reports, from freight car loadings to party policy discussions, were screened, translated, and sent off to the Army commanders and to Washington.

Agent reporting also covered Soviet military targets within East Germany in detail and depth: the location and movement of units, equipment, airfields. Some agents managed to supply vital information on Soviet strategic targets high upon the list of priorities: bacteriological-warfare testing on the Baltic island of Rügen, uranium production and transport in the Joachimstal area of the Harz Mountains, samples of nickel-wire mesh employed in the Soviet production of fissionable uranium through the gaseous diffusion process. Indirect contact was also made with German rocket specialists in the Soviet Union who were allowed to correspond with families they had left behind in East Germany.

THROUGH THE IRON CURTAIN

Direct entry into the other European satellites was not so easy. The Iron Curtain was a formidable obstacle, and the agents willing and able to cross it were limited not in number, but in proper education and useful contacts "inside."

The Iron Curtain was not built overnight. The Soviet Union had thirty years to seal off its frontiers with a foot-by-foot control of its borders, especially in the west and the south. It took years to split Europe along the 1,000-mile stretch from Stettin to Trieste. Along the new frontier, much of it mountainous and wooded terrain, sector after sector was sealed off with miles of single and double barbed wire fences, much of it electrified. Watchtowers were closely spaced, woods and brush cleared, strips plowed to show footprints, mine fields planted. Constant patrols with trained dogs chased anyone—coming from the east or the west—who triggered the elaborate alarm system. No safe houses existed along the border, for all but the most reliable inhabitants had been removed from the border zone.

The obstacles to entry were matched by the hazards encountered once inside. Internal controls exercised by residence and work permits and a ubiquitous police soon matched the rigor of the system inside the Soviet Union itself. Soviet officers ran the satellite security services. There were no resistance groups in Eastern Europe after the Czech coup, or none that could be trusted. There were no lists of pro-Westerners who would risk harboring a spy. There was little chance for an agent to live underground, or camp out, or stay at an inn or hotel. Above all, the new Communist regimes had rapidly whipped up their populations to be on the lookout for Western spies.

In the early days agent candidates were available by the thousand. Up to 1948–49 there were so many gaps in the Iron Curtain that refugees literally poured through, whole families, on foot, pushing their baby carriages loaded with household goods. As the holes were plugged, only the more adventurous and courageous made it out, chiefly young unattached males, the most likely candidates for going back in as agents.

Though it would seem unlikely that a man who has just escaped at risk to life and limb from "Communist oppression" would risk his neck again on an even more hazardous trip, there were many volunteers. The fight against the Communists was a strong motive for some, escape from a dull refugee camp life for others, but material incentives perhaps played the greater part with most: a job, good pay, preferential treatment in resettlement, help in obtaining a visa.

The principal mission of the CIA stations in Germany, Austria, Greece, and Turkey was to establish resident agents in Eastern Europe, to send in agents who could recruit residents inside to serve as continuing sources of intelligence on their areas. Yet the CIA carried out as well a large share of missions designed to look at a specific airfield, barracks, or factory in the satellite areas.

At their simplest, such operations involved sending back in a refugee who had reported an installation of interest to the CIA. He knew his way around and what to look for, and he often was able to find a place to stay overnight with either an old friend or a relative. In most cases the agents came back in short order with their tidbits of visual observation and local chitchat. The long-term missions offered greater problems. There were two possible approaches to recruiting a well-placed source inside an Eastern European country: to send in a man to recruit someone he knew, or to send in a suitable courier to recruit a stranger who, on the evidence we had, was strongly opposed to the Communist regime. It was necessary of course to ensure that the courier who made the approach would be accepted as a legitimate messenger from the West.

In one case a Czech major who had defected in 1951 from a regional military command headquarters in eastern Czechoslovakia recommended two of his fellow officers as strongly anti-Soviet. A properly documented courier with several missions to his credit was sent in through the barbed wire and reached the command headquarters by train. He recognized one of the two officers from the major's description and showed the officer a picture of the major's child to identify himself as a friend and an authentic messenger.

The two officers accepted him and talked to him freely about the morale of the Czech Army and the attitude of its officers to the now politicized Czech General Staff. They gave their personal estimates of the degree of Soviet confidence in the reliability of senior Czech officers. The courier returned to his base with a detailed appreciation on these and other matters. His report was of burning interest to the American command, who were eager to determine whether the Czech armed forces would be a reliable Soviet instrument for offensive action in the West. The reports from the two officers made it clear that they would not.

The case of Jiri, also a Czech, had a human twist. An engineer from Prague, Jiri had decided to escape when the Czech security services began questioning some of his friends about his political views. Since he was engaged to be married, he went alone to reconnoiter a safe route across the border over which he could later take his fiancée. He got through without difficulty and made his way to a refugee camp in Bavaria. He now wanted to go back and bring out his fiancée.

A case officer was sent to the camp, and Jiri offered to carry out an intelligence mission inside in return for any help the American might give him.

His mission was to contact and recruit a high-level Czech government official whose willingness to work against the regime had been reported by an earlier escapee. When Jiri heard his name, he laughed—the man was an old friend of his family's. He agreed to make the contact first and then get his fiancée. He calculated that it would take three days to accomplish both missions.

On a moonless night in May, Jiri went back under the barbed wire at the same place he had come out.

Three nights later a reception team was waiting for Jiri and his fiancée to reach the wire and give them any help they might need. Toward midnight a figure appeared on the other side of the fence—no patrols were due on the Czech side for another ten minutes. First one, then a second, then a third figure crawled under the fence and through the tall grass to the country road where the team was waiting. The first was a girl, the second Jiri, and the third the Prague official.

Jiri had made his contact without incident, but when his host learned of his mission, he begged Jiri to help him escape then and there. It was his only chance, for he was beginning to feel the security heat as well, and Jiri did not try to talk him into staying. It was a satisfying event. We lost a possible resident agent, but we gained a defector with an enormous amount of information on the party and government situation in the Czech capital. Jiri gained a wife.

Once recruited, a resident agent had to be given secure communications. Two-way radio contact was ruled out. The recruiter could not lug a radio set across the border, cache it, find his target, get the set, brief the new resident on the use of the set, ciphers, and signal plans, and return. Nor would an urban resident be willing to risk operating such an incriminating device in an area equipped to detect illegal transmissions. The few sets that did operate within Eastern Europe were in the hands of rural residents who hid their sets in a barn or manure pile when not in use and, who rarely came on the air. Their only value was to transmit early warning indicators from nearby rail or air traffic.

In most cases communications were maintained by letter with concealed or coded messages to "friends" in West Germany or Canada—a slow and unreliable method of contact. Safer, but even slower, was the "dead drop"—a cemetery, hollow tree, kilometer stone, public toilet, church graveyard, or public park where the resident placed his reports. Couriers serviced these drops on an irregular schedule.

The handling of resident agents was carried out with care and the losses were rare. It was in the routine cross-border operations aimed at tactical targets that the hazards ran high and failures were legion. Some agents were caught or killed on the way in or out. Some who got through were arrested because of suspicious behavior or were turned in by the people they were supposed to contact. But the most damaging losses came from the aggressive counterintelligence operations of the satellite security services.

It was child's play for the Czech and Polish services to send out their own agents as bona fide refugees to report on the mechanics of Allied handling, the émigrés involved, the kind of screening carried out. With this information on hand, they were able to insert agents into the refugee stream tailored to the Allied interest. Once recruited by Allied intelligence, these "agents" carried out their missions with great success, bringing back precise reports of mostly misleading information and glowing accounts of the resident agents they had recruited. As the counteroperations progressed, the East European security services were often able to get their agents hired as spotters or interrogators at the processing centers or even as employees in the clandestine training areas.

They were thus able to learn the identities of Western cross-border agents even before they were dispatched. They were also able to get the names and targets the Western services were working on. In addition, they were able to turn around, or double, legitimate Western agents who were arrested and persuaded by personal or family threats to return with false information and accept another mission.

Oskar L, for example, was a reliable agent of the Berlin base who had completed several missions into Poland. On what was supposed to be his last mission to Warsaw, he was to recruit a senior official of the Ministry of Heavy Industry.

Oskar returned to West Berlin three days late with a packet of Polish steel production statistics for the first half of 1950. During Oskar's debriefing he had to account for all the time he was on his mission—hour by hour. He described how he had gone to his contact's apartment on the first evening, only to be informed that he had just left on a three-day inspection trip for his ministry.

What to do with the three days? He decided to look up an

old girl friend in a suburb of Warsaw who did not know that he had fled the country a year before.

She was glad to see him, and he spent the next two nights with her. On the third day he called again at the ministry official's apartment, found him at home, and persuaded him to cooperate.

He embellished his story with details on the official's apartment, the girl friend, the buses he took, etc.

After the debriefing Oskar told his case officer he wanted to go on another mission. His offer was somewhat surprising for he had stipulated before his Warsaw mission that this would be his last venture before he emigrated to Argentina with American help.

The next day Oskar was informed that he would be given a lie-detector test. His answers to two questions proved that he was lying. "Did you spend two days and nights at your girl friend's apartment?" "Yes." The needles leaped. "Were you arrested during your mission?" "No." The needles leaped again.

His case officer took Oskar off the machine, gave him a drink, and persuaded him that the truth was best for both of them. Oskar confessed that he had been arrested by two plainclothesmen who had the official's apartment under surveillance. He spent the next three days in jail under interrogation and gave the police details on his mission, his employers, and his training. To save himself from ten years in prison, he agreed to go back to Berlin, take on another mission, and report to the police when he returned. If he did not return, his parents in a small village outside Warsaw would get the ten-year sentence.

To protect his parents we played it straight. Oskar was sent back to Warsaw to contact the steel ministry official, ostensibly to get more information from him. We never heard from him again, but there was a good chance both he and his family thus escaped imprisonment.

No estimate can be made of how many bogus agents were

dispatched into Eastern Europe by Western services during these years. The hazards of being penetrated were, of course, recognized, but the closest possible screening, the most careful interrogation and assessment, could not uncover every planted agent. The CIA units involved not only took elaborate precautions to protect the security of their own operations, but did what they could to assist American military intelligence units with name checks, lie-detector tests, and data on the satellite security services. It was a losing battle, as we were to find out in North Korea and North Vietnam.

No claim can be made for a significant return on the heavy investment in these cross-border operations any more than on the airdrops in the Soviet Union. They were started at the insistence of understandably apprehensive military commanders, and they developed their own momentum in the atmosphere of an audacious undertaking against great obstacles. The hard work in documenting and training an agent, the excitement of his successful dispatch, the tension in awaiting his return, the despair at his loss—these often contrived to cloud case officers' judgments on the value of the intelligence their agents were producing.

To dismiss these operations as a total failure, however, is perhaps too smug. We must remember the tenor of the times: World War III was coming, and such operations were the only means of reaching the target. There was, as in the operations into the Soviet Union, a positive by-product: the first generation of CIA operations officers was learning its trade by doing, by developing know-how, both in what to do and what not to do.

But there is no question the operations lasted far longer than they should have. For more than five years the CIA in Europe spent most of its resources on wartime tactical intelligence. For a strategic service initially designed to place long-term agents at key points in a hostile camp, it was a wasteful diversion.

CHINA AND NORTH KOREA

With the Communist takeover of China in the fall of 1949, the second circle extended to the Pacific, for Communist China was then, against all common sense, viewed as a Soviet "satellite." Mainland China became a denied area, curtained off by coastal controls except in the southwest and in Tibet. Illegal operations were the only means of access.

After the Japanese surrender in September 1945 our OSS stations and bases in China were called upon for a time to develop intelligence sources on the activities of the Soviet military forces in northern China. However, as it became increasingly evident that the Chinese Communists were continuing to extend their control of the countryside against the Chinese Nationalists, the Communist-held areas became the main target for espionage operations. These areas, even without fixed border-controls, were effectively denied to outside observers, and the Pentagon required hard data on the location and movement of Communist military units to supplement the sporadic information supplied by the refugees who fled the advancing Communists.

The rapidly changing military situation on the mainland allowed only limited opportunities for penetrating the denied areas. Some refugees were sent back on quick turn-around missions, but CIA's main effort was devoted to finding Chinese civilians who had legitimate reasons for moving into and out of the Communist-occupied areas. Several score of these agents produced a fair amount of tactical information on local military units, living conditions, and civilian morale, but were understandably incapable of providing an overall view of Communist military capabilities, much less Communist intentions.

Several strategic intelligence operations were launched, but they were rendered ineffective by the rapid Communist advances in many areas. Arrangements were made, for example, with a tribal leader in the Ordos Region of Inner Mongolia to establish a permanent base for collecting intelligence in return for the supply of tube wells to irrigate the arid tribal farmlands. Mongol agents were recruited, trained, and equipped with radios, but time proved too short to set up an operating base. Several stay-behind agents with radios were established in other areas not yet overrun by the Communists, but they survived only briefly.

Just as the Communist victory in 1949 created an urgency for military intelligence on China, so the division of Korea into the Soviet-occupied North and U.S.-occupied South in 1945 had created a new urgency for military intelligence in that area. Agents supplied a steady stream of information on Soviet and North Korean military activities and described the role of the Soviet "advisers" who ran both the Communist Party and the armed forces of their easternmost satellite. As early as February 1947, for example, a young Soviet sergeant who had defected to the Americans was carefully briefed and sent back into the Soviet zone. Posing as a loyal Soviet soldier, he moved about freely, talked with troops from a variety of units, and noted everything he saw. He made eight successful missions in the next ten months and produced the bulk of all the Army's information on Soviet troops north of the thirty-eighth parallel that year.

As 1949 ended agents brought back repeated warnings of preparations for an attack on the South. These generalized warnings lost their urgency with constant repetition, however, and no agent forecast the actual offensive of June 25, 1950.

After the outbreak of the Korean war the CIA performed espionage missions assigned by the UN command. South Korean fishing and cargo vessels were used to infiltrate South Koreans behind the North Korean lines. A combined CIA-Navy team secretly reconnoitered the islands off the coast of Korea near Inchon occupied by the North Koreans in preparation for the Inchon landing in September 1950. CIA case officers went along on the Inchon invasion to contact their agents in the area and dispatch them across the lines during the American advance to Seoul. Some reached Pyongyang, the North Korean capital, in early November, but were forced to withdraw on its capture by the enemy.

The main crunch in the Korean war came with the introduction of Chinese forces, and the key figure in providing firsthand evidence of the military situation north of the Korean-Chinese border was a CIA agent. A former high-ranking Chinese Nationalist officer, he was dispatched to the Chinese mainland in the summer of 1950 to assess the military situation in the north. He had been born and brought up in Shanghai and had served with the Nationalist forces in various provinces, including the northern area. Many of his officer colleagues had defected to the Communists before the defeat of the Nationalist armies, and he hastened to get in touch with those he could locate. From his conversations with them, and from his own observations, he was able to establish with some precision the number and distribution of Chinese Communist troops along the Manchurian-North Korean border. His detailed reports, as well as others from Chinese Nationalist sources in the fall of 1950, gave fair warning to the UN command of the imminent Communist crossing of the Yalu River in November 1950.

Although General MacArthur later denied having seen any reports depicting a buildup of Chinese forces along the Yalu, President Truman stated publicly that he had seen and read CIA reports on Chinese troop concentrations in the area which the General either had not read or had ignored.

Once more the strategic approach through the second circle failed. In the hot war in Asia, as in the Cold War in Europe, CIA operations responded mainly to the tactical requirements of the military commanders.

4

TO RUSSIA BY VISA

The early history of CIA espionage in the Soviet Union and its satellites was featured by the transition from "illegal" to "legal" operations. These terms were part of our in-house jargon. "Illegal" was the term used for our airdrop and cross-border operations in direct violation of another country's sovereignty. "Legal" operations, on the other hand, involved the use of agents with normal access to the target area: diplomats, tourists, delegations. Both sets of operations were, of course, illegal in the normal sense.

Even during the illegal phase of operations into the Sino-Soviet orbit, many of CIA's sources in the inner circle were Soviet or other nationals who were temporary or permanent residents. They had no need to cross frontiers surreptitiously or carry forged papers; they moved about legally.

Most of them were recruited in the course of our local operations around the periphery of the Soviet Union. In West Berlin, for example, one of CIA's local contacts in the early fifties was a young German who worked as a courier into East Germany.

During his trips into East Berlin he began a romance with an East Berlin girl, a university student from an educated middle-class family. One day he informed his case officer that his friend had received a scholarship to study in Moscow for two years. She was, according to him, basically pro-Western and could use some money.

A meeting was arranged in West Berlin, and she agreed to accept a passive observer mission during her stay in the Soviet Union. She was trained in observation and reporting and briefed on Soviet counterintelligence practices in Moscow. She was assigned specific targets of technical interest in and around Moscow, and was instructed to report her observations only in person during her summer vacations in East Germany.

She proved to be a cautious but determined agent. Her principal feat was the collection of samples of earth, water, and plant life within the restricted area around the Mozhaysk atomic site near Moscow and their safe delivery to her Berlin contact on her summer holiday. Ingenious, if not foolhardy, she capped her student career in Moscow by including some radioactive pine cones from the same area as decoration for a Christmas gift parcel she sent by normal international mail to a friend in East Germany.

Other "legal" sources within the Soviet Union were a by-product of our counterintelligence work in the Munich area against the KGB headquarters in Karlshorst. A Ukrainian nationalist, for example, was visited by an East German woman with a letter from his family in the Ukraine. He reported the visit to the CIA and agreed to cooperate with the KGB in order to protect his family. After a period of supplying some innocuous émigré gossip to his KGB case officer, he was invited to Karlshorst for a personal meeting. During his stay with the KGB he was given a trip to Moscow and Kiev to see his family—and to solidify his loyalty to the KGB. An alert observer, he came back to Munich with useful observations on both cities.

At the time, these marginal legal activities were only inci-
dental to the larger illegal airdrop and cross-border programs
of the early fifties. In 1954, however, our illegal operations
virtually ceased, and our work began to focus on exploiting
legal access to Soviet terrain.

Within a year of Stalin's death in March 1953, the climate
of the Cold War thawed slightly. The new leaders in Moscow
were faced with the immediate problem of succession at
home and with riots, verging on revolution, in East Germany
in June 1953. In Europe tension eased as the new leaders
began negotiations that would eventually (in 1955) culminate
in an Austrian peace treaty and withdrawal of Soviet troops.
In Washington a Soviet military move seemed "less imminent." Western Europe had not succumbed to its domestic
Communist parties, and Greece and Turkey were intact.
The Korean armistice was signed in July 1953. Above all,
Stalin's successor, Khrushchev, now spoke in more moderate
terms, and even looked favorably on a proposed summit meeting.

Khrushchev's relaxation of internal restrictions on the
Soviet citizen was accompanied by an easing of controls on
foreign visitors. Soviet officials abroad, virtually caged in
compounds under Stalin, slowly became accessible to social
contacts. Soviet scientists and scholars began to appear at
international conferences outside the Soviet Union. The isolation of foreign embassies in Moscow became less stringent,
the police surveillance less obtrusive. Delegations of foreign
professionals for the first time crossed the thresholds of
Soviet laboratories and scientific institutes. Collaboration
with the West on such nonmilitary projects as the International Geophysical Year brought face to face scientific men
who had not up to then been permitted even to correspond.

The thaw did not, however, curtail the Pentagon's demands for secret intelligence on Soviet weapons, advanced
research, and technical capacity. Only the urgency of early
warning diminished.

Khrushchev's thaw provided the conditions for "legal operations," the gathering of intelligence by foreigners with legal documents and proper Soviet visas. These legal travelers were not spies in the narrow sense. They were untrained, they did not seek out classified information or secret military installations, they did not try to recruit Soviet citizens. They provided an easy and inexpensive means to look at visible intelligence targets in the main metropolitan areas and along the main transportation routes. As the number of visitors to the Soviet Union increased, tourist reports and tourist cameras began to produce "instant intelligence" of interest to the Pentagon.

The new tourists were a global assortment, and many were happy to cooperate in a purposeful legal enterprise. There were Americans, western Europeans, and third-world nationals. There were government officials, visiting diplomats, East-West traders, chess players, church leaders, athletes, ordinary tourists. There were port-callers, both American and foreign. They did precisely what every Soviet-sponsored tourist or official visitor during and after World War II had done abroad as part of normal routine: observe and report. In this case, however, they were all volunteers.

It took a great deal of painstaking work to determine what travelers were planning to visit the Soviet Union and where they planned to go. In each case, once the travelers' routes were clear, a simple kind of triptych was prepared for each one with points of interest for observing or photographing: a specific factory, railroad yard, or port installation, construction sites, civil aircraft, or liquid oxygen tank cars. They bought samples of Soviet merchandise or picked up any electronic gadget available for sale. They were briefed on their tasks and warned to avoid any behavior that might bring a charge of spying. They were told what kind of physical surveillance, bugging, or provocative approaches they might encounter.

A major task for the intelligence analysts in Washington was to convert the technical requirements on atomic energy, guided missile, and aircraft production installations into simple demands for visual observation from trains, planes, or roads that could be carried out by a traveler with no particular technical education. This they did with great competence. The color of the smoke coming out of a specified factory chimney or the color of a sandpile outside a specified plant was enough to give them the answers they wanted.

The Pentagon's main intelligence concern in the mid-fifties was the state of Soviet missilery. The running controversy between the Air Force and other intelligence agencies over the "missile gap" was fanned into flame by the firing of the Soviet Sputnik on October 4, 1957; many of the observers who visited the USSR in the next two years focused on missile targets guided by detailed instructions on specific missile installations.

Photographs of missile installations taken from civil, non-jet airplanes were of the greatest value. Tourist cameras produced the first "small format" aerial photographs of the SA-2 surface-to-air missile systems spotted earlier by the U-2s. They uncovered SA-2 systems deployed in previously unreported locations. They provided stereophotos of a missile assembly plant and storage area. Their coverage extended to broader areas: from aircraft serial numbers that resulted in new American estimates of Soviet aircraft production to the first photos of several classes of Soviet submarines.

Not all visitors were equally productive. An American chess player was asked to answer some simple questions after his match with a Soviet opponent. In three hours' play the pair did not exchange a single word, and our American friend did not remember his opponent's name or what he looked like.

And then there was romance. A young American graduate student, officially contacted in Paris, made his trip, fell in love with a young ballerina, and later married her.

The coverage of observable targets by legal travelers peaked in 1958–60 and contributed no small share to closing the "missile gap" of the last Eisenhower years. It also contributed many minor and some major items of information on Soviet long-range bombers, nuclear propulsion systems, manned space flight, and bacteriological warfare capabilities.

During those years not only were more and more outside tourists briefed to look and report, but individual Westerners, mainly Americans, were recruited by the CIA to go to the Soviet Union on a prearranged itinerary and report in depth on the key target installations that were emerging from earlier observer and U-2 reporting. In some cases one man was sent on a trip to cover a single target. In others an individual was given a set of requirements generally suited to his professional competence.

The men sent in on these "mounted" operations were much more qualified than the ordinary tourist who was asked to take a photograph or two. They almost all spoke Russian and had some knowledge of the USSR. Many were academics—graduate students or professors who were eager to see, usually for the first time, the country of their specialization. They were carefully screened before being invited on the expense-paid visit, and those who were accepted received a week or more of intensive briefing before they took off. Many were young, with a sense of adventure. Settled scholars were more cautious, but equally cooperative.

These tourists provided an extraordinary amount of information on high-priority targets. They supplied thousands of photographs of facilities for the production of intercontinental ballistic missiles and of the sites at which ICBMs had been deployed. They photographed more than a dozen SAM missile sites. They described an "unusual" submarine, one of the first Soviet nuclear subs, and a missile-launching destroyer. Their streams of reports on aircraft markings doubled the Pentagon's estimate of the production of one type of aircraft. They located scores of missile support facilities and direction-finding antennas.

The tourists contributed substantially to our ability to keep track of the early stages of the Soviet antiballistic missile (ABM) program: the construction of a new testing range, an institute involved in a 1956 antimissile test, activity in and around several ABM sites in the Leningrad area. These installations were also described in some detail by returning German technicians who had worked in institutes or plants connected with ABM development and by several agent sources.

Up until 1960, the Soviet internal security services, mainly the Internal Directorate of the KGB, took an almost benign view of these foreign visitors. A stubborn Western professor who insisted on photographing an off-limits military installation for his own private collection was handled most politely by the police observing him—they treated him like a wayward child. In 1958 and 1959 some of the more active travelers were quietly arrested and expelled without fanfare. The KGB was perfectly aware of the CIA program. They simply chose to turn a half-blind eye on eager tourists who did not go too far.

The technical intelligence requirements of the time extended far beyond missiles and military hardware. The analysts in Washington were relatively ignorant across the whole range of Soviet industrial production—facilities, output, technology, bottlenecks. What they needed were the products themselves, and these were obtainable both inside the Soviet orbit and, from the mid-fifties on, outside.

Consumer goods like typewriters were available to foreign tourists in the big cities. The serial numbers of Soviet-made boxcars and civilian airplanes could be observed both in Russia and in Eastern Europe. Soviet trade fairs often included products of Soviet technology that could be examined and photographed. Out of these routine collections of Soviet materials, the analysts were able to extract annual production figures, availability of machine tools, alloys employed, etc. As more and more Soviet manufactures reached foreign markets, Soviet industrial capacity could be sketched in ever more precise fashion.

In 1955–56 Soviet military equipment suddenly became accessible outside Russia and the satellites. Part of Moscow's new program to develop friendly relations with third world countries involved the provision of military aid, and military equipment began flowing into Indonesia, India, the United Arab Republic, and into Afghanistan, Iraq, and Syria. Here, on the ground, were many of the key items of Soviet military hardware in whose technology and performance the Pentagon had an overriding interest: machine guns, antitank guns, artillery pieces, antiaircraft systems, the latest MIG fighters. The Pentagon wanted samples, specifications, performance capabilities.

The value of the target weapons were graded by the armed services. Reward money in tens or hundreds of thousands of dollars was assigned for the procurement of priority items. CIA used its contacts abroad to get not only specimens but training and equipment manuals for such sophisticated equipment as the most advanced Soviet ground-to-air missile systems.

During the sixties about ninety percent of the Soviet matériel supplied to the Department of Defense came from CIA agent sources. The principal instrument for getting this matériel was local military sources handling or servicing the equipment in the countries to which it was sent. In some of these receiving countries the Soviet connection was politically unacceptable, and indigenous officers could sometimes be prevailed upon to provide the United States with information against "the enemy." Other cases required the painstaking development of general staff or civilian contacts with access to this highly classified information.

The value of this secret procurement program was substantial. Not only did it afford evidence of the advanced technology available to the Russians, but specific data on specific weapons permitted the Pentagon's research and development program to invest its funds more efficiently. In our missile and antimissile programs, in our submarine and antisubmarine technology, in our tank and antitank work, in

our aircraft and antiaircraft development, precise knowledge
of Soviet weapons saved billions.

During the fifties and sixties no sources on Soviet industry
and technology were left untapped by the Pentagon, the State
Department, and the CIA. One of the projects that fell
within the mission of CIA was the inspection of mail from
the Soviet Union to other parts of the world.

Various arrangements were made in friendly countries for
the screening and examination of the mail that came through
Soviet censorship, but the most systematic program was carried out in New York. The mail-cover operation started in
1952 with the recording of information on the outside of
envelopes. But within a year the technical facilities were in
place to open and close envelopes and examine or copy the
contents without leaving any indications of tampering.
Throughout the fifties this painstaking sifting and examination of mail from the Soviet Union produced thousands of
items of information on technical, industrial, and administrative topics. As the mail-intercept program developed and
the requirements for positive intelligence on Soviet targets
decreased, both the mail-cover and intercept work concentrated more on counterintelligence—looking for leads to
Soviet intelligence connections with American residents.
These intercepts were of principal interest to the Federal
Bureau of Investigation.

Twenty years later the intercept program was declared
"illegal and improper" by the Rockefeller Commission.
Though several attorneys general and postmasters general
approved the program over the years, it clearly violated federal law. The pragmatic reasons for starting this work in the
atmosphere of the early fifties is understandable. Its continuance to 1973 is less so.

The Khrushchev "thaw" that had facilitated our intelligence gathering operations during the fifties came to an
abrupt halt at the end of the decade. The boom was lowered
in May of 1960.

On Sunday, the first of May, Francis Gary Powers took off

in a U-2 plane from Pakistan on a nine-hour flight to Norway, most of it over Soviet terrain. Thirteen hundred miles into Russia, flying at 65,000 feet, he was making a ninety-degree turn to the north over the industrial complex of Sverdlovsk when his plane went down.

Four days later Khrushchev announced the shooting down of an American plane to the Supreme Soviet, and let Washington come up with its lame cover story of a missing weather-observation plane. He said that Powers was "alive and kicking," that he had confessed, and that he would be tried for espionage.

On May 11 President Eisenhower assumed full responsibility for the U-2 flight. He had personally approved the Powers mission—in spite of the fact that he was to meet with Khrushchev at a summit conference in Paris on May 16. Angered by Eisenhower's refusal to apologize for past "aggressions," Khrushchev boycotted the Four Power session after the first day and withdrew his invitation to the President to visit the Soviet Union. Then he threatened to solve the Berlin problem by signing a separate peace treaty with East Germany. The thaw congealed.

Within the Soviet Union the border guards increased baggage checks, internal surveillance of foreigners was intensified, and tourists were arrested for taking illegal photographs. The campaign against American espionage and agitation featured massive publicity for Soviet "vigilance," the arrest and trial of Soviet citizens allegedly recruited by American tourists, and the arrest, trial, and expulsion of at least a dozen tourists, mostly American. This new hard line against the United States curtailed many of our intelligence operations, particularly those involving tourists.

The U-2, however, signalled a major breakthrough in our reconnaissance of the Soviet military capacity. Technology replaced human sources—illegal agents, legal travelers, random visitors, correspondents—to produce *visible* evidence of Soviet and Warsaw Pact capabilities.

The desirability of photographic reconnaissance of the

Soviet Union had been recognized since the late forties when propeller airplanes dropped the first American agents into the Ukraine. The jet engine helped the CIA achieve its goal: a high-speed, high-altitude airplane capable of photographing 125-mile strips of Soviet terrain with exact definition.

Plans for the U-2 plane were approved by the Air Force in December 1954, and it was built and tested under secure conditions during the next two years. Assigned to Germany and Turkey in late 1956 as "meteorological squadrons," the U-2s were first employed to photograph Soviet border areas, to take atmospheric samples, and to observe test rocket launchings.

Soviet air defenses tracked the U-2 flights from the beginning and sent up missiles that could not reach their target, for the essential purpose of the U-2 was to reduce the chance of interception to zero. For almost four years these flights eluded interception—and Soviet diplomatic protests. When, finally, Soviet countermeasures caught up with the elusive target in May 1960, the U-2 program had produced without loss of life invaluable information on the major military and industrial targets in the Soviet Union and Eastern Europe.

The CIA, rather than the Air Force, was assigned the task of developing, building, and operating the U-2s because of the overriding need for secrecy. The CIA handled the contracts with the builders, recruited the pilots, and secured the secret bases abroad through arrangements made with local security services. The intelligence directorate of the CIA set up a secure system for processing the photographic take and distributing the results to a narrow circle of need-to-know units in the intelligence community.

Illegal spy flights reached their zenith with the launch of Tiros 1 (Television and Infra-Red Observation Satellite) in April 1960 and of Midas (Missile Defense Alarm System) the following month. The succeeding generations of reconnaissance satellites opened up the earth's terrain to continuous live observation. In the process illegal flights became legal.

They became an internationally accepted mode of spying for the simple reason that no nation could take effective action against them.

In the past fifteen years the U-2 and reconnaissance satellites have been the main instrument for early warning and for the detection of military-industrial structures. They are an essential element in verifying Soviet compliance with missile or arms agreements. Their eyes and their ears play an increasingly refined role in recording visible, audible, or electronic events within the Soviet Union.

They cannot, however, record what goes on beneath the roofs of the military research institutes they photograph. They cannot record the conversations or supply the minutes of committee meetings in the Politburo, Central Committee offices, or General Staff headquarters. They cannot record the *intention* of the Politburo to send offensive missiles to Cuba or tanks to Angola. They cannot, in short, reach into men's heads to determine their thoughts, plans, and goals.

For these invisible targets men are still needed—members of the Soviet establishment with access to classified information in the normal course of their careers. The Russians need their men in Washington. We need ours in Moscow.

5

RECRUITING RUSSIANS

Some of the best spies are often men who have volunteered their services. They simply walk in or write in, say what they have to offer, explain the reasons for their action, and propose a deal.

A Soviet official who, for whatever reasons, wants to work for the Americans makes his approach as directly as possible and supplies immediate proof that he is the man he says he is and that he has firsthand information (ideally, with samples) of real value to American intelligence. A "walk-in" of any sophistication knows that he must allay the immediate suspicion that he is a phony or a provocateur sent by Soviet intelligence.

The most productive CIA Soviet agent of the fifties (whom I shall call Major B) recruited himself quickly and expertly in Vienna during the Allied occupation of Austria. The most valuable Soviet agent of the sixties, Colonel Penkovsky, recruited himself with great difficulty in Moscow and London.

TWO AGENTS-IN-PLACE

On New Year's Day 1953 a short, neatly dressed man handed a letter to an American vice-consul about to enter his car with a girl friend in the international sector of Vienna. It read: "I am a Soviet officer. I wish to meet with an American officer with the object of offering certain services. . . ." The letter specified the time and place for a meeting, at which the Russian satisfactorily identified himself as a major assigned to the Vienna office of Soviet military intelligence—the GRU. For the next six years Major B was the key CIA source on Soviet military matters.

I took a particular interest in the self-recruitment of Major B because he had been hailed by some of my colleagues as an example of a real "ideological" agent, a Russian who had come to us purely out of principle. In conversations with the operations officers involved and from reading his case file, it was clear that Major B had a strong sense of social injustice. Born in 1923, the son of a peasant, he lived through Stalin's collectivization program and retained an enduring hatred for the regime's continuing mistreatment of the poor peasants. Yet it was his own personal circumstances that triggered his act. He was being criticized by his GRU chief for recruiting only a few useless agents, one of whom, a Serbian woman, he had taken on as his mistress without informing his boss. When his wife and child arrived from the Soviet Union, he began to run short of the money needed to support two establishments.

Only late in his first conversation with a CIA officer did he disclose, almost casually, that he had offered his services because he had "an affair to straighten out" and that he came to CIA only "as an extreme measure." Political principle is rarely the sole or main reason for the transfer of a man's allegiance, and Major B was no exception.

He and one CIA case officer met secretly once or twice a

month in comfortable middle-class surroundings, where their sessions often lasted eight or nine hours. They became intimate companions with a strong mutual affection. B found in his case officer the only man he had ever been able to talk to in his adult years about his feelings and anxieties, his job frustrations, and his attitude to his bosses and the regime. After one of their many discussions about the relative merits of the CIA and the GRU, B expressed his feelings about the two services:

> This is what I like about your organization. You can find time to drink and relax. It is an entirely human approach. You have respect and regard for an individual. With us, of course, the individual is nothing, and the Government's interest is everything.

As the years went by, his secret contacts with the CIA became "nerve-wracking." The GRU, apparently growing suspicious, asked him to return to headquarters.

In his last meeting before going back to Moscow he felt shaky but remarkably confident. He was urged by his case officer to defect, but he refused: "I am not the man for that." Arrangements were made to meet him in Moscow if he so wished.

Major B was apparently arrested in February 1959, shortly after his return to Moscow, but the Soviet authorities kept his arrest quiet in order to use him against the CIA. We continued the contact in the hope of keeping him alive, but immediately after an emergency meeting with him in October 1959, the CIA case officer was arrested. After attempting to cajole him to work for the GRU, the Soviet security officials released him on the basis of his diplomatic immunity. According to an official Soviet announcement, Major B was executed shortly thereafter.

Major B was the most valuable source of Soviet military intelligence of the time. He provided technical specifications on Soviet conventional weapons, including the first information on several new Soviet tanks. He furnished detailed order of battle data and tables of equipment for Soviet tank, mechanized, and rifle divisions. He reported large increases in the number of amphibious vehicles and armored personnel carriers a full eighteen months before they were spotted by other sources. His other firsts included the description of several tactical missile systems and reports on the existence of Soviet nuclear submarines, a new heavy tank division, and Soviet Army tactics in the utilization of atomic weapons.

This one man's reporting had a direct and substantial effect on U.S. military organization, doctrine, and tactics, and saved the Pentagon at least a half-billion dollars in its research and development program.

The second agent-in-place, unlike Major B, was a well-educated aristocrat—the most publicized of CIA agents: Oleg Penkovsky. The son of upper-class pre-Bolshevik parents, he was a brilliant man who became a full colonel at the age of thirty. He was sophisticated and extravagant, with a taste for luxuries from white nylon sheets to good porcelain and fine ladies. Not merely articulate, but voluble, he was a dynamo of energy. He hit like a cyclone.

His first approach to the Americans resembled that of B in Vienna. After reconnoitering the American Embassy in Moscow for several days, and noting that all visitors were being photographed from a KGB safe house across the way, he strolled along the unlighted banks of the Moscow River, and at 11 P.M. on August 12, 1960, he approached a pair of obviously American tourists taking a walk. As an earnest of his bona fides, he gave them some hitherto undisclosed details on the shooting down of the U-2 plane the previous May—fourteen rockets had been fired, there had been no direct hits, one near-burst had brought it down, etc. He then handed them a letter to be delivered to the American Embassy.

The letter offered his services to the United States "for the ideals of a truly free world and of democracy for mankind." It

stated that he had "very important materials on many subjects of exceptionally great interest" and wished to transmit
them to the Americans through a dead drop whose description he enclosed or through a drop designated by the Americans.

In the atmosphere of the time, with the antispy crusade in
full swing, this approach by an anonymous stroller along the
Moscow River was read by the embassy and by Washington
as a possible KGB provocation, a clumsy effort to implicate an
American official in espionage as another proof to the Soviet
citizenry of the need for vigilance. Accordingly, no attempt
was made to establish contact.

Fortunately, Penkovsky was persistent. In December,
under cover of his civilian job in the State Committee for
Science and Technology, he asked a visiting British scientist
to deliver a package to the American Embassy. The scientist
refused. Penkovsky then actually passed a bulky sealed envelope to a Canadian trade official who, equally skeptical,
returned it intact.

Finally, on March 10, 1961, Penkovsky told a member of a
British commercial delegation led by a Mr. Greville Wynne
that he would soon head a Soviet delegation on a return visit
to England. He handed Wynne some papers and a letter. The
letter was addressed to the President of the United States and
the Queen of England.

On April 20, two British and two American intelligence
officers sat down with Penkovsky in a London hotel and let
him talk. He explained that various personal factors had entered into his decision to work against the Soviet regime. His
principal motivation, however, was his overwhelming fear
that Khrushchev, then at the height of his power, would use
his atomic weapons to destroy the human race. He hated
Khrushchev and the system. Khrushchev *was* the system,
and he had to stop him from the threatened holocaust. It was
an *idée fixe* possible only in a brilliant mind.

Over the next two years, through carefully arranged contacts in Moscow, Penkovsky supplied Western intelligence with the most valuable strategic military information produced by an agent since World War II.

His detailed reports on Soviet strategic offensive and defensive capabilities provided a firm basis for American estimates on Soviet ICBM strength, on Soviet ABM capabilities, and on Soviet doctrines of strategic and tactical nuclear warfare. He provided comprehensive details on Soviet medium-range missile systems, unique data on tactical surface-to-air missiles, and details on antimissile systems and locations. On ten separate occasions between mid-July 1961 and September 1962 Penkovsky supplied timely and valuable comments of senior Soviet generals on Khrushchev's announced effort to force the Allies out of Berlin.

Largely through Penkovsky, when the Cuban missile crisis came to a head in October 1962, President Kennedy *knew* the realities of Soviet missile capability (it was inferior to the American) and could safely work on that premise. Further, the data provided by Penkovsky on the medium-range missile system deployed in Cuba by the Russians permitted American intelligence to make precise estimates of the construction stages and the dates for operational readiness of the Soviet missiles—a crucial factor in the timing of the American responses. Pentagon concern over a Soviet countermove against Berlin in response to the American action against Cuba was moderated by his reporting.

Without Penkovsky's reporting the Soviet-American confrontation over Cuba would have been an even more precarious event than it was.

By that time, however, Penkovsky was apparently already under Soviet surveillance. There is no definitive evidence on what led KGB counterintelligence to suspect him, but it is likely that he was under close investigation in the summer of 1962 and placed under KGB control by mid-September. In May of 1963 he was tried in open court, and, according to official report, later executed for his espionage activities.

ACCESS AND APPROACHES

There have been other, less valuable Soviet walk-ins over
the years, and countless East European volunteers, as well as
a few Chinese. Each CIA station abroad is prepared to
handle their abrupt, and welcome, appearance as securely
and critically as possible. To establish a walk-in's authentic-
ity, or bona fides, requires fast, competent action in inter-
rogating him, checking out his statements, and determining
the nature of his access to classified Soviet diplomatic or
intelligence information. Only then can the operation start
with the arrangement of secret meetings acceptable to both
sides.

Walk-ins simply require efficient reaction. Recruiting a
Soviet official requires a persistent, long-term effort. From
the late forties on CIA has concentrated many of its resources
on spotting and recruiting Soviet officials who are judged to
be both vulnerable and valuable. The main factor in this
effort is their accessibility: How open are they to Western or
third world contacts? As the Cold War waned and slowly gave
way to the present state of official détente, CIA access to
Soviet officialdom abroad steadily improved.

In the postwar years under Stalin the physical isolation of
Soviet installations outside the Soviet Union and the social
isolation of Soviet officials made them all but unreachable.
Soviet embassies and trade missions in Western capitals were
fenced-in compounds where the postwar crop of Stalinist
officials not only worked, but ate, slept, and drank. Their
families normally were kept hostage in Moscow.

When Soviet officials began appearing at diplomatic receptions in the early fifties they were for the most part a crude
lot, reliable but incompetent party hacks, cautious insecure
men who dressed badly, talked badly even through interpreters, and were badly versed in foreign ways. The man in the
baggy trousers became a stock caricature in the West. A few
were gradually permitted to live in private residences outside

the official compound, but no Soviet official was allowed to have a nonofficial contact with a Westerner.

With Khrushchev's thaw and the opening up of Soviet diplomatic interest in the third world, the quality and the way of life of Soviet officials abroad changed radically. More and more of the new breed of Soviet bureaucrats were assigned abroad—carefully selected men, well trained in area and language studies, capable of acting with self-assurance outside their own closed society. Many of them were graduates of four- and six-year courses in international affairs. Many had behind them practical careers in economics, engineering, or journalism. The intelligence officers were the products of rigorous KGB and GRU schooling. As the years went by, many became specialists in their country or region of assignment. These men today are comfortable and effective at a dinner party of corporate executives in New York City or a bankers' luncheon in Bonn.

The most talented among these officials were those working for the KGB—and they became the principal CIA targets.

As scores of new Soviet embassies and trade missions opened up in Asia and Africa, as old missions expanded, KGB officers swelled their ranks. They came with broad missions, not only to recruit agents for political and military intelligence, but to engage in political action and secret propaganda operations, to help organize student and labor groups, to subsidize politicians and government officials, to select students for the Friendship University in Moscow. They recruited foreign office clerks, legislators, student leaders, ministry of education officials, journalists and newspaper editors, security service officials, policemen, businessmen, junior officers and soldiers.

They were assisted in their task by the East European intelligence services, whose officers followed the flag of their expanding embassies and trade missions abroad. The Polish and Czech intelligence services were especially helpful to Moscow with their unique access to ethnic groups not open to Soviet contact. Even in the late sixties the Rumanian intelligence service cooperated with the KGB in spite of the semi-independent line followed by the Rumanian Foreign Office. After the Soviet-Cuban rapprochement in 1968 the Cuban Intelligence Service began close cooperation with the KGB.

As Soviet intelligence officers became more gregarious, they became more accessible. They cultivated the social acquaintance of local government officials and businessmen, Western and third world diplomats, and American Embassy officers. They joined social and athletic clubs, lunched and dined out, threw caviar-drenched parties. They could be approached at diplomatic receptions or fashionable restaurants. The KGB clearly was willing to expose its new breed of officers to Western scrutiny as the price it must pay for increasing the range of its own operations.

The easiest, and least productive, CIA recruiting exercise in these early years (our files on Soviet diplomats were still rather thin) was the "cold approach," a flat proposal that he cooperate with us to a man about whom we knew very little.

There was, to start with, the "nickel pitch." A CIA officer telephoned a KGB official whom he did not know and suggested the official work for American intelligence. If the Russian did not hang up at once, the caller would make a specific proposal, often involving a large sum of American dollars, and suggest a safe meeting place. Normally, the Russian said "No," sometimes profanely, often nervously. Even the turndowns had some psychological value: Why was *he* selected for CIA attention? If he reported the call to his superiors, they would have to ask themselves the same question.

The nickel pitch was mainly a game, but other cold approaches were more sustained, as the following two cases illustrate. In both the scenario was played out on a railroad train. These approaches, like all our operations, were written up in detail by the case officers involved, both for the record

and for the benefit of other operations officers. I read the
contact report of the first railway case and talked at length
with the case officer who had made the approach, a warm
volatile man with more than a touch of the Slavic soul himself. His story impressed me as a human document displaying
a simple political loyalty most Westerners are likely to over-
look. It is worth retelling.

A Communist attaché in a European capital had come to
the attention of the local CIA station because he had made no
observable contacts at all during the first year of his assignment. He was a man with a peasant face and peasant de-
meanor, in his mid-forties, unmarried. Every effort to meet
him and size him up failed. The only facts we knew were the
items on his visa application.

A few weeks before the end of his tour we discovered that
he planned to go home by rail. We had his train and his
compartment number, and placed a fluent Russian-speaking
CIA officer in the next car. He departed on schedule and
promptly locked himself into his private compartment.

As the train reached the Austrian border, a series of
passport control and customs officials knocked on his door,
inspected his passport and baggage, and moved on. Within
minutes there was another knock. Again he unlocked his
door, this time to a man who greeted him in Russian and
forced his way into the compartment.

"I just want to talk to you for a while. Have no concern."

A two-hour conversation followed as the train rolled
through the Austrian countryside. It was a very human talk.

The CIA officer proposed that the attaché work on behalf
of the Americans after returning to his home assignment. He
discoursed on the main themes: the threat of war, the aggressive nature of the Soviet regime, the values at stake, the high
purposes of the Western Allies. He emphasized the uncer-
tainties of life in a police state. He held out the prospect of a
safe and prosperous life in the West after he completed his
assignment.

The attaché's reaction was disarming. He thanked his visitor for showing so much concern for an official of such low standing and insisted he would be in no position to supply any information that would be of real value to the West. He then explained very simply why he would not be disloyal to his country or his party:

"I lived in a small village. My father was an uneducated man who earned his living by working on a railroad crew that inspected and repaired the roadbed over a twenty-mile stretch. Each day, ten hours a day, he worked with his back. If it had not been for the party—and the war—I would be doing the same thing.

"When the Germans came, I went into the woods and joined the partisans. I was only a boy, but they used me to carry messages and get food from the nearby villages. The leader of the partisans was a young Communist who liked me, and when the war was over, he recommended me for an award. The local party official arranged for me to get my high-school education. I worked hard, and the party sent me to a technical college. After that they gave me an assignment in Defense, and then one day they asked me to take this assignment abroad. It was something I never could have hoped for.

"So you see why I cannot do what you ask. I owe my life to the party. I am an educated man because of the party. I have lived in the West because of the party. If it had not been for the party, I would be working on a road gang like my father. I can never be disloyal to the party."

He clearly meant what he said, and the parting of the two men was almost affectionate.

Another approach to an official on his way home was more comic than human.

On this occasion the target was a sophisticated senior diplomat on whom CIA had been working during the entire course of his two-year assignment. He had certain weaknesses: a taste for high Western living, an interest in European women, and (we thought) an uncertain status in his home ministry—mainly because he was Jewish. Although he had been active in the social life of the diplomatic community, we had found no way to approach him directly. Several cold approaches elicited no reaction whatever: letters sent to his home, a message delivered through a non-European diplomat, telephone calls for a meeting. He knew he was being chased.

At the end of his assignment he went home by rail. Two CIA officers were placed on the same train, and two attempts were made to talk to him: once by a knock on his compartment door, once in the dining car. Both were rebuffed.

The last train stop before it crossed into Soviet-controlled territory was in West Berlin. The CIA officers determined to make a final attempt. They got off the train as the passport officials got on and found a large advertising placard. On its back they lettered a message in block capitals and carried it from the station to the track on which the train was waiting.

As they came alongside the diplomat's compartment, they waited. After a few minutes he got up from his seat to take a stretch and looked out on the platform. They immediately displayed their sign:

YOU ARE IN REAL TROUBLE. COME WITH US.

He looked at the sign, smiled, and thumbed his nose at his would-be recruiters.

These are the failures one can recount. There were isolated successes in a decade of cold approaches, but their recital, however vague, could only accrue to Soviet benefit.

The most substantial CIA effort from the mid-fifties on was devoted to the recruitment of Soviet or satellite senior intelligence officers whom we had come to know well, directly or indirectly, over the years of their service abroad.

These efforts were directed at officers who were judged to be vulnerable to recruitment for specific personal reasons. Their vulnerability was assessed on the basis of broad-ranging profiles reflecting their personality, living habits, and social attitudes. The information that went into their profiles, often collected over a period of years, was obtained from innumerable sources: reports on and surveillance of their movements, associations with Western or neutral diplomats, police reports, and any so-called "access agents" who had dealings with them: travel agents, real estate men, printshop salesmen, etc. In some cases double agents—Soviet or Polish agents turned by the CIA—were able to provide insights into the temperament and political attitudes of their case officers on the other side.

In selecting vulnerable targets during the fifties many naïve assumptions underlay some of the judgments on what made a Soviet, Polish, or Czech intelligence officer a likely candidate for recruitment. These assumptions were at least in part provoked by the Cold War mentality of the time and its distortions of Soviet reality. Experience proved most of these notions flatly untrue—notions such as the following:

—A Soviet official who enjoys the fleshpots of Western living must be unreliable and highly suspect by his own security people. False: Like Americans or Germans, Russians or Poles make the most out of a foreign assignment without moral qualms.

—A Soviet case officer is in serious trouble with his superiors when he loses or mismanages an agent or when he is exposed in public. Afraid of being demoted, sacked, or sent back to Russia for a term in labor camp, he will seek a way out. False: Like other services, the KGB and GRU accept a modicum of incompetence and indiscretion as a fact of life.

—A Soviet case officer who is a heavy drinker, whoremaster, or homosexual is an easy mark for recruitment. False: Drinking and adultery are not confined to capitalist societies, and homosexuality is a greater handle for blackmail against an American than a Slav.

—A bureaucratic upheaval in Moscow headquarters, as in Beria's fall in 1954, will impel case officers in the field connected with, say, the Beria clique, to find a way out of returning to Moscow. True only in rare instances.

—If a Soviet official makes disparaging remarks about life in Russia or about Stalin or Khrushchev, he is a disloyal citizen. False: Even in Russia, criticism is not a sign of treason.

Operations based on these premises normally failed.

A thirty-five-year-old KGB Latin American specialist was assigned on his first tour to Central America. Fluent in Spanish, a good dancer, and an ostentatious flirt, he cut a wide swath in the society of a small city with a small upper class.

Surveillance reports began to build up a picture of frequent drunken excursions, and identified some of the local women, mostly married, with whom the KGB officer was carrying on a series of sporadic affairs. It was assumed that the Soviet ambassador, a stern and straitlaced Russian, would not have approved had he known of his subordinate's private behavior. It was rumored that the KGB security chief in the embassy was concerned.

At a diplomatic reception where everyone in town was present, a CIA case officer made a point of engaging the KGB officer in conversation. In quiet tones, the American diplomat quickly ran down the dates and women involved in his recent assignations, and capped his talk with the name of a known homosexual with whom the KGB man had recently developed a close association. The KGB officer listened impassively, sipping his drink. When the pitch was made—"If you will cooperate with us, we'll keep all this quiet"—he nodded, politely rejected the offer, and moved away. He completed his tour without breaking off his drinking or philandering.

A KGB officer with an even more checkered career abroad proved to be equally impervious even under the stress of more aggressive CIA measures. Highly talented, fluent in four languages, with three foreign assignments behind him, he also had a weakness for alcohol and women. He had been in some kind of trouble on each of his overseas tours. In Paris he had run through a string of mistresses and got into several publicized brawls. During his assignment to Washington he was drunk in public on several occasions, and he made the front page by being involved in a motorboat collision on the Potomac. His professional competence must have exceeded his private vices in the eyes of his superiors, who continued to post him abroad.

Their patience, however, was finally beginning to run out. Sources within the Soviet Embassy informed CIA that he was now being carefully watched by his own security people and had been informed by his ambassador that this was his last overseas assignment. A brilliant but fundamentally unstable man, by now addicted to the behavioral freedoms of living abroad, he was at this point in his career judged to be vulnerable.

CIA put on the pressure. Shortly after the fall of Malenkov in 1954, the CIA planted an article in a local newspaper on the dismissal, in the course of which the KGB officer was described as a protégé of Malenkov whose future was now imperiled. About the same time a sum of money was deposited in his name in a New York bank, and the deposit slip sent to him at his embassy. Finally, a book about Stalin's purges in the thirties was mailed to his home. In it was a letter suggesting that he work for the Americans until the end of his tour and then defect to the West.

He did not react to the invitation, nor change his way of life. Several attempts to reach him on the telephone were rebuffed. He departed for Moscow several months before the end of his tour.

The success of a recruitment proposal is often contingent upon the confidence the target official has in the man who makes the proposal. A professional intelligence officer is almost neurotically sensitive to any approach as a provocation: Either the other side is trying to provoke him into behavior that can ruin his career, or his own side is simply testing his loyalty by setting up a tempting scenario. Nor is he willing to entrust his own security, if not his life, to any man whose competence or discretion he does not completely trust.

Carefully tailored approaches, using a non-American diplomat as intermediary, have often been successful in at least bringing the KGB officer into direct contact with the CIA for a face-to-face discussion.

Since the mid-fifties these direct contacts between CIA and KGB case officers have become more frequent. Both sides, of course, are committed to the same end: to size up the other man, to wring from him any political intelligence worth reporting, and to let him know he is welcome to change sides. In many of these encounters the question naturally arises as to who is getting the most from the other, but there are tangible profits to the CIA even when the relationship does not lead to a recruitment. These encounters have permitted our case officers to become personally familiar, and therefore more sure-footed, with their adversaries. They have also provided political insights into Soviet thinking that cannot be gained in any other way. On one occasion, for example, a doctrinally sophisticated KGB officer analyzed the Chinese commune experiment in depth and provided the political analysts in Washington with a perspective they could not create on their own. In another case, a realistic and persuasive account of long-term Soviet interests in the Near East by a KGB Arab specialist served the same purpose.

The ultimate goal of these contacts of course, was to explore for psychological weaknesses in any of these KGB officers that might provide an avenue for recruitment. In some cases the direct personal approach led eventually to several defections from KGB ranks. In a handful of cases during the sixties it led to clean-cut recruitments.

Such direct associations between CIA and Soviet case officers, each interested in recruiting the other, provide easy opportunities for provocation. On more than one occasion in the past ten years the CIA has gone out of its way to provoke a Soviet recruitment proposal to teach the KGB a lesson—and conversely.

A CIA case officer had been intensively courted by a local Soviet official to the point where he was considered ready for a proposal. A KGB officer flew down from Moscow to make the pitch without causing a local stir. When the three met under carefully arranged circumstances, the CIA officer proceeded instead to pitch the Moscow visitor and his local Soviet friend. Another face was added to the CIA files, and the local KGB residency became more restrained in its chase after Americans.

In a reverse play, a KGB case officer let himself be attracted by two CIA officers and buoyed up their hope of recruiting him by making the right sounds. He invited both to dinner in a local restaurant, in the course of which he led them on to make an offer of political asylum. Outraged, he assaulted both. The free-for-all was stopped only by the arrival of the local police. The incident made the front page the next day, and the KGB got a good propaganda play out of the nefarious and bungling Americans.

Many of these CIA pitches, even when unsuccessful, left one important residue: If, later, the Soviet officer changed his mind, he knew whom to get in touch with—a man whom he had come to know well.

It is through approaches like this, time-consuming and persistent, that the CIA has scored some of its most valuable penetrations of the Soviet diplomatic and intelligence bureaucracy. Even a one- or two-year penetration of a Soviet Embassy can provide classified information going far beyond the parochial concerns of the embassy itself: broad policy reports from the Soviet foreign office, party correspondence from the Central Committee, new directives from KGB or GRU headquarters in Moscow. All roads do not lead to Moscow, but in a highly centralized and disciplined bureaucracy most spokes lead to the hub.

The climate for recruiting professional Soviet intelligence officers has improved in recent years as a new breed of younger officers has entered both the KGB and the GRU ranks. Some of these young men have inevitably been affected by the growing expression of dissident opinion in the Soviet Union and have more open minds about the virtues and vices of their own and the Western world. One cannot make too much of the generation gap in Moscow, though it certainly exists within the establishment middle class, but even a slight openness or curiosity or restlessness makes the quarry more susceptible. These young men are the senior bureaucrats of tomorrow, and through them the closed society they inhabit may develop a few more cracks.

6

THE THIRD CIRCLE

The most widespread, persistent, and productive operations of the CIA in its first twenty-five years were directed against the "third circle"—the scores of Communist parties, both legal and underground, actively at work on all continents. In those years thousands of Communist Party members were recruited to report on their own parties, their contacts with other parties, and their relations with the Soviet, Chinese, or Cuban party. Hundreds kept Washington informed of Communist Party espionage and terrorist actions. More than a score provided firsthand reports on conversations with top party leaders in Moscow and Peking.

The fear of "international communism" preceded even the threat of a Soviet military strike in the late forties. The Communist threat was ever present in one form or another: insurrectionary and electoral challenges in France and Italy; an armed insurgency in Greece; an increasingly powerful Communist Party in Iran; the first wars of national liberation in Malaya, Indonesia, and the Philippines; the ousting of the Nationalists from the mainland in China.

Revolution was in the air throughout Eurasia.

All these actions were read as part of a worldwide conspiracy engineered out of Moscow. The parties were Stalin's puppets, for Stalin gave orders to the Italian leaders, determined the course of the civil war in Greece, called the timetable for insurrections throughout Asia. It was he who dictated the "general line" for the entire "movement." For many observers the Comintern, the Third Communist International, established in 1919 and officially dissolved in 1943, was still effectively operating to achieve the "world revolution."

The myth of a Communist monolith persisted for fifteen years: a solid global network of disciplined revolutionaries dedicated to the fight against capitalism, imperialism, colonialism. Only America could keep the network from spreading.

Stalin's personal power and a substratum of organizational fact supported the image of the monolith. It was no myth that up to the mid-fifties the Soviets exercised direct and mostly unchallenged control of the Communist parties outside Yugoslavia and China, securing their obedience through the dispensing of secret funds, which most of the parties needed to survive. As the West European parties began to flounder in the immediate aftermath of the war, Stalin established the Communist Information Bureau in September 1947, in effect bringing the French and Italian parties under organizational control.

The notion of a crackproof Communist monolith was fortified by Washington's ignorance of all things Communist. Hardly a man in government had read Karl Marx or Lenin. No desk officer in State or Defense could state the principal theses of Marxist-Leninist theory or outline the organization of a Communist Party. No one knew how an underground party operated, or even the mechanisms by which legal parties communicated with each other and with Moscow.

The handful of men in the CIA who began working on the party target in 1946 shared in this profound ignorance. We had very little to go on.

What we needed even to visualize the Communist Party

target was garnered in the next several years from police, security service, and Allied occupation sources throughout the world: how a party is organized, how it recruits and trains its members, what it takes to go up the promotion ladder, what the sources of disaffection are among its members, how it keeps its "classified" records, how it guards against infiltration by the police, on and on. It was clearly impossible to recruit a Communist about whom one knew nothing, to penetrate an organization one did not understand, to ask knowledgeable agents intelligence questions.

The main focus of our work up to 1948 was elementary fact gathering abroad and detailed research and analysis at home. Studies were issued to educate case officers in the doctrine, structure, and psychology of the party. A compendium of Marxist-Leninist theory in forty pages of nonjargon English, an outline of the party's organizational structure, a glossary of party terminology, the mechanics of party financing, a list of Comintern personalities still alive and functioning, a description of current insurgencies—these background studies, combined with the increasing number of Communist contacts abroad, served to make our officers reasonably surefooted.

Two human facts impressed me in my early reading on communism and Communists.

In the German writeups on Communist Party activities and their interrogations of captured Communists, I saw countless educated and uneducated Europeans who were willing to give up their lives for their cause. Any man willing to work in the Communist underground in Hitler's Europe had to be courageous and devoted. I felt profound respect for an ideology that could promote that kind of response.

A second fact is not unrelated: the capacity of a few well-organized men to get things done. Lenin's greatest contribution to the Communist movement was not, I felt, his theoretical or political analyses, but his constant stress on *organization*. Ten disciplined men can get more done than a hundred well-meaning activists in loose cooperation. The best parties, for revolution or elections, are not the largest but the most tightly organized parties.

A third fact of life served to distort the American view of Communists then as now: the American Communist Party. The CPUSA is the worst party in any industrial nation. It is a pathetic political instrument. Staffed by many offbeat or oddball individuals, vilified for fifty years as un-American and anti-American, penetrated wholesale by the FBI, it operates on the farthest fringes of American politics.

This image of a Communist Party cannot be transferred to Europe or Japan. In the early fifties a British security official told me that the then secretary-general of the British party was eminently qualified to be prime minister—had he not been a Communist, he would probably have become prime minister. A French security official made the same point in a different way. He said that his service expected most of the brighter university students to go through "a Communist phase," but that fortunately many were sobered by the prospect of earning a living, and only a few decided to make their careers in the party.

CIA's intelligence target was not the broad range of party activities, but the parties' secret operations. More than ninety percent of the information required by the political analysts on an openly functioning Communist Party can be gained from public sources. This kind of straightforward intelligence lies within the province of the State Department, for it requires only the normal methods of diplomatic reporting to secure relevant information on a party's personalities, policy shifts, propaganda activities, labor and student organizing, party fronts. The minutes of Politburo meetings (if they are kept), confidential instructions to subordinate party committees, or "official use only" resolutions of party conferences and congresses are useful to the political analyst, but not essential in evaluating party programs or electoral prospects.

The focus of CIA operations was on three aspects of party work:

The activities of illegal, or underground, parties, like the Spanish and Thai parties today, and the Portuguese party only yesterday.

The mechanisms by which both the legal and the illegal parties* are funded.

The secret activities of legal parties: Most parties support a highly restricted program to penetrate the police and the armed forces and to carry out espionage operations for their own purposes. Many legal parties also maintain a parallel "illegal apparat" or secret organization that goes into action when the party is banned.

Penetrating the legal parties turned out to be a fairly easy task, for even a well-organized and well-disciplined party has endemic weaknesses: personality clashes, ideological fights, internal witch hunts. These weaknesses are magnified in parties that do not have a strong foothold in their societies or are struggling to survive under the harassment of the police or security forces. Waves of dissension and disillusionment have accompanied all the shifts in Soviet policy from Lenin's New Economic Policy to the Soviet invasion of Czechoslovakia, from Stalin's irrational hunt for Titoists after the rift with Yugoslavia to the Chinese rift with the Soviet Union. Add to these the generation gap between the old-line Stalinist bureaucrats and the committed young party members, and the monolith proves somewhat shaky.

A Communist Party can be penetrated in two ways: by "seeding" a young man in a party cell and guiding his career upward, or by recruiting a party functionary as an agent-in-

---

*Communist Party use of "legal" and "illegal" adheres to the normal sense of the two terms. A legal party, as in France or Great Britain, is simply another public political organization. An illegal party is one that is prohibited by law. Every illegal party tries to become legal so that it can become a more effective force in its society.

place. The first is easy but time-consuming and often non-productive. The second is more difficult, but reaches the secret sectors of party work more quickly.

PLANTING AN AGENT

To plant an agent with good career prospects requires a detailed knowledge of the party's "entrance requirements," the types of sponsors it values for a new recruit, and what kinds of workers it needs. Well-run Communist parties are always hungry for talent: stenographers and bookkeepers, writers and editors, stump orators. In a small party young men with the right qualifications can reach the front office in a few years. In the larger parties of industrialized countries (France, Italy) or populous countries (Brazil, Indonesia), moving up will take longer, but the right man can move ahead swiftly even though the top positions are monopolized by the older bureaucrats.

To sponsor the right man is the principal challenge. He must not only have a desirable specialty, but be bright, hard-working, and personally ambitious. He must also be able to get some kind of equivocal satisfaction out of doing a good job in an organization to which he is disloyal.

Once in the party, the plant can begin to work at once. He can keep his eyes and ears open to spot easygoing or undisciplined party officials, to pick up cell gossip on the higher-ups, or to report on disaffected members in times of organizational or ideological stress.

It is the principal concern of the case officer to do what he can to advance his cell member's career. One way to do this is by moving his man from the provinces to the capital city, thereby raising the level of his access to party circles. For example, an agent planted in a provincial city finds himself doing nothing but routine chores like handing out leaflets or attending public meetings. He clearly has nowhere to go. His case officer gives him money to move to the capital and get a job in a local advertising firm. Now in a big city cell, he rubs shoulders with the bright young men around party headquarters and is occasionally singled out for special party assignments. The party begins to exploit his business travel as a cover for conducting sensitive party business and maintaining secret liaison with other fraternal parties.

Another way to advance an agent is by making him a competent student of Marxist theory. Party leaders constantly endeavor to raise the "political consciousness" of their members through lectures, seminars, short courses, and self-study programs. Their efforts are often fruitless, because the capacity of ordinary party members for abstract thought is no greater than the average worker's or businessman's capacity for philosophy or dogmatics. If the planted agent does his homework and is drilled by his case officer on the basic essentials, he often comes to the attention of the district or national leaders who are hungry for a serious student of Marxism-Leninism. Once near the front office, his prospects become bright.

RECRUITING AN OFFICIAL

A Communist Party official can be recruited in two ways—directly by a CIA officer or through a native intermediary.

In many operating environments—where an American is instinctively suspect—it is more secure and psychologically advantageous to use a native intermediary as a principal recruiting agent. The best such agents are former party members who still have amicable relations in party circles—not turncoats or anti-Communists, but "honest" ex-Communists who are still leftists, still Marxists, still activists. Activists who have been expelled from a bureaucraticized party for "excess militancy" or "recklessness" make the best agents.

They find in espionage work some of the enjoyments of the secret life that were formerly one of the party's strongest appeals.

Among dissatisfied Communists leaving the party in any country there are always some who want to strike back, rehabilitate themselves in the eyes of the public or the authorities, or regain their self-respect by acting as individuals under their own steam. Among many ego and money play an equal part.

The left-wing local journalist with a reputation for keeping off-the-record confidences also offers certain advantages as a recruiter. Not only is he an avenue to high-level party information, but he can recruit—as a source for himself and for modest payment—a clerk in the party's front office or a university lecturer on close terms with party leaders.

A former comrade from the old days, a local reporter who makes a small loan to a party clerk, a businessman with a brother in the interior ministry, a Socialist politician who needs material for a speech on land reform, a young radical with police contacts—in each case a party official will cooperate more willingly with an identifiable fellow citizen than with a foreign diplomat whose hand behind the scene he cannot detect.

There are no shortcuts for a CIA officer to recruit a Communist official face-to-face. He must first make a careful and detailed collection of information on his target, much of it procurable only from agents already in the party—his character, friends, income, personal tastes, position in the party. He must get reliable firsthand assessments of the likelihood that the official will accept a low-key approach by a foreigner. He must determine the least threatening method for arranging an introduction.

A cold or clumsy approach can only alert the party. Most parties are highly security conscious, especially in regard to their secret or illegal activities. In the best parties a security section watches party activists closely, maintains lists of "suspects," and investigates rumors or odd contacts of party members that might reflect the attention of the local police or the CIA. These professional counterintelligence units will follow up on newspaper leaks of party secrets, make damage reports on arrested party members, interrogate suspect members. Members in sensitive positions are watched most carefully—contact men with the Soviet Embassy, couriers, safe-house keepers, any worker in an illegal apparat.

Why have innumerable Communist officials agreed to work for the American imperialists?

Most of them are educated "bourgeois intellectuals," not industrial workers or farmers. They have complex human psyches and are subject to the same complex motivations as non-Communists, but by and large, the younger men are more open than their elders.

A few cases from different cultures will illustrate, but by no means exhaust, the complexities of the "Communist mentality":

An African official in touch with Soviet and Chinese propaganda personnel becomes friendly with a French-speaking American businessman who is eager to get an "education" in African ways of thought and life. The American is human, personable, and compatible, and the African finds himself drawn into a series of conversations that often turn into long bull sessions about politics as well as life. The African gradually comes to realize that he has no firm ideological commitment to Marxism and that he has been exploiting the Communist Party simply to satisfy his own personal needs for power and status. The issue becomes a simple one: Why not exploit the capitalist camp as well? He agrees to cooperate with the American. A sensitive man, he recognizes that the Soviet and Chinese officials treat him like a paid servant, and he can now work off some of his resentment in the awareness of his superior double role.

A talented journalist, a member of a Chinese-dominated party in Southeast Asia, has spent nine years of his life in prison. In his late thirties, he is still dedicated to the national liberation movement in his own country and deeply opposed to his own pro-Western government and to "American imperialism." On his release from prison, he receives no help of any sort from his party comrades, but accidentally meets a friendly American official. He accepts some food and money to tide him over and in return agrees merely to discuss the problems of his party and his own personal experiences in it. As the conversations progress, his feelings of intense devotion to the Chinese party gradually turn to a skeptical questioning of the real motives behind Peking's willingness to support his party with money and arms for an armed revolution. Basically a nationalist, he concludes that the aim of the Chinese is to dominate the peoples of Asia, using the local parties as instruments. He finally agrees to report on the pro-Chinese elements in his own party and on the content and mechanisms of Chinese assistance.

A restless young Arab, educated in Europe, rebels against his wealthy father and takes up with a circle of intellectual Communists. He finds in Marxism a comforting framework for his rebellion against the bourgeois system, and joins the party out of mixed motives: to gain an identity, to satisfy his intellectual pretensions, to assuage his guilt at being rich by helping the downtrodden. After several years of propaganda work, he becomes frustrated by his monotonous career and increasingly disillusioned by the gulf between the party and the impoverished masses. He meets a sympathetic American with whom he develops a personal and intellectual relationship, and is offered a generous salary as a "consultant" on developments within his party. Considering himself an honest Marxist, he accepts, not as an "agent" for the West, but as an instrument for combating the reactionary thinking of his comrades. He will use Western money for a higher Marxist purpose.

A young Communist activist in a Western country has a job close enough to the central workings of his party to feel the attractions of power. He sees the party as a vehicle for fulfilling his personal ambitions, and he is frustrated by the old-line Stalinists who still run the party. After a flattering approach by an American political writer who seeks his view on national developments, he agrees to contribute to a study of Soviet policy toward the capitalist world. He makes it clear that he is not acting against his own country or party, but against the Soviet and Chinese interest, and accepts the view that the United States, a powerful country, has never hurt him or his country. He also accepts a generous payment for his services, for part of his ambition is to achieve financial security. As his involvement deepens so does his rationalization: Bolshevism has nothing to tell the people, for it is purely Russian and a failure; reporting on his own party is right because it helps the U.S. government support the liberal wing of his party against the old-line reactionaries. Political reasoning meshes with personal interest to create an acceptable self-image.

The combination of youthful idealism and the generation gap has played an increasing role since the fifties in weakening party loyalty among these and many other "honest Communists." These eager enthusiasts with a thirst for action see the party as the best instrument available for achieving social justice. They find in Marxist rationalism a persuasive analysis of life-as-it-is and what life will (inevitably) become. Once in the party they easily become disillusioned with the conservatism and incompetence of the leadership, the curtailment of talk as well as action under party discipline, and the gradualist, go-slow strategy of building a mass party laid down by Moscow in the mid-fifties.

The information produced by these and countless other Communist agents in the fifties and sixties covered a broad spectrum of political intelligence on party policies and personalities that gave depth and detail to what the political analysts in Washington learned from the open sources available to them.

Reports on the illegal activities of these parties, and on the illegal or underground parties, were naturally less voluminous. The recruitment of party couriers proved the most productive source of secret information. A single party courier is able to supply the names or descriptions of the various persons he is sent to, the secret meeting places, and copies of the messages he is delivering. In one case a teen-age truant, who joined the party during a brief legal period and then was recruited by the CIA, became a trusted inconspicuous courier for the underground apparat and carried out dozens of trips to more than a score of other parties. He was given the names and addresses of people to contact, an agenda of subjects to be discussed or materials to be delivered, addresses to be passed on for mailing secret correspondence. In most cases he met directly with the foreign party leaders, briefed them on the situation in his party, and was briefed in return. A single itinerant source was thus able to provide detailed information on the strength and prospects of more than half a dozen underground parties in the third world and their relations with the Soviet and Chinese parties.

Other sources close to or in the party's illegal section have produced information on such matters as party penetrations of the local security service or the armed forces, underground caches of arms and wireless transmitters stolen from the army, secret contributors of funds to the party, the location of underground presses, and the mechanisms for the secret distribution of propaganda leaflets, etc.

More politically significant coverage has been that on the illegal parties operating in the dark—either after a period of legal existence, as in Brazil, or during a period of continuous underground life, as in Spain. In the first case penetrations of the party can often be maintained even when the party goes underground. A party that has been illegal for a long period offers greater difficulties, but the CIA has succeeded over the years in developing sources within many illegal parties. When one of them emerges from its underground life, its leaders, strength, and intentions are already well known.

Hard facts about the secret actions of individual Communist parties have been the main product of CIA's party operations, but our major concern throughout has been to use sources in the third circle as a window on Soviet or Chinese activities and political intentions. Only when our agents have reached the right spot in the party hierarchy have they been in a position to penetrate the inner circle.

From the mid-fifties on, well-placed party agents began to contribute high-level political intelligence on the problems and the thinking of the Soviet leaders in Moscow as well as unique inside slants on Peking's views on the world and on the Russians.

After Stalin's death, and more emphatically after the Twentieth Party Congress in 1956, the relationship of the Soviet party with its fraternal parties abroad shifted drastically. Stalin gave orders to the foreign leaders; he did not reason with them. Under Khrushchev, dictation and direction were replaced by discussion and persuasion. The long-term result was to convert foreign party leaders into men to negotiate with, to convince, persuade, cajole, threaten. Within a few years the Soviet party was forced into even more intense political huckstering by the threat of the Chinese party to split the movement. Some parties were up for the highest bidder. Not a few leaders were ready to revenge themselves on Moscow for Stalin's rudeness. Small parties had to decide between Peking's revolutionary line and Khrushchev's peaceful road to socialism.

Accordingly, the tone and content of Soviet party leaders' discussions with foreign leaders visiting Moscow became more substantive and businesslike, and began to reflect Soviet power politics on both the party and government level. Party visitors from Europe and the third world came back from attending international meetings in the Soviet bloc with interesting sidelights gained in their bilateral talks with

Soviet representatives. The monolith became a web that could occasionally be pierced.

The most dramatic product of party operations came shortly after the conclusion of the Twentieth Party Congress: the verbatim text of the off-the-record speech denigrating Stalin that Khrushchev delivered to a closed session of the Congress. Its publication in the Western press, with Khrushchev's rich rhetoric intact, had profound effects throughout the Communist world and gave the West graphic evidence of the drastic shift to de-Stalinization within the Soviet party. Although the substance of the speech would in due course have been passed along to subordinate party units in the Soviet Union and to the membership of foreign parties as a shift in "the general line," the intensity of Khrushchev's attack and the fact of its procurement by Western sources added to its impact on political and governmental circles from Left to Right.

The first inside information on the nature of the growing rift between the Soviet and Chinese parties came as early as 1958 from party leaders visiting both capitals. Two separate sources reported border differences as the principal source of friction. They and others who had conversations with Central Committee members cited most of the Soviet and Chinese themes that were to become part of the public Sino-Soviet polemic some years later.

With both the Soviet and Chinese parties eager to line up the foreign parties on their side as the rift widened, foreign Communists were able to monitor the situation in Moscow and Peking. Their reports came, directly or indirectly, into CIA hands:

A foreign secretariat member in Moscow for medical treatment is given a series of political pep talks by various Soviet Central Committee members. He makes detailed notes and reports his observations to his fellow members in the secretariat when he returns to his own country.

A junior official of an Asian party is dispatched to Peking to find out what is going on. He is given full-dress treatment by the Chinese and makes a written report on his return.

A foreign Communist official attending an international conference in Peking is invited by senior Chinese officials for private talks in which they run down, item by item, the Chinese charge sheet against the Soviet party. He returns home via Moscow, where he is debriefed by Soviet officials on what the Chinese told him. He is then given a detailed briefing on the errors of the Chinese and on the correct positions he should take in his own party on both the Chinese and Soviet sides of the dispute.

Marginal contributions to the political workings of the Communist mind have also come from direct contacts with senior party officials. In many embassies abroad the task of keeping in touch with opposition political leaders, both in Europe and in key third world countries, is assigned to CIA officers, who normally maintain these unofficial contacts out of public view. Their conversations often range across a wide political spectrum—from party policy and intraparty differences to the Soviet or Chinese relationship. The reports that evolve out of these talks are in no respect "agent" reports, but they provide the political analysts in Washington with a broader perspective on Communist Party thinking than can be obtained solely from the party press and speeches.

An astute senior CIA officer, familiar with European politics for twenty years, develops a personalized relationship with a party leader. For several years the two men exchange views on the national political scene, with the party official furnishing keen analyses of the trends within his party (and of the Left generally) and of the impact on party thinking of Soviet and American policies in Europe.

In one case a CIA officer proposed that his Communist friend provide precise sources for the statements of fact he was making in return for any help he might wish from the

Americans. His refusal to become an "agent" was polite: "I've been in the party for over thirty years, and I will not be disloyal to my comrades. Don't ask me for my sources and we'll keep on talking."

In another instance the leader of the Soviet wing of a non-European party offered, through an intermediary, to discuss the developing split within his party. The ensuing discussions provided an insight into the various factors involved in the dispute during an active phase of the Sino-Soviet competition for adherents in the world movement.

Sometimes these brushes with Communist Party leaders come close to constituting a deal. During the sixties several other pro-Soviet leaders probed their CIA contacts to determine if the Americans would be willing to assist them against the growing influence of their pro-Chinese opponents in the party. In a long discussion I had one night with a senior party official on the state of the left in India, he discussed the rift in his party between the Soviet and Chinese factions and gingerly inquired about Washington's possible interest in supporting his pro-Soviet group. These were the days when the peaceful Soviet Communists were considered "good" and the revolutionary Chinese "bad," and as a practical politician he hoped he could garner American support for good Communists. His polite suggestion was politely rejected.

As the more significant Communist parties become serious political forces on their own national scene, as they have in France and Italy and may in India and Spain, the priority for secret operations shifts from their illegal activities to their domestic plans and intentions. Although the general shape of their political stance is evident from open sources, it is naïve to assume, for example, that the Italian party conducts all its affairs in the open and that nothing more is needed than to read its leaders' speeches and digest party publications.

Each party has within it a closed sector of party leaders, the actual policy makers who work out in private the party's tactical programs and contingency plans and who determine the party's reactions to changing situations. These leaders also control the use of the party's unofficial resources: its illegal apparat, its secret connections with other domestic parties, its clout in the labor unions, etc.

Only agent operations can penetrate this closed group and round out a realistic picture of the party's real strength and its longer-term intentions. Only penetrations at a high level can, for example, produce a solid insight into one of the most crucial areas of European politics: the future plans of the Italian Communist Party. Both the Soviet and Italian party leaders are faced with delicate and complex problems on the issue of Communist participation in an Italian government. Their conversations, in Rome or Moscow—private assessments of the situation, contingency plans, policy responses to Western initiatives—can at the least give the White House a less cloudy view of the future of NATO and the European Economic Community.

7

ESPIONAGE: THE GLOBAL BEAT

In the mid-fifties American foreign policy became increasingly global—and thus too CIA intelligence operations. The growing power and influence of the Soviet Union, the emergence of China on the world scene, the rising tide of revolutionary action, the increasing force of the Left in the third world as well as in Europe became objects of immediate concern in Washington. Mideast tensions, troubles on the Indian subcontinent, strife in the Indochina states, Castro's revolutionary program for Latin America, events in the Congo, Ghana, and the Portuguese colonies, the spurt of Chinese activity abroad in the early sixties, coups and countercoups on four continents—all became grist for Washington's intelligence analysts.

The overall effect on CIA's intelligence operations overseas was a steadily increasing focus on current intelligence reporting, on the day-to-day coverage of behind-the-scenes plans and intentions of governments both friendly and unfriendly, of the secret forces at work on presidents, dictators, juntas, cabinets, and legislatures. Political intelligence exceeded military intelligence in bulk if not in value.

The so-called "hard"—military—targets of the first decade retained their priority, but as the sixties progressed, more and more agents were recruited to cover the "soft" targets: behind-the-scenes political and economic activities in the key capitals of the third world. In recruiting agents for these third world activities the CIA found a surfeit of willing collaborators.

Not all were "agents" in the narrow sense of men recruited and paid to carry out precise tasks. Many were simply "confidential contacts"—politicians, labor leaders, journalists, all ready to supply information for favors received (an occasional drink, help in expediting a visa or getting a son into an American university).

The sources of the best reporting, however, were agents who worked for CIA on a fixed salary, contacts who could be called upon to provide "inside information" on impending events of interest to Washington: a new treaty, a cabinet shift, a threatened coup. They carried out specific assignments and produced documents or oral reports. Each had his reason for what he did.

Many worked for the CIA because they wanted to be on the American side. Many saw in the United States the main source of help and support to their own countries. Many just liked Americans and enjoyed their company. There were other motivations: political self-interest, excitement, social resentment, tribal hatreds, an uncle in Detroit, a liking for good talk—and money. Some were quickly recruited: "I thought you'd never ask." Others agreed to cooperate only after patient development by a case officer they had learned to trust. Others walked in to offer their services. Every agent of every service is a psychological study in himself.

Most of these agents commit no crime in working for a foreign intelligence service. Espionage is a criminal act in most countries outside the Sino-Soviet area only if it is directed against the classified information of that particular country, if it involves its own official secrets. A journalist spying on Communists or Soviet diplomats, a CIA officer trying to recruit a KGB officer in Paris or Djakarta, a businessman reporting on the progress of a trade deal with Moscow, a politician or labor leader retailing private information on his competitors—none of these is violating espionage laws. They are not committing misdemeanors, much less felonies, unless they disturb the peace.

In those countries, mostly unfriendly, where secret government actions are of serious interest to American policy makers, the most useful agents are those with direct access to the cabinet, foreign office, or military staff of the regime in power. These agents *are* breaking the law, and it is on their account that espionage has been characterized, somewhat loosely, as "making a man become a traitor."

A rare agent is a traitor in his own eyes. Why do men commit criminal espionage?

A foreign office clerk in a newly born nation where patriotism is a meaningless term smuggles out cables for money. An Arab junior officer hates the Russians in his country and reports classified information on the Soviet role in supplying his armed forces with equipment and advice. Where tribalism, not nationalism, rules, there can be no conscious treason against the state. Where religious sectarianism rules, there is a higher law than secular statutes. There are many faces to "treason," and only the solid citizen in a stable democratic society can call them all black.

Whatever their source, however easily or strenuously obtained, agent reports are of maximum value when they supply unique information that permits the policy makers to act intelligently in a specific situation. A large percentage of all reports from abroad serves mainly to keep Washington generally informed on what is going on in the world. It is only the reports on matters of immediate and urgent importance that help the decision makers take informed action. Crisis situations and impending coups are constant priorities for CIA coverage.

CRISES

Agents cannot be produced overnight to supply secret coverage of unanticipated events, but since the main crisis areas have been clear from the late fifties on (the Middle East, the Asian subcontinent, and Southeast Asia), a concentrated effort was made to develop military and political sources in camps of actual or potential warring states.

In ground situations involving the location and movement of troops, armor, aircraft, and mobile missiles technical coverage plays a fundamental role. Observation from U-2 flights and satellite photography fix the visible ground facts with accuracy and precision. The monitoring of electronic ground signals and communications at all military levels provides an insight into the activities of both army and air force units. Yet, as we have seen, these mechanical spies have a crucial limitation: They can see and hear only what is going on at any one moment; they cannot forecast what will happen tomorrow or next week. Only human agents can report human plans.

A case in point is the Arab-Israeli war in October 1973. With both sides on the ready, massive photographic and electronic instruments were keeping hour-by-hour track of the situation on the ground. But the question remained, Would the Egyptians and Syrians attack?

Several CIA agents in excellent positions on the Arab side did in fact report in concrete detail the Arab intention to attack the Israelis and, as the crisis intensified, specified the approximate time of the attack. These were only isolated reports, however, in the vast amount of information coming into Washington from all sources. They also ran counter to the prevailing prejudice among the policy makers in Washington and Tel Aviv: that it made no sense for the Arabs to start a war they could not win. As it turned out, the Arabs did not start the war to win it, but to restore their shaken morale and improve their bargaining position.

The failure of analysts and policy makers to pay adequate heed to agent reports is nothing new in the espionage business. Stalin refused to believe a dozen reliable agent reports on the German plan to invade the Soviet Union because he was convinced that Hitler would first issue an ultimatum. The White House refused to believe reliable secret reports that India would forcibly take over the Portuguese enclave of Goa because the policy makers were convinced India would not use armed force to achieve its ends. Some intelligence analysts will not believe an agent report unless it is backed up by information from identified sources. Some policy makers select only those reports that bolster their own policy positions. These are attitudes any intelligence service faces, and there is little it can do about it except argue the case for a report's reliability. Perhaps this is one reason Prime Minister Churchill insisted on reading "raw" agent reports as well as the "finished" intelligence estimates in which they were homogenized.

Another crisis, the Soviet invasion of Czechoslovakia in 1968, illustrates the limits of technical intelligence—and of secret agent operations as well. A year earlier the leader of the Czech party, Alexander Dubcek, had begun a series of liberal reforms to establish "socialism with a human face" in his country. His experiment finally achieved a degree of party democracy and public freedom of expression that Moscow could not tolerate.

In June 1968 the Warsaw Pact powers were carrying out large-scale military maneuvers in East Germany, Poland, and Czechoslovakia that were closely followed by Western cameras and electronic monitors. While the maneuvers were under way, on the night of August 20–21, a large force of Soviet, Polish, Hungarian, Bulgarian, and East German troops moved into Czechoslovakia, arrested Dubcek, and restored a hard-line regime.

The invasion was not anticipated by Western intelligence. Although technical intelligence kept close track of what was happening on the ground up to the night of August 20, it could not of course anticipate what might happen in the next twenty-four hours. Agent reports from Communist Party sources had indicated that the Russians would move into Czechoslovakia if troops were needed to avoid the breakdown of Communist Party control, but they could not confirm that the Russians had actually made that decision. Since Moscow's decision to move in was a last-minute and, according to Khrushchev, reluctant one, only a Western agent inside the Soviet or Warsaw Pact general staff that day could have forecast the invasion—and even then only by a few hours.

Overhead photography has even greater limitations when military movements are virtually invisible, as in the jungle trails of Laos, or when the action takes place in remote places like Yemen or along the Tibetan-Indian border, or when there appears to be no reason for reconnoitering a hitherto quiet spot on the earth. In these cases human agents are virtually the only source for early warning.

The performance of CIA agents in situations of this sort cannot be measured in terms of wins and failures. If agents are in the right spot at the right time, they can describe secret actions and sometimes predict future moves. If public information is confused or misleading, they can often answer the salient questions. If there are no agents in place when events occur suddenly, there can be no secret reporting.

Reports from agents in Cuba first alerted Washington to the preparation of missile sites in 1962. Although these reports were imprecise and inconsistent, they helped stimulate a series of U-2 overflights that finally provided clear evidence of the sites' existence.

On the Asian subcontinent each of the various wars between India and Pakistan was forecast with some precision by agent reporting. The Chinese invasion of India's Northeast Frontier in 1962, however, came as a surprise to all but the Chinese.

Secret agent coverage of events in less crucial areas of

continuing tension has been more easily achieved: the various border conflicts in Latin America, the progress of the revolutionary movements in Portugal's African colonies, the Eritrean rebellion against the Ethiopian regime, the course of the war in Yemen, etc.

The value of this crisis reporting to the policy makers varies enormously. In crises where the White House can or must take action, as in Cuba, a few reports can be invaluable. In most cases, however, Washington can do no more than keep an eye on distant crises, and both technical and agent reporting simply keep the White House informed and alert.

COUPS

The crown of intelligence reporting in Washington for many years has been to get a scoop on a coup. White House and congressional concern with coups began early.

On April 9, 1948, during the Ninth International Conference of American States, Secretary of State George Marshall was forced to flee a violent antigovernment and anti-Yankee demonstration in the streets of Bogotá, Colombia. The riots were touched off by the assassination of a leftist leader that same morning. The assassination itself was unplanned and therefore unpredictable, but the CIA was severely criticized for not giving early warning of this "South American Pearl Harbor." In the climate of 1948 (the Communist takeover of Czechoslovakia, Communist drives for power in France and Italy, the beginning of the Berlin blockade), the incident was read by the policy makers as a deliberate extension of the Cold War to the Western Hemisphere, as an act of "Soviet Russia and its tool, international communism." As Governor Thomas E. Dewey, the Republican presidential candidate, put it: "If the United States had the adequate intelligence service it should, it would have known about Communist plans for the Bogotá uprising in advance."

Out of this "intelligence failure" came an unspoken requirement that the CIA predict all coups anywhere. Coupitis reigned in the intelligence community for the next twenty years, and constant warnings of impending coups came from sources throughout Asia, Africa, and Latin America. A great many of the reported coups never came off, but the intelligence community could pride itself on having correctly forecast some that did.

An ironic aspect of Washington's continuing concern with coups is that in almost all cases the American government cannot or will not take any action on the basis of coup reports. There have been hundreds of coups in the past thirty years, many of the most marginal concern to the American interest, and yet the intelligence agencies compete to report them first. The simple fact appears to be that no American President likes to be surprised by any dramatic event anywhere even though he can do no more than watch it happen.

The most unrealistic demand on any intelligence service is the precise prediction of an upcoming event. Operators are not prophets. Not even Khrushchev himself knew during his Crimean vacation that he was about to be deposed by his Politburo colleagues. Not even Chou or Mao could know when he would be stricken with sudden illness or death. Signs of senility or serious illness can, of course, be reported by agents, and Washington has been preoccupied by the health of foreign leaders to a ridiculous degree.

The group action required for a coup makes it a more practical intelligence target than a sudden change in leadership, but accidental circumstances often intervene to make it impossible for the coup leaders themselves to predict the hour and day of the action.

Iraq is the title holder for frequency of coups per decade, and illustrates the difficulty of predicting such actions.

The coup of July 14, 1958, that ended the monarchy in Iraq came as no great surprise to Washington, though its precise timing was not forecast by anyone. Rumors of army plotting had been circulating for months in Baghdad. A week before the coup agents reported: "Things are really moving now." Neither CIA agents nor the Iraqi plotters could tell *when* the coup would take place, for the timing depended on a fluke.

Two brigades of Iraqi troops under the command of one of the army plotters were ordered to move from one part of the country to another via Baghdad. Through an oversight the normal order to remove their ammunition during transit was not given by the king, and once in the capital the troops seized the palace and vital installations.

Since not even the brigades' commanding officer knew the preceding afternoon that he would carry out the coup the next day, no agent could have reported it before midnight.

There are instances, however, when precise prediction is possible.

A later coup in Iraq, the result of long-term plotting by the radical Ba'th Party, was forecast in exact detail by CIA agents. Agents in the Ba'th Party headquarters in Baghdad had for years kept Washington au courant on the party's personnel and organization, its secret communications and sources of funds, and its penetrations of military and civilian hierarchies in several countries. The Ba'th plan was to take over Iraq as a base, then Syria, and finally the western bastion in Jordan, giving the Ba'thists control of the Fertile Crescent.

CIA sources were in a perfect position to follow each step of Ba'th preparations for the Iraqi coup, which focused on making contacts with military and civilian leaders in Baghdad. The CIA's major source, in an ideal catbird seat, reported the exact time of the coup and provided a list of the new cabinet members.

CIA reporting on the Iraqi coups illustrates the diplomatic-intelligence bind that underlies all coup reporting. To call an upcoming coup requires the CIA to have sources within the group of plotters. Yet, from a diplomatic point of view, having secret contacts with plotters implies at least unofficial American complicity in the plot. This sensitivity has increased over the years as almost any coup anywhere has been uniformly ascribed to the CIA or the State Department.

The bind on the intelligence operators is a tight one: The ambassador normally wants to know who is plotting what, and when the plot will come off, but he does not want the CIA station to be in touch with the plotters for fear of diplomatic involvement. In many cases, therefore, the choice is between involvement and ignorance. One cannot read a conspiracy from a distance.

DRUG TRAFFIC

In the mid- and late sixties two fresh targets joined the list of CIA priorities: international drug traffic and political terrorism.

The main burden of combating international traffic in hard drugs falls upon the police and internal security services across the globe. In Washington the agency with primary responsibility for detecting and neutralizing the illegal entry of hard drugs into the United States is the Drug Enforcement Administration of the Department of Justice, whose representatives abroad are in touch with appropriate elements of foreign police and security services. From 1968 on, when the White House first raised the drug traffic to a high-priority target for CIA, its operators abroad have made occasional but vital contributions to the work of DEA.

These have varied from independent agent operations against drug traffickers, to putting pressure on foreign government officials or security services to use the government's resources to clamp down on growers and shippers.

A CIA agent reported the existence of an opium-processing factory in a remote border area in the Golden Triangle of Southeast Asia. The report was passed to local law-enforcement officials who professed to be skeptical and—for whatever reason—took no action. As a last resort the local police chief was taken on a helicopter ride directly over the factory. Faced with incontrovertible evidence, he closed it down.

In another case in the same area a senior government official was reported to be a linchpin in a heroin-smuggling chain. CIA agents supplied hard evidence of his role, and the information was passed to the proper officials. The police were unwilling, or unable, to take any action against a man in his position. The CIA station embarked on a publicity campaign in the local press that raised enough furor to force the government to act. The official was dismissed, and the protection of a key sector of the smuggling chain was at least temporarily destroyed.

CIA agents in a dozen countries have identified drug traffickers, their laboratories and transshipment points, the couriers they employ. Controlling heroin traffic appears to be one of the insuperable tasks in the modern world.

TERRORISM

An even more challenging target for security services throughout the world is the growing tide of political terrorism. Where the terrorists have a secure geographical base from which to operate, like the Palestinian guerrilla and terrorist groups, they are virtually inaccessible. Where they are outlaws in their own country, as in Latin America, they are almost equally difficult to get at.

In the past ten years more than five hundred people have been killed by political terrorists, among them sixteen American officials abroad. Hundreds more have been kidnapped, and in only one case out of five have the kidnappers of foreign diplomats been caught and punished. Latin American terrorists have been the most active, but such groups as the

Baeder-Meinhof gang in West Germany, the Japanese "Red Army" group, and a variety of Palestinian groups have often made the larger headlines.

Together these groups form a kind of global archipelago of small islands of outlaws living apart from the societies they intend to destroy by violent action. They are almost all anti-Communist, for they dismiss the conventional Communist parties as nonrevolutionaries who work within the established social structure. The goal of many internal terrorist groups is simply to establish a society without an establishment—much of their thinking goes no farther than that.

Counterterrorist work is both difficult and dangerous, for the targets of political terrorists are uncountable: *any* American business executive or diplomatic official in Latin America or Africa, for example, a rich American or European Jew anywhere, any bank or corporate headquarters in a large city, etc. To give all possible targets individual protection is beyond the capacity of police or security agencies. Only in the case of airplanes have security measures been even partially effective, for the number of flights and terminals, though large, is limited.

The professional terrorist group selects its targets at random, avoids any kind of pattern, and determines its own timing. It has no fixed headquarters, no approved tables of organization, no party cards or other documents, no regular publications, no visible ties with the society around it. It is a shifting free-wheeling outfit. Any contact with it requires a password.

There is only one way to secure prior information on a terrorist act, and that is to have an agent or informant within the terrorist group itself. It is a difficult job, for terrorists are highly sensitive to police attention and observe the most stringent security precautions to protect themselves.

In Latin America, where terrorism has been a way of life for decades, the hard-core terrorists who plan and carry out the actions are unrecruitable even if they can be identified. They are mostly young men, totally radicalized, who can see only extreme solutions to the problem of social injustice in their own societies.

The action center of an urban terrorist group can be reached only gradually from the outside, for terrorists depend on the support of many other people to survive: people with safe houses for living or meeting, couriers for transmitting instructions, men who will get and supply guns, explosives, or false papers, etc. It is here, outside the hard core, that agents can be planted or informants recruited to supply information for money. Only a support agent who performs well and builds up trust is likely to be invited to join the inner circle.

There are various routes into the outer circles.

The local Communist Party is one avenue. It can provide the names of former party members who have become disillusioned with the party's nonviolent program and left to join the terrorists. Since the party is hostile to the terrorists, it often makes an effort to keep track of its renegades—and a CIA agent in the party can find out where they are. In most cases it is necessary to track down a Communist-turned-terrorist by working through his former friends, residences, etc. In rarer cases an agent can discover the means by which a party member can join the terrorists—and then he himself can make the jump.

The main reservoir for agent recruitment against terrorists is among the more radical students and young jobless professionals. Spotters in these groups often pick up word of a man who has left town to join the terrorists. In some cases the spotter himself can offer his services to someone in the outer circle.

These plants are not easy to come by. A young leftist student comes to the U.S. Embassy to inquire about a visa. He is eager to make out, one way or another. He is offered an escrow account for his cooperation, and joins the terrorist fringe. Another young man, a country teacher, comes to the city, becomes cynical about his chances, and halfheartedly joins a radical teachers' union. He is ready for anything. Another teacher, after a trip to North Korea, becomes cynical about socialism, communism, and any other ism, but he continues to play his radical role. All three eventually come close enough to the action center to report planned terrorist actions.

Although the goal of many terrorist groups is simply to destroy the society around them, many are true revolutionaries who aim at power. Small terrorist actions cannot achieve that end and the next step is to create an outlaw state within the state that will grow strong enough to destroy the state. In this stage terrorist groups become extremely vulnerable.

The Tupamaros of Uruguay are a case in point.

In their early stages they formed an action core loosely structured in the old Bolshevik tradition into military, intelligence, finance sections, etc., under the leadership of a political inner circle of a few men. The inner core was surrounded, first, by an outer circle of supporters who supplied safe houses, acted as couriers, or changed money and, second, by a looser political organization of sympathizers who were the main financial contributors. The group itself carried out a variety of actions, from kidnapping or assassinating political and government figures to raiding banks and police arsenals—both to get money and weapons and to make a psychological impact. They carried out propaganda operations—by rushing a factory and forcing the workers to listen to a lecture, or by taking over a movie house and putting on a propaganda film for the benefit of their captive audience. They also made efforts to penetrate such hostile organizations of the establishment as the police, the army, and government offices.

The hit-and-run Tupamaros remained an elusive target for

the security services. It was only when they resorted to building up a paramilitary arm to destroy the establishment by force that they became vulnerable. Once they began to recruit and train their own military units in the remote countryside, their troops and stores of ammunition became a more or less static, locatable target. The army was called in, and the Tupamaros were destroyed. The broad lesson is simple: Once the professional terrorist group becomes an armed movement, it can be destroyed with relative ease by an adequately armed state.

Latin American terrorists are genuine outlaws, and although terrorist groups have connections with groups in other states, they are mainly domestic threats. The Palestinian terrorist groups, on the other hand, operate on an international scale. They enjoy the security of a safe base of operations. They have a generous reservoir of recruits among the Palestinian refugees. They have easy access to funds, arms, and explosives. Skilled fanatics, they are among the most competent and security-minded political terrorists on the current scene.

The penetration of these groups is particularly difficult. The only systematic approach is through the recruitment of young Palestinian students living outside the Arab states. Palestinian students in foreign capitals are always organized and frequently participate in local demonstrations on behalf of the Palestinian cause. They are therefore identifiable and can be approached under various pretexts by both the CIA and the KGB. Occasionally the CIA is able to recruit a Palestinian from the outer circle who can supply information on the inner core and its planned actions.

A Palestinian doctor, a Christian with a Western education, developed a personal relationship with a sympathetic and intelligent American with whom he could talk out his deep frustrations. It turned out that he worked in a Palestinian office as middleman between the Palestinians and local

Soviet officials. He was number three in the office under two Muslims who had cars and money and who were not very bright. He had gradually decided that in the long run the Palestinians would be losers in the Middle East and that he had no future in his present work: "Why am I doing what I'm doing? Why should I be loyal to those who are not loyal to me?"

He willingly accepted a proposal to report to his American friend what he learned about terrorist plans and the Soviet connection. A door had been opened in the blank wall of his future—he now had a purpose in life.

Another Palestinian, also a frustrated intellectual, walked into an American Embassy in the Middle East and asked to see an embassy officer. In a four-hour conversation he described himself as a disillusioned member of one of the Palestinian groups and recited his past history in detail. He supplied the names of contacts and front groups from Quebec to San Salvador, outlined Palestinian connections with extremist left groups in Israel, and described the working personnel of his own and other terrorist organizations. Convinced that the Palestinian cause had no future, he offered to take up his old contacts and involve himself on the fringes of the revolutionary movement. Mainly interested in money and his own future, he was a smart man who performed admirably. In his own eyes he was a heroic figure.

Most political terrorists work on a small scale: an explosion, a murder or a kidnapping, a squad-size raid. There is now emerging the possibility, if not the likelihood, that a new small-scale weapon with a large-scale effect will become available to the most enterprising terrorists. As nuclear materials proliferate and the technology of producing a small atomic bomb can be mastered by amateur engineers, the ambitious terrorist need only steal a small amount of fissionable material to come up with his ultimate weapon: a small package that can destroy a city. He will possess the ultimate form of political blackmail, and no one can forecast what the reaction of a government to the threat of its use will be.

JOURNALISTIC ESPIONAGE

As the tempo of events in the third world has increased, the intelligence requirements laid down by Washington's intelligence community have grown by leaps and bounds until they now cover all the nations of the globe. Inevitably, more and more effort has been placed on keeping routine track of behind-the-scenes internal developments in third world countries of no particular importance to the U.S. interest.

This increasingly large-scale coverage of internal political and military events in countries of no strategic importance became a feature of Washington's global coverage in the sixties through both open and secret means. What is going on in Sierra Leone? In Paraguay? In Chad? In Singapore? In Liberia? These are all proper questions for American journalists to report on and for the political and economic officers of American embassies to examine through local papers and by talking to local politicians and professors. They are not, however, proper targets for agent operations. Agent reports on important events in marginal countries or on marginal events in important countries add little to the effectiveness of foreign policy decisions.

During the sixties the U.S. intelligence community became a global city desk to support America's role as global policeman. The intelligence analysts wanted to know what was going on everywhere. They set requirements and priorities that justified the collection of almost any information. Good researchers are omnivorous, and the man on the Sierra Leone desk wants to know as much about what is going on in Freetown as the Hungarian specialist about affairs in Budapest. In the intelligence sector, as in the media, the information explosion brought rapid communication of more and more information of lesser and lesser interest.

American intelligence has become an all-source glut in Washington.

Every twenty-four hours, seven days a week, the brain of the global policeman monitors the world's words and blips and photographs slices of its surface. The intelligence community records and translates thousands of foreign radio broadcasts, reads some ten thousand newspapers and periodicals, excerpts and indexes thousands of names and places. American embassies forward hundreds of memoranda of conversation, piles of financial and economic statistics, crop reports. Military attachés describe equipment, culverts, maneuvers, generals. Satellite cameras record thousands of frames, and hundreds are blown up, analyzed, and interpreted. Monitoring stations record millions of electronic signals: ship to shore, ground to air, radar and counterradar, missile launchings. Open and coded messages are intercepted by the million. Some are broken and read. Others remain cryptic.

Secret reports from overseas agents are only a fraction of one percent of the total. Yet there are far too many. A strategic intelligence service can be of vital help to the policy makers on vital decisions. If it loses itself in minor events, espionage competes with journalism, and its news dies quickly and without profit to the nation's security.

8

COUNTERESPIONAGE

Counterespionage* is often touted as the aristocratic sector of secret operations. In the romantic image the counterespionage man is pitted against his fellow professionals on the other side who are trying to get his nation's secrets. His job is to foil them. It is a true adversary relationship unlike the espionage situation, in which two men work together to purloin secrets. Most spy stories are not about spying but about counterspying.

Counterespionage (CE) work often requires hard, persistent, analytic labor and poses an intellectual challenge. The

*Counterintelligence, the broader term, covers any action or information on individuals or groups judged hostile or dangerous to a society. These can range, as in the United States, from Communist and New Left militants to the Ku Klux Klan. Under President Nixon they included Democrats, radical students, and hostile journalists. Counterintelligence work normally involves collecting information, investigation and surveillance, and running informants. It can also involve taking action, as in the FBI's Cointelpro, or counterintelligence program, of the sixties—harassment, intimidation, denunciation.

Counterespionage operations, on the other hand, are exclusively concerned with the activities of a foreign intelligence service.

better the opponent, the more challenging the task. For almost thirty years the KGB has been the principal adversary of
the CIA. For more than fifteen years the American target has
been the top priority for the KGB.*

The KGB has in its ranks some of the most brilliant, patient, and careful case officers in the world today. They have
been formidable opponents—and become more formidable
each year as East-West intercourse broadens and deepens.
Détente provides them with a favorable climate for the preliminary contact work essential to the recruitment of a well-
placed agent.

The operating advantages of this confrontation are all on
the side of the Russians. They can act almost with impunity
in the open societies of Western Europe and the United
States. Their case officers reside, not by the score but by the
hundred, in the major Western capitals. They have at their
command tens of thousands of aboveboard "special" contacts
built up over the years, not only political leftists, but government officials, politicians of the center and right, journalists,
professors.

Recruiting Europeans or Americans to work against their
own governments is easier than recruiting Russians or Poles
to work against theirs. Planting an illegal agent in the United
States, though requiring time and technical expertise, is
child's play compared with recruiting and handling an agent
able and willing to work for the Americans in Eastern Europe
or the Soviet Union. Secret communications in an uncen-
sored, uncontrolled Western society are safe and simple.
Sending a courier from Europe to North America, or conversely, costs only the air fare. After years of operating

---

*Although Soviet intelligence has worked on the American target from the ear-
liest days in Berlin, Vienna, and Tokyo, the KGB was officially given the priority
mission of penetrating classified U.S. installations in 1959. In the fall of that
year, on Khrushchev's personal order, Alexander Shelepin, then chief of the
KGB, held a secret conference of senior KGB officials in Moscow and laid down
the law: The United States, as the Main Enemy, is your main target.

against the Soviet Union I would find it a vacation to run a KGB net in the West.

American concern about Soviet intelligence started before the war with Japan ended—and before the founding of CIA. The alert within the intelligence community came in the fall of 1945 when President Truman was informed by the Canadian prime minister that Soviet espionage operations out of Ottawa had reached deep into America's bomb secrets while the war with Germany was still going on.

Igor Gouzenko, code clerk in the office of the Soviet military attaché (and head of the GRU station, or residency), had decided to seek political asylum in Canada rather than return to the Soviet Union at the end of his tour. He was disgusted at the spectacle of his country's spying on its allies during the war with Hitler.

His attempt to defect led to a hair-raising drama. No one had heard about Soviet defectors at the time, and no one apparently understood what he was trying to do. He left his apartment with his wife and child, and he then visited one police and newspaper office after another. By the time his strange behavior came to the attention of the Royal Mounted Police's intelligence branch, the Soviet Embassy had been alerted to his disappearance, and a Soviet strong-arm squad had taken over his apartment and was waiting for him to come back. Alert to the danger, Gouzenko and his family returned to their apartment house that night, but stayed in the apartment of a neighbor friend. Here he finally made contact with the Canadian authorities and reached safety.

Gouzenko brought with him a rich variety of GRU files and documents that gave us our first close-up look at the internal operations of a Soviet intelligence residency: the operational notebooks of the GRU case officers, samples of cable and pouch communications between the Ottawa residency and its director in Moscow, methods of accounting for operational funds, etc. Out of these documents and follow-up investigations came the names of Canadian and American agents working for the net and of top-level Canadian Communists who had helped the Russians. The net's priority mission was to get information on our development of the atomic bomb. What Moscow had already obtained and precisely what information it was still seeking emerged clearly out of Gouzenko's documents.

In 1946 American intelligence was almost totally unequipped to counter the Soviet espionage effort. It had no direct contact with the Soviet services in Europe or the Far East and few sources to fill the vacuum.

Many of the men who began working in counterespionage from the late forties on had learned their business under British tutelage during the war. The counterespionage branch of the OSS was established in 1943 at British suggestion to assist in the cleanup of Nazi intelligence services after the war. The American officers recruited for this work were trained in England, picked up the CE jargon, and learned their craft by watching the British handle their double agents into Nazi intelligence in England, Lisbon, and Stockholm. The staples of CE work are the same in peace as in war: the principles of security in one's own operations, the analysis of hostile organizations and their methods of operation, the techniques of surveillance and interrogation, and the handling of penetration and double agents. A handful of these men formed the nucleus of CIA's work against the KGB.

It took the CIA some time to catch up with the Soviet CE target. Now, thirty years, scores of Soviet defectors, and hundreds of penetrations later, the computerized CIA central file has amassed a rich supply of name-data within and around Soviet, East European, Cuban, and Chinese intelligence operations. It provides the data bank against which the name of any agent, agent prospect, or suspect hostile agent is checked; the heart and core of every defector interrogation; a register of foreign case officers, false passports, accommodation addresses, photographs, handwriting specimens, etc.

With this buildup of file support information there slowly came gleams of light.

An espionage service is vulnerable to penetration at three levels: its headquarters staff, its case officers abroad, and the agents on its payroll.

The ideal goal for any service is to have an agent high up in the headquarters of a hostile service: for the CIA, an agent in the KGB Foreign Directorate in Moscow, for the KGB an agent in CIA's Directorate of Operations. The KGB has succeeded at least twice in penetrating European services near the top: for a time the counterespionage chiefs of the British and German intelligence services were KGB agents. Up until the time I retired in 1970 there was no evidence that the KGB had any agents within CIA headquarters itself.

DOUBLE AGENTS

The most accessible level of Soviet espionage is, of course, the agents they recruit and run abroad, and the routine CE operation is to turn or double KGB agents against their employers.

In the early years we doubled KGB agents both to protect our own operations, such as the Munich-based airdrops, and to find out what Soviet intelligence was up to in Europe and the Middle East. Mostly low-level, these doubles were able to supply information on the personality and competence of their KGB case officers, on Soviet intelligence requirements, and on communications techniques from secret writing to microdot readers and high-speed radios.

Several episodes have stayed in my mind from those early days in Munich.

One episode I recall with mixed feelings was an initiative taken by my CE chief and belatedly reported to me. A Georgian double agent of ours had been requested to go to Karlshorst to meet the KGB officer who had been running him through an East German courier. A very mild man, the Georgian was petrified at the thought of being interrogated by the Russians and sure that his anxiety would arouse Soviet suspicion. To convince him that his fears were groundless, his case officer offered to give him a polygraph examination, asking him the questions he could expect in Karlshorst. The machine would record his responses and he could see for himself if his nervousness showed. During the examination the needles wiggled drastically, but the case officer took the graph, went into the lab, and came back with another polygraph recording with no telltale wiggles. Reassured, the Georgian went to Karlshorst, handled himself coolly, and came back in the good graces of the Russians—and with a new self-confidence.

Another CE gimmick I approved beforehand, greed being what it is. A Soviet courier whom we wanted to recruit was meeting an agent of ours the next day. I agreed that the agent's case officer could break into the meeting and plunk ten thousand dollars in greenbacks on the table in front of the courier. My only admonition was to make sure the courier did not grab the bundle and run. Ogling the green, the courier agreed to cooperate with the rich Americans—to start with, on a very modest salary.

There was also the dilemma that faced my finance officer. We made it a practice to take from our doubled Soviet agents any money they received from their Soviet case officers—we did not want them beholden in any way to the other side. He appeared one day in my office with the first batch of Russian money in his hand, and complained that there was no way he could handle it in his accounting: No secret service was supposed to *make* money, and no account had been set up for cash receipts. It took CIA headquarters almost a year to arrange a proper procedure for listing income.

In the late fifties the large-scale and often blunderbuss Soviet approach to recruiting agents in the third world gave CIA even richer opportunities to ferret out Soviet agents in the key capitals.

Some were volunteers, either because of a pro-Western slant or because of the parsimony of their Soviet case officers. For example, in one Asian country an army captain dropped in on the U.S. military attaché and announced that he was a Soviet spy and wanted to work for the Americans. After careful interrogation by a CIA case officer on his past work—he had a most sensitive target—and the reasons for his shift in allegiance, he was recruited to continue his work. For the next two years he made his regular visits to his Soviet case officer and dutifully reported his intelligence missions and his other contacts. The material he provided the KGB, though carefully screened, appeared to satisfy his Soviet employer. What he gave CIA exposed some particularly valuable Soviet secrets.

In the absence of such walk-ins, leads to a Soviet agent can come in a variety of ways. The surveillance of a KGB case officer, by our own people or by a friendly security service, sometimes leads to observing a rendezvous with one of his agents, who can then be tailed and identified. A CIA Communist Party contact can report on a colleague who appears to be in close touch with an officer in the local Soviet Embassy. One doubled agent occasionally leads to the identification of another Soviet agent.

Although many of the Soviet agents we recruited in third world countries were used by the KGB for low-level missions, they served a useful purpose in familiarizing us with Soviet personnel and practices in a new operating area. In Africa, the Near East, South Asia, and Latin America hundreds of double agents served to identify Soviet and satellite case officers, their targets, and their meeting places. Much of this information was passed to local security services and provided the basis for the almost countless expulsions of Soviet and East European "diplomats" that reached a peak during the late fifties and early sixties.

Routine double agents are of great value to internal security agencies who are looking for evidence of espionage on the part of a resident diplomat. They are of limited and parochial value to a foreign intelligence service, for they require far too many man-hours for the minor results achieved. Since the KGB runs thousands of agents, turning them on their case officers could easily consume most of the resources of a Western service.

By the mid-sixties, as the CIA stations abroad became thoroughly acquainted with Soviet intelligence personnel and practices in their areas, the limited value of double agents led to a sharp decline in their numbers. There is also a constant hazard involved in the role of the double agent. Not many agents are able to play the role of double. Calm duplicity is not a common quality outside of con men. The ideal double agent must appear stable even under stress, for he cannot afford to get rattled with his Soviet handler. He must be intelligent, for a stupid agent can easily trip himself up. He should be a good talker, for fluency is in itself persuasive. He must enjoy not only the secret life, but the excitement of playing one side against the other. It is only natural that double agents provide better material for spy fiction than straight spies.

AMERICANS AS KGB TARGETS

Since the main Soviet espionage effort is to plant or recruit agents in the policy levels of the departments of state and defense, or in their communications centers, and in such intelligence organizations as the National Security Agency, the CIA, and the FBI, the KGB has made a determined effort to recruit American citizens abroad. Most Soviet approaches to Americans attached to our embassies are automatically reported to the CIA station. Upon occasion an American who is approached may be encouraged to continue the contact if he or she is agreeable and judged able to play a double role.

Recruiting a government employee is the most direct means of getting access to his government's classified information. Just as the CIA has concentrated on the recruitment of Soviet, East European, and Cuban officials abroad, the KGB's American specialists have focused their attention on Americans abroad who work for federal agencies. To counter this effort is a major CE task for the CIA.

It is a statistical fact that the KGB has recruited more American citizens to work for Moscow than the CIA has recruited Soviet citizens to work for Washington.

The KGB advantage is obvious. The party selects with great care all personnel sent on foreign assignments or "unofficial" travel. Their behavior and contacts abroad are closely monitored by Soviet Embassy security officers.

American citizens, on the other hand, can leave their country and travel abroad without screening or restraint. Tens of thousands reside abroad for two years or longer as employees of the U.S. government. Among them thousands, both civilian and military, have normal access to classified U.S. information. Most of them, especially military officers and foreign service personnel, will be given classified assignments on their return to the United States. They form a large reservoir of possible agent recruits for the KGB.

The KGB prefers not to recruit Americans within the United States, since they are keenly aware that their officials in Washington and New York are closely watched by the FBI for any signs of clandestine contacts. The principal Soviet activity in this country, both for intelligence and nonintelligence personnel, is to spot likely recruits who may at some time prove susceptible. A dossier on a potential agent can be exploited in an approach to him when he is traveling abroad.

The KGB is convinced that Americans like to work abroad because they make more money through higher salaries, rental allowances, and tax breaks, and that Americans will do almost anything for money. Money, according to the Soviet view of capitalist society, is the only means by which an American can ensure his personal independence and fulfill his material and spiritual needs. This wisdom, however cynical, is a lesson learned by the KGB in its dealings with many Americans abroad.

In almost every overseas capital there are one or more KGB officers devoted to recruiting Americans for eventual return to the United States. They are aware that Americans tend to let their guards down in a foreign environment. They talk more freely, mix more easily with foreigners, and treasure a new acquaintance in a strange city.

In most cities the KGB sets up routine nets of local nationals or third-country diplomats to keep an eye on Americans and spot likely prospects. Anyone in contact with Americans can be useful—bartenders, restaurant owners, real estate or travel agents, local businessmen, members of the jet set, as well as local employees in the American Embassy or USIA. Many of these "support agents" are natural intermediaries for striking up an acquaintance with an embassy clerk or American businessman as a preliminary to introducing them to "my Soviet friend."

The favored KGB targets are junior employees of the U.S. government, both male and female: code clerks, secretaries, and Marine guards in the embassies, enlisted men in the armed forces. These are, in the Soviet view, not only "second-class citizens," but politically unsophisticated and lonely. Many are unmarried and spend their off-duty time with each other at home or in a few bars or cafes. These young Americans form a coherent social group that can easily be joined by an attractive local citizen or a gregarious young Soviet official out for fun.

Code clerks have top priority for the KGB for their access to cryptographic materials and machines. Secretaries and file clerks are valuable for their access to classified documents. Marine guards are mainly of interest for the ease with which they can plant listening devices while on night duty.

Some Soviet approaches are extremely crude, like the drunken second secretary who barged in on a code clerk having dinner with his date in a restaurant and noisily offered to make him rich for life for his cooperation. Most, however, are carefully planned, and some are contrived to keep the Soviet hand from showing right up to the final pitch. I recall a case from the thirties in which Soviet intelligence spent seven years and more than a million dollars to get a man into the code room of a Western foreign office.

In the late sixties several hundred cases of direct approaches by Soviet officers were reported each year by American official personnel stationed overseas. Other approaches came to our attention from both the surveillance work of friendly local security services and from reports of our own agents.

The cases that follow come mainly out of the voluntary reporting required by embassy regulations, and stress the espionage techniques of the KGB rather than CIA's counterespionage response. Some Americans "recruited" by the KGB have been run as double agents, both abroad by the CIA and on their return to the United States by the FBI, and any hint as to their identity can only profit the KGB.

Over the years the KGB has displayed a special interest in female embassy employees who might be vulnerable to a sexual approach:

A Soviet visitor to a West European trade fair telephones a secretary of the local American Embassy and delivers a letter from a distant cousin of hers in Latvia. Pleased with the letter, the secretary accepts the attractive visitor's invitation to dinner, and after a few more dates she succumbs to his charms. When it is time for him to return home, he introduces her to a local friend as a channel for keeping in touch with him in Moscow. Perhaps alerted by his smooth style, the secretary tells her story to the embassy. The local friend turns out to be a seasoned KGB officer whose assignment was clearly to recruit her for the Soviet service. He is more closely watched thereafter to identify his other contacts.

An American file clerk is visited by a Soviet third secretary who gives her a story about bringing a message from a mutual acquaintance, a Soviet civilian whom she had met on a Black Sea cruise five years before. The lonely clerk takes the Soviet official as her lover, but her suspicions mount and, stricken by guilt or patriotism, she decides to report the contact to her superiors.

Occasionally the KGB will go to great lengths to stage an elaborately constructed romance:

Eleanor, an attractive twenty-five-year-old file clerk working in a sensitive area, has recently been transferred to the American Embassy in The Hague from a previous European assignment, where she was spotted by the KGB as a desirable recruit.

Upon her arrival at The Hague, Eleanor meets an attractive young American named George at an embassy club dance. He tells Eleanor he was born in Singapore and became a naturalized American citizen after World War II. He has worked since then as a construction laborer in the States and as a merchant seaman. He got off his ship at Amsterdam to look for a job in Europe.

George rapidly cultivates Eleanor in a whirlwind romance, and the two become engaged. He then moves to West Berlin, ostensibly to get a temporary job through a friend of his, but actually to make contact with his Soviet case officer in East Berlin. He stays constantly in touch with Eleanor by phone and mail, and she visits him twice in his West Berlin apartment.

An accident intervenes: George is badly banged up in an auto accident in *East* Berlin, and Eleanor rushes to visit him in the hospital. Before she leaves, George gives her a roll of film and asks her to leave it at his apartment in West Berlin. On her way out of the hospital, she is arrested by the East German police, frisked, and accused of spying. The police interrogate her, with occasional slaps in the face, and she finally admits George gave her the film.

Somewhat demoralized, she is taken to a compound to which George has been brought, also apparently under guard. In a brief exchange when the guards are looking the other way he tells her he has been working secretly for a Western intelligence service and begs her forgiveness for involving her. At that point a uniformed KGB officer enters the room and promises to let both George and Eleanor go free if she will work for Soviet intelligence in Holland. Eager to save her lover, she agrees and is released.

Both the embassy security officer and the CIA station, alerted by her trips to Berlin, interrogate Eleanor on her return. She reluctantly narrates the course of her romance with George, and even more reluctantly accepts the fact that George is a Soviet agent and that the romance was a fiction worked out in Moscow to lead to her entrapment. George is arrested when he comes to The Hague to handle his new "recruit," for it is clear that Eleanor is in no state of mind to carry on the operation as a double agent for the CIA.

American businessmen or technicians abroad are considered fairly easy marks. Capitalist businessmen, according to the KGB script, are willing to cooperate with the Russians in order to develop markets in the Soviet Union for their products, and technicians are ready to accept money for furnishing information about, or blueprints of, the latest American industrial equipment. In both cases, there is an immediate intelligence return from a recruitment, but in the case of the technician there is the additional possibility of penetrating a scientific or industrial research establishment in the United States when the technician's overseas tour is over. Here is a typical approach:

A Soviet couple meets an American technician and his wife in the capital of an Arab country which practices prohibition. On his first visit to the American's home the Soviet official brings along a house present of five bottles of whiskey. The Soviet wife offers to give Russian lessons to the American wife, in the course of which their kitchen talk leads to the Soviet wife's offering gifts of flour and other commissary items. As their social intimacy progresses, the KGB official makes a modest proposal that the technician request certain specified computer data from his home office. He also talks about money, suggesting that the Russians will be glad to provide him with enough capital to set up his own business in the States. The CIA station, alerted to the continuing contact through its surveillance of Soviet Embassy personnel, intervenes and gets the full story from the technician. He is then encouraged to carry on the contact, for whatever requirements the KGB places on him will produce evidence of Soviet technological knowledge—and ignorance—in a sensitive field.

On rare occasions the CIA has attempted to plant an American on the KGB abroad. In these "dangle" operations a likely prospect is brought to Soviet attention. A direct offering rarely succeeds. For example, a "dangle" visits a Soviet Embassy to get a copy of *Soviet Land,* attends a Soviet film showing, or takes the initiative in developing a friendly contact with a Soviet official. Any experienced case officer, Soviet or American, is properly skeptical of any action in which he himself has not taken the initiative.

A more effective means of breaking down this skepticism is to have the name of a dangle come up in the reporting of a Soviet agent under CIA control.

The cashier in an American Express office recruited by the KGB is asked to report on Americans working in the local embassy. The KGB officer expresses interest in anyone who might provide information on a U.S. Air Force base in the vicinity. The cashier suggests a junior employee whom the KGB officer proceeds to develop socially and finally recruits without much trouble. Both services now have a new agent.

Since the United States is dangerous operating terrain for the Soviet services, they are particularly careful to avoid agents "planted" on them in the States. They minimize the risk by making new contacts only when they are proposed by a reliable and tested Soviet agent or by going after an attractive target they have themselves selected. Once a prospect is singled out, his background is thoroughly checked, he is surveyed before and after his meetings with his Soviet contact, and care is taken to arrange meeting places that can easily be watched for signs of hostile surveillance.

For the same reason an American agent recruited by the KGB abroad is put in touch with a Soviet case officer on his return to the States only after he has been tested and proven completely trustworthy. He must have gained the full confidence of his case officer by carrying out his instructions with discipline and performing his intelligence tasks well. He is placed in situations abroad that are bound to expose any signs that the CIA is alert to his existence. He must, in short, be guaranteed "clean" by his overseas handler.

The extent to which the KGB, or the GRU, has succeeded in penetrating the departments of State and Defense and Washington's intelligence agencies through Americans recruited abroad is bound to be a matter of intelligent conjecture. The counterespionage operator can be sure only about what he knows—agent X arrested, agent Y being run as a double. Beyond these hard facts he can only guess at the extent of his own ignorance.

What has led many Americans to spy for the Russians? Not politics or ideology, but human weakness: mostly the need for money, often neurotic anxiety, occasionally blackmail. Since a large number of Americans are easily accessible to Soviet intelligence abroad, recent proposals that the CIA not be permitted to survey or investigate any Americans abroad except at the explicit request of the FBI simply make no sense. Since the CIA has the exclusive responsibility for counterespionage operations abroad, just as the FBI has at home, it must be free to investigate any possibly improper connections of Americans with Soviet, East European, Chinese, or Cuban officials. It is in the earliest stages of "agent development" that such contacts are most open to observation, and it is then that the countereffort can most easily frustrate the recruitment of an American as an agent. To wait for actual evidence of espionage can only promote the KGB interest.

KGB OFFICERS AS CIA TARGETS

Far more valuable, and far more difficult, than doubling Soviet agents is the recruitment of a Soviet case officer in place, the prime goal of offensive CE operations. The case officer not only knows his own agents, but he knows at least something about the sources his fellow case officers are running. He can provide an intimate look at the other members of his station, at its layout and files, at the intelligence directives from the Moscow headquarters. He will, someday, if all goes well, work in that headquarters.

Identifying Soviet case officers under official diplomatic cover in foreign capitals offers no great challenge. A combination of filework on his previous assignments, his freedom of movement outside the embassy, and surveillance of his social contacts normally distinguishes him from his legitimate diplomatic, trade, and journalist colleagues. Once tagged, the Soviet or satellite case officer is given the full treatment—by the CIA station or by the CIA in conjunction with a friendly security service. His movements are surveilled on foot and by car, his comings and goings monitored by watcher or camera, his telephone tapped, and on occasion his office or residence bugged. Keenly aware of operating in a hostile environment, however, a Soviet case officer rarely leads a surveillant to an agent rendezvous or a dead drop he is servicing.

The main outcome of this local CE work has been the building up of ever sharper profiles on individual KGB officers: their personalities, habits, methods of operation, etc. It is on the basis of these profiles that the decision is made to focus on a vulnerable target. Many of these time-consuming approaches have failed to achieve their final end, but a few

KGB officers have for a time worked for the capitalist enemy.

KGB officers under official cover are relatively easy to spot. It is the Soviet intelligence officer under unofficial cover, the professional operating as a private citizen in a foreign country, who poses an almost insuperable challenge to Western intelligence and security services. It is the invisible Soviet "illegal," operating on his own in Bonn, Zurich, or Chicago, who confounds detection.

The most highly trained and carefully prepared of all intelligence officers operating in the world today, the illegal lives as a private citizen under an assumed name with false documents and a bogus life history. He is a case officer who recruits agents, not an agent himself, and his communications are directly with the desk in Moscow that sent him on his mission. Only in rare cases is he permitted to have direct contact with a Soviet diplomatic installation in his area.

The rationale for developing a network of illegals parallel to and separate from the KGB's legal residencies is typically Soviet: in time of war, or when diplomatic relations are broken off in time of peace, the KGB will be able to continue its operations even after its official representatives are withdrawn. It is the same rationale that led Lenin to insist that every legal Communist Party also construct a parallel "illegal apparat."

An illegal Soviet network normally includes a chief and one or two assistants who alone have direct contact with him. One or more local intermediaries, or cutouts, are employed to make contacts between the Soviet case officers and their native agents, none of whom (ideally) know the identity of the Soviet officers they are working for. A fully staffed network includes a Moscow-trained radio operator who maintains two-way communications with KGB headquarters. The chief himself also possesses a locally bought shortwave radio receiver by which he can receive coded instructions from Moscow. International couriers are dispatched by the Moscow desk to deliver instructions or equipment and to pick up bulky or diagrammatic intelligence that cannot be sent by radio.

Each illegal requires an expensive investment in time and operational support. His preparation can go on for three to seven years before he is even dispatched to the country in which he will operate. He is almost always a Soviet citizen, often a career intelligence officer. His training is rigorous: three or more years acquiring a language, or languages; an up-to-date familiarity with his country of assignment; and at least a year of tutorial instruction in intelligence work in a Moscow apartment. He practices his trade, spotting potential agents or using his radio, in a safe area like East Germany, and builds up his fictitious life history by visiting the places he has purportedly lived or worked in. He takes on his final identity, complete with forged papers, only after he has changed his identity and papers at least once during his residence in the West. Once he has reached his final destination (for most recent illegals, the United States), he may spend years establishing himself as a normal American citizen or legally admitted alien.

A favorite Soviet device in creating flawless identities is to make use of the birth certificates of citizens whose deaths have never been placed on the public record. Shortly after World War II the KGB began to investigate the fate of families from the Baltic states and other areas now under Soviet control who had emigrated to Canada or the United States in the early 1900's and then returned to their homelands. Children born of such families before they reemigrated automatically became Canadian or American citizens with local birth records. Many such families who returned to the Soviet Union were wiped out during the war, and all trace of them and their children was lost—except in the files of the KGB. It is an easy matter to bring such a child, now ostensibly grown up, back to life: The man who is to assume the identity of the dead child gets in touch with local Canadian or

American authorities, reclaims his earlier citizenship, and requests a copy of his birth record. The birth certificate entitles him to a Canadian or American passport. It is an almost unassailable procedure, but occasionally even the most carefully assumed identities are uncovered.

A suspected illegal picked up in England seemed to be a bona fide Canadian on the basis of an initial check made with the Canadian authorities. During his imprisonment while under investigation he underwent a medical examination. Soon thereafter the Canadian authorities sent further information regarding the circumstances of his birth to London. For once the Russians had slipped up: The documents of the person he claimed to be indicated that he had been circumcised at birth. The illegal had not.

The second key requirement in the preparation of a Soviet illegal is the slow and careful building up of his legend, or bogus life history. After he leaves the Soviet Union, he may become a salesman or a photographer and live in two or three countries, thereby building up his story with legitimate jobs, residences, and passport entries. An illegal often spends years constructing a new verifiable identity to add legitimacy to his false documents. Illegals who *have* succeeded in settling down as private citizens in the United States or Western Europe provide Western security services with their greatest challenge. No amount of systematic investigative work can lead to their detection. No culling of immigration files is likely to expose a bogus immigrant.

The only direct source on the identity of a working illegal is a Soviet intelligence official, a defector, or an in-place CIA agent who has participated in the preparation of an illegal— either in his training, in tailoring his documents, or in dispatching him to the West (most often via Berlin). Without such exposure from inside his own service, the illegal is safe—unless he cracks up on his wearing solo assignment or accidentally comes to police attention.

The most notorious Soviet illegal uncovered in the United States, Colonel Rudolf Abel, had an assistant, also an illegal, whose true name was Reino Hayhanen, born a Finn. On him the KGB imposed the identity of one Eugene Maki, the son of Finnish immigrants to the United States, all of whom had returned to Finland and disappeared during the war. Hayhanen, posing as Maki and living in Finland under that name, wrote to the town in Idaho where the Makis had lived and procured a certified copy of "his" birth certificate. With it he was readily issued an American passport in Helsinki with which he eventually entered the United States as a bona fide American citizen.

Hayhanen did very little useful work in the United States for five years after his arrival. Both Abel and his Moscow desk were clearly dissatisfied with his performance, and Hayhanen knew it. When he received a message from Moscow in March 1957 to come home on a secret visit, he found the invitation ominous. He felt guilty not only about his own poor operational record, but about his secret marriage to a Finnish woman during his preparatory period in Finland—a marriage he had not reported to his superiors. On his way back via Europe he got cold feet and walked into the U.S. Embassy in Paris on May 6, 1957. He told the CIA everything he knew about his boss and provided operational details of Abel's and his own work that led to Colonel Abel's arrest and conviction in federal court. Colonel Abel, a seasoned and disciplined operator, never talked and waited for Moscow to secure his release. He was later exchanged for the American U-2 pilot Francis Gary Powers, and lionized in the Soviet Union for his unknown exploits.

The main function of the CIA in countering the introduction of Soviet illegals into the United States is to intercept them abroad. Leads to illegals abroad have come from a wide variety of sources: friendly security services in Europe, agents within the Soviet intelligence bureaucracy, Soviet defectors, and illegals in desperate circumstances who walk in and identify themselves.

Occasionally an illegal bungles, but even then, he is not always discovered.

In the case of Colonel Abel, as it later turned out, a minor accident might have exposed him even before Hayhanen's defection, had the Brooklyn police been as alert as the police authorities are in Moscow. Abel ran a photographic studio in Brooklyn, and one day on leaving his apartment building he happened to drop a coin out of his pocket—a nickel. A small boy playing on the steps picked it up and began to play with it. He noticed it was very light, and after monkeying with it for a while, he managed to slip one side of the coin out of the other: It was hollow (Abel had used it to pass microfilm to and from his agents). The boy showed his find to his parents, who were suspicious enough to take it to the police as a possible counterfeit. The police took no further action.

In the past fifteen years Soviet illegals have become a flourishing arm of Soviet intelligence. In the early sixties the list of known and suspect illegals operating in the West numbered roughly a hundred. By 1970 more than a thousand were known to be operating throughout the globe. It is a reasonable judgment that illegals, and not official Soviet residents, are now handling the most sensitive Soviet agents in the upper reaches of the Western civilian and military establishments.

DEFECTORS

In the past twenty-five years of Soviet-American political competition Moscow has lost out drastically on one front: the loyalty of its diplomatic and intelligence officers. Scores of Soviet intelligence officers and hundreds of East European diplomats and intelligence officers have sought asylum in the

West. During these years not a single CIA or American Foreign Service officer has sought asylum in the Communist
world.

The majority of Soviet defectors* have been intelligence
officers—and for a good reason. The intelligence officer in
any service is the most knowledgeable about security practices in his own embassy, and as a trusted case officer in his
daily work, he knows his way about town. He is in the best
position to make a safe contact with a Western service and, in
what will probably be his last secret operation, not to get
caught. He may plan his defection for years, or for a few
weeks, but he can carry it out as a professional operator.

In the postwar years in occupied Germany and Austria any
Soviet, Pole, or Czech official who wanted to go West generally had no trouble. If he could arrange an official visit to
East Berlin, he simply went to West Berlin and turned himself in to a local army post. He was immediately placed under
CIA protection, and flown out to safe quarters in the
Frankfurt area. The reception of defectors in Vienna was
equally easy to arrange, but without an American-controlled
airfield in Vienna proper, the defector had to be transported
secretly across the Russian-occupied zone.

For a Soviet official to defect from a European or third
world capital, knowledge and care are needed. He cannot
break his pattern of behavior or show any signs of unex-
plained nervousness. If he does not take a direct but un-
noticed route to a Western embassy, if he is not acquainted
with its normal reception practices, if he does not know
whom to ask for, he is running serious dangers of delay,
exposure, and arrest by his own counterespionage colleagues.

In the record of Soviet defections that misfired no failure
cost the West more than the case of the KGB officer Konstan-

---

*In American intelligence parlance a "defector" is a man whose knowledge is of
substantial interest to the intelligence agencies in Washington. He is given special treatment not accorded the ordinary political exile or émigré.

tin Volkov, who walked into the British Embassy in Istanbul in 1945 with an offer of valuable information in return for political asylum. Volkov urged that extreme caution be observed in forwarding his proposal to London since, he asserted, the KGB had two agents in the British Foreign Office and a counterintelligence agent in the British service. Unfortunately, the "counterintelligence agent" was Kim Philby, and he was the man who handled the London end of such matters as Soviet intelligence defectors. Moscow, alerted by Philby, pulled Volkov out of Istanbul. Had Volkov succeeded in his attempt, his information would have uncovered Philby and robbed the KGB of its most productive postwar agent in the West.

The roster of Soviet intelligence defectors since the early fifties runs into scores. The first high-level Soviet defector after World War II, an MVD colonel who came out in May 1950, provided a rare combination of positive and counterespionage information, for the MVD (the Ministry of Internal Affairs) at the time was responsible for the Soviet atomic energy program. In addition to filling large gaps in Washington's knowledge of the organization and personalities of the Central Committee and Council of Ministers in Moscow, and even larger gaps in CIA files on Soviet intelligence headquarters, he provided information on uranium production, processing, and research that forced a sharp upward revision of U.S. estimates of the Soviet atomic energy program.

For the next twenty years, at varying intervals, more than a dozen Soviet intelligence officers and scores of high-ranking East European intelligence officers were among the hundreds of Communist officials who came over to the West. Why did they flee?

The climate for the highest-level defections has often been set by the drastic power shifts, party purges, factional rivalries, and doctrinal revisions endemic in the Soviet satellite system. Each has produced losers who are demoted, imprisoned, executed, or threatened.

During Stalin's purge of "national communists" after Tito's defection in 1948, the main victims were Communists who had spent the war years in Moscow and were installed in the new regimes by Stalin himself. Many were Jews, particularly in Poland, Hungary, and Czechoslovakia. Under Khrushchev it was the turn of the discredited Stalinists, some of whom fled to the West even though not assured of an enthusiastic welcome. Czech Communists were especially vulnerable: those with a bourgeois background after the Communist takeover in 1948; "national communists" in the purge of Titoists; discredited Stalinists in the Khrushchevian "thaw"; rightists in the brief Dubcek interim; "liberals" after the Soviet invasion of 1968.

Many of these men fled to the West to escape imprisonment or death. Others, some of the most valuable intelligence officers among them, had no such clean-cut reason for changing sides. What led these men to abandon their elite career, their loyalty to their country, and in some cases their family?

The question has intrigued the American service for years. Various committees of psychologists and psychoanalysts have addressed themselves to this enquiry, basing their analysis on the case histories of Soviet defectors and agents-in-place. If a psychological profile of a potential defector or recruitable agent in Soviet ranks could be drawn up with any precision, it was reasoned, the CIA could then begin to search actively for the right "type" and not simply wait for him to walk in. Unhappily, no one has come up with any useful indices. Each man's act is a case unto itself.

There are few "ideological" defectors in the strict sense: men who are disillusioned with Marxism-Leninism or prefer the political and economic premises of Western thought. There is an occasional man who defects on grounds of principle, out of moral or emotional distaste for the actions of his government, but the common notion that a Communist "chooses freedom" because of the greater satisfaction of living in a democratic society is both naïve and self-serving.

What many defectors choose in giving up their well-paid jobs abroad is freedom from personal trouble. They leave job, home, and country for the same reasons that prompt ordinary citizens in other societies to walk out of their houses and start a new life—anxiety in the present and fear for the future. They may be anxious about poor job performance, threatened demotion, or punishment. They may be frustrated by a disagreeable boss or a nagging wife. They may be seduced from the drab life of their homeland by a glamorous Western capital with its restaurants, entertainments, and available women.

The short-term intelligence profit from Soviet and East European defectors has been immense, and exceeds in scope and detail the reports produced by agents-in-place. Political and military defectors can be leisurely debriefed in safe surroundings by Western intelligence experts in every field of their knowledge. They can be asked thousands of questions—to check out information on hand, to clarify puzzles, to evaluate their former colleagues, to analyze party policies or the intricacies of Moscow-Warsaw or Berlin-Prague relations, etc. But once fully debriefed, they are soon out of date, and only agents-in-place can provide ongoing reporting.

A defector from an intelligence service has the most durable value. His interrogation, for example, may profitably last for years. A jog to his memory may bring out deeply buried associations: the past career of a case officer, an address in Switzerland, a report from a "prime source" in a European government. A long-forgotten allusion can lead to the identification of another Soviet agent in the West. Some intelligence defectors have also been of great value as consultants or advisers, in interpreting personnel shifts in their former services or analyzing a peculiar turn in a Soviet operation under current scrutiny.

Usually intelligence officers who intend to defect go about their task with professional care. Aware that their value to the Western services is directly proportionate to the amount of information they possess, they often load themselves with a rich trove:

A senior East European intelligence officer who planned to defect on his next official trip to the West spent months selecting key documents that passed over his desk and placed copies inside a hollow tree in a public park through which he walked every night on his way home from the office. He defected at the beginning of a long holiday, and his service was not alerted until several days after he was in CIA hands. The delay gave the CIA time to empty the drop and speed the documents to Washington before the local service knew it had lost one of its most valuable men.

The top KGB defector of the early sixties had decided years before to leave his service. A man with a remarkable memory, he internalized operational and agent information up to the moment he left. He was able to provide the names of more than eight hundred Soviet case officers and identifying data on a score of Soviet illegals operating in the West. In addition he brought with him several original documents with details on current KGB operations in Western Europe.

During the Cold War an important by-product of defection was its exploitation for political propaganda. The Communist defector was hailed in the West as testimony to the fact that even an able and respected official found life "behind the Iron Curtain" insupportable. Stories of corruption, deceit, and poverty inside the "people's paradise" were played up for the benefit of the third world, and American congressional subcommittees periodically used them to indict the "Communist system."

The counterpropaganda blast from the Soviet side, for home and foreign consumption, was equally mechanical. The defector was an embezzler, a drunkard or wife beater, an immoral man with only the lowliest reasons for flight.

Intelligence defectors, on the other hand, were and are normally kept under close wraps. The lives of KGB or GRU defectors in particular are in danger, for if they remain scot-free, they pose a bad example to their former colleagues. There have been no recent assassinations of former Soviet intelligence officers, but it is a standing task of Soviet counterintelligence officers abroad to run down the new identities and residences of Soviet defectors resettled in the West. A great deal of care has been taken to foil their search.

It is from these men, safely sequestered, that the CIA has obtained the most valuable contribution to its CE effort: leads to Soviet and East European agents operating in the West at the time of their defection. They have identified hundreds of Soviet agents, mainly in Europe, many in NATO, who were arrested or monitored for further leads. The impressive list of exposures of Soviet penetrations of European intelligence services in the 1960's is directly or indirectly traceable to the items of information they were able to furnish.

Following up the leads supplied by intelligence defectors has always been a priority CE task. Both speed and care are required.

The road from the first vague lead furnished by a defector to the final identification and arrest of a Soviet agent is often a long and tedious one. In hardly any case can a defector supply the name or exact identifying data on a Soviet agent he has not himself been running. He may have seen a document or two that came from a Soviet agent in the West. He may have overheard some vague reference to an agent by a colleague. Many of these leads are followed up for years: patient file work, continuing investigations, questions put to new defectors, checking out names around the world—the CE specialist cannot know when the pieces of the puzzle will fall into place and finger a man in the Western establishment.

Precise leads from defectors can and must be followed up with the utmost speed. When a KGB officer is known to have come into the hands of a hostile service, the immediate response is to protect the agents or communications the defector may give away. Agents are told to move or to lie low. Mail drops or safe houses go out of use. Staff officers under official cover are withdrawn from the embassy. If the lead to a Soviet agent in the West is not quickly pursued, he will be warned to cover his tracks, play safe, or disappear.

In cases of leads from CIA agents within Soviet services, the priority concern is to protect the agent-in-place. The defector is in safe custody. The agent is on the firing line, and any information he supplies that can conceivably be traced back to him may lead to his death. The GRU officer in Europe who provided the CIA with such rich military information in the fifties also identified more than sixty GRU agents in Austria and more than forty in Germany. No immediate action could be taken on most of his leads without throwing suspicion in his direction. When an agent is lost, any service will look for a leak from its own ranks. When the identity of the agent is known only to a few officers, the weak link is soon found.

One of the highest prices for such abstention was paid by the Soviet service to protect an agent of theirs in the British service. George Blake, who had been recruited by the Russians during his imprisonment in North Korea during 1950–53, participated in the planning of the joint British-American enterprise, the "Berlin tunnel," before his own departure for Berlin in early 1955. The tunnel permitted Western technicians to tap some of the high-security Soviet military telephone lines in East Berlin. The Russians were faced with the alternatives of foiling the operation and possibly losing a key penetration agent of the British service, or protecting Blake by allowing the British and Americans access to classified information of distinct value to the West. They chose the latter course, allowing the operation to go on from May 1955 to April 1956 when a Soviet maintenance crew "found" the tunnel.

On rare occasions, when a service learns that the other side is coming close to identifying one of its own highly placed agents, it will attempt to divert the other side's attention to one of its own agents of lesser value. This practice is more common with the KGB than with the Western services.

Only in counterespionage operations will a service give up one of its own foreign agents to the other side. In no case will a service sacrifice one of its own case officers for any end whatever. "Termination with prejudice" means murder only in fiction or a romantic press. Counterespionage, it has been said, is not an occupation for altar boys. Nor is it a career for criminals.

The crucial element in any intelligence service is its counterespionage component. Without effective counterespionage no service can protect its own operations from penetration or exposure, and no government can keep its own secrets. One fallout of the recent CIA investigations was the virtual destruction of its centralized counterintelligence staff and the loss of many senior CE operators. Only a few CIA operators have, over the years, concentrated on counterespionage work, for most case officers are temperamentally more suited to espionage and action operations. Here the American impulse to act, to get something done, has a wider theater, and the bureaucratic rewards for a good operation are normally greater. The defensive role of the CE analyst is essentially negative: to examine our operations for evidence of hostile knowledge or penetration. Even a small number of experienced and highly critical minds can protect us from being duped by our own uncritical enthusiasm for action.

9

COVERT ACTION: PROPAGANDA

The transformation of the American intelligence service into an all-purpose action instrument for secretly executing presidential policies began with the start of the Cold War.

The March 1948 crisis led not only to the war scare and the urgent requirement for early warning of Soviet military intentions, but to the determination to counter Soviet expansion with some of its own weapons. When President Truman, a practical politician, saw that Stalin could not be bargained with, he decided to fight him, to "stop the sons of bitches no matter what." His main instrument for stopping the sons of bitches was a new agency to carry out covert action operations against the enemy.

On June 18, 1948, the National Security Council issued a directive establishing a new agency to carry out covert political, psychological, economic, and paramilitary operations to counter the "vicious covert activities of the USSR." It listed a broad variety of specific actions: propaganda; economic warfare; preventive direct action, including sabotage, antisabotage, demolition, and evacuation measures; subversion against

148

hostile states, including assistance to guerrillas and refugee liberation groups; and support of indigenous anti-Communist elements in the threatened countries of the free world.

The new agency, the Office of Policy Coordination (OPC), was to operate under the policy direction of the departments of State and Defense. Although independent of the director of the Central Intelligence Agency, it was housed within CIA for administrative support. The charter for covert action was given to a new separate organization rather than to CIA apparently because the National Security Act of 1947 was construed to make CIA responsible only for espionage and counterespionage.*

It was an odd arrangement, unique among Western secret services, and did not survive for long. From its founding on September 1, 1948, until August 1, 1952, the OPC worked as an independent service alongside the intelligence service (the Office of Special Operations). Its chief was appointed by the secretary of state and its directives for covert action came from the departments of State and Defense and the Joint Chiefs of Staff. Then in 1952 the two operations agencies were merged into a newly baptized Clandestine Services, and OPC became an integral part of CIA.

The four years during which two American secret services operated side by side were featured by duplication and confusion. Both maintained liaison in Washington with State and Defense, though for different purposes. Both collaborated with European security and intelligence services for executing different tasks. Both often made contact with the same

---

*Even before the founding of OPC, however, the National Security Council, at its first meeting in December 1947, instructed the CIA director to initiate a secret propaganda campaign as part of an overall anti-Communist information program directed mainly to Europe. This first American covert action came out of a recommendation by the Department of State that the U.S. government counter Soviet covert operations with a program of its own. It is generally conceded to have played a useful role in the successful outcome of the Italian national elections the following April.

groups or individuals overseas for intelligence or action purposes.

There were other causes of friction between "the two sides
of the house." The new OPC operators were looked upon as
amateurs by the "old" professionals. They spent their time
and money the easy way—by buying the cooperation of
friendly Europeans or Americans to carry out simple tasks
like founding radios or subsidizing newspapers. Untrained,
often able to speak only English, they could never handle,
much less recruit a foreign agent in the professional sense.
They had "contacts" or "friendly collaborators," not agents,
and the semantic quibble reflected a professional put-down.
Moreover, the new action operators, recruited in haste, were
well paid, often more generously than their contemporaries
on the espionage side. The rivalry was also bureaucratic. The
action men of the OPC were given more spectacular tasks
than recruiting a spy or countering a KGB operation. They
had a large and rapidly expanding budget (espionage is a
relatively low-budget operation). And they received much
more attention from the top levels of State and Defense and
from the White House. All the pressures were clearly designed to subordinate intelligence to action operations.

The creation of OPC was a pragmatic decision. No questions of morality or legality intruded into the Cold War climate of the time. Senior State Department officials provided
the main stimulus, with the Pentagon adding its encouragement. On the one hand, the Communist takeover of Czechoslovakia in February 1948 had made American diplomacy
aware of its own impotence. On the other, the victory of the
Christian Democrats over the Communists in the Italian
elections that same April—at least partly due to substantial
covert American support—encouraged them to view covert
political action as an effective instrument.

There were other persuasive reasons for Washington to
create a "third arm" for fighting the Russians. The White
House was thenceforth able to direct anti-Soviet propaganda

without being officially responsible for its content, to exert political pressure abroad without involving its diplomats, and to carry out military actions without committing the armed forces.

Another critical advantage was the freedom the Executive enjoyed in planning and executing large-scale secret operations without congressional approval for each action. Even in its preimperial phase, the presidency was seen as the only institution capable of fighting the men in the Kremlin.

The effect of this decision was to create an organization similar to the wartime Office of Strategic Services. We now had a peacetime secret agency involved in both intelligence and covert action.

President Truman's role in making this vital decision has been obscured by his apparent denunciation of covert operations years later. The critical remarks he supposedly made in a syndicated article that appeared on December 22, 1963, have often been quoted: "I never had any thought when I set up CIA that it would be injected into peacetime cloak and dagger operations. . . ." In a conversation with President Truman the following April, the then CIA Director Allen Dulles brought up the President's published statement, and recalled to him some of Truman's own decisions authorizing covert operations in Italy, Greece, Turkey, and the Philippines. After reading the article Truman expressed puzzlement and said, in effect, that the story was all wrong and gave a very unfortunate impression. Apparently, the article had been written by David Noyes, his former White House assistant, and not read by the President himself who was then in his eighties.

Covert action operations cover a broad front: dropping arms and money to guerrilla groups, supplying funds to a political party or leader, subsidizing a labor union, funding an editor or giving him an outline for an editorial, supporting an ostensibly private radio or magazine, supplying an airline ticket, taking a man to dinner.

Conventionally, and bureaucratically, they fall into three types of action:

Psychological warfare, or psywar: to carry out secretly sponsored propaganda, anti-Soviet or pro-Western, or to create radio stations or publications that appear to be sponsored by the Russians or Communists.

Political action: to use secret contacts and funds in order to affect the political situation in another nation (*a*) by supporting a friendly government or party against its political opponents, or (*b*) by supporting opposition forces against an unfriendly regime. The first, (*a*), is an adjunct to conventional diplomacy; (*b*) is subversion.

Paramilitary operations, or unconventional warfare: to support or stimulate armed resistance elements in their homeland against the regime in power, or to employ irregular troops to invade a country and unseat its regime—or a combination of both.

All covert operations, therefore, are broadly political in attempting to shape the domestic power structure of another nation without war. Covert action is the extension of diplomacy by other means.

Covert operations became an integral part of the counteroffensive against Soviet "expansionism." Two forms of action were called for: a positive program to build up anti-Communist elements and an aggressive effort to weaken the Communists both inside and outside the Soviet orbit. The first tactic, a kind of benign intervention, sought victory, in George Kennan's words, "within ourselves in our Western world." The second sought to fight the Communists on their home ground—simple subversion. Both reflected the underlying nature of America's overall containment policy: to stop the fire from spreading, not to put it out. Covert, like open, political action was therefore fundamentally defensive.

In practical terms the new action charter of 1948 called for operations designed to:

• Contain, or retard, the spread of communism in the "free world" by supporting non-Communist governments threatened by a Communist takeover and by strengthening democratic political parties, labor unions, and cultural organizations.

• Counter Soviet propaganda by funding anti-Soviet groups and publications and building up democratic international front groups.

• Fight the Communist regimes on their own terrain by supporting resistance movements inside the orbit and by weakening the loyalty of their citizens through radio broadcasts, leaflets, and Western literature.

The President maintained control of his third arm through a subcommittee of the National Security Council (most recently known as the Forty Committee and the Operations Group) that reviewed all covert action proposals of any size or sensitivity and made its recommendations to him through his national security adviser, the subcommittee's chairman. Proposals for covert action were originated by the departments of State and Defense and by the CIA itself. In some cases the White House initiated its own proposals.

The rationale behind the U.S. government's taking actions without accepting official responsibility was expressed in the theory of "plausible denial." Plausible denial requires that no covert operation can be traced back to the U.S. government: to the White House, the State and Defense departments, *or* the Central Intelligence Agency. It means that an operation, even if it is blown, can be denied as an officially sponsored act without the government's being caught in a barefaced lie.

This "deniability" was sought in a variety of ways. Funds were passed to foreigners through secret contacts. Private organizations were established, both in the United States and abroad, ostensibly by private citizens with private money, and funds funneled to them through dummy foundations and benefactors. Official Americans participating in "unofficial" actions acted as private citizens. Proposed covert operations were equipped with cover stories supplying an innocuous explanation. The aim always was to find proxies.

Stalin himself was a great practitioner of plausible denial.

In 1933, negotiating for recognition with President Roosevelt, he disclaimed any responsibility for the Third Communist International in the face of hard fact. He and his successors to this day deny any responsibility for the direction of Communist parties they subsidize and whose leaders they openly haul to Moscow for periodic international congresses. However implausible, these denials serve to simplify Soviet diplomatic relations with other countries, including the United States.

President Truman's covert action operations rarely came to public notice in his day, and plausible denial required little more than "no comment." Under President Eisenhower covert action entered its heyday, and the fifties were the decade of a broad-ranging covert action program. Alternately restraining and spurred on by his secretary of state, John Foster Dulles, Eisenhower sanctioned action operations in Iran, Guatemala, and Cuba, extended the covert propaganda mechanisms started under President Truman, and intervened in countless domestic political situations where "communism" appeared to be a threat.

Even before he became secretary of state, Dulles had become a public proponent of covert action against the "Red menace." In November 1950 he advocated "stimulating guerrilla and insurrectional activities" in mainland China, as well as "stepping up subversive activities within areas of Soviet control." Reading the Soviet program in South Korea as a combination of "terrorism, fraudulent propaganda, infiltration, and incitement to civil unrest," he emphasized that Soviet communism was succeeding because of its capacity to conduct "indirect aggression" and the absence of any "counteroffensive." He saw the task of the future to set up "strains and stresses" within the "captive world" that would eventually permit parts of it to regain independence.

In a 1952 *Life* article he repudiated the "negative, futile, and immoral" policy of containment and sounded the call for "liberation" of the captive peoples of the Soviet empire. During the 1952 Republican campaign General Eisenhower promised to "peacefully bring about freedom for the captive nations." Dulles repeated the promise, omitting "peacefully."

In the early fifties CIA's covert operations were literally the front lines of the American containment effort. They pierced the enemy's lines, tested his ground defenses, turned his émigrés against him, beamed subversive propaganda to his people, and promoted armed resistance within his borders. It was a picayune effort compared to the Soviet open and covert offensive against the United States and Europe, but it was the best Washington could do. As the fifties went on more and more covert operations were assigned to CIA because State and Defense did not want to do them in the open or because the simplest and fastest way to get something done was to assign the job to the secret arm.

The mood of the White House in the mid-fifties is best reflected in a top-secret report submitted by the second Hoover Commission to President Eisenhower in September 1954. It urged the continued desirability of "an aggressive covert psychological, political, and paramilitary organization more effective, more unique, and if necessary, more ruthless than that employed by the enemy. . . . We are facing an implacable enemy whose avowed objective is world domination by whatever means and at whatever cost. There are no rules in such a game. . . . We . . . must learn to subvert, sabotage, and destroy our enemies by more clever, more sophisticated, and more effective methods than those used against us. . . ."

The next year a National Security Council directive reaffirmed the Executive's commitment to covert operations. It instructed the CIA to continue creating problems for "International Communism," to reduce its strength and its control worldwide, and to "increase the capacity and the will of . . . peoples and nations to resist International Communism." It specifically reaffirmed CIA's authority to "develop underground resistance and facilitate covert and guerrilla operations."

By 1953 there were almost fifty covert propaganda and political action operations in Europe and the third world. They continued to grow in number and costs into the mid-sixties, and then began to decline.

Propaganda operations are the easiest and least dangerous of all covert actions. During the Cold War years talented collaborators were available by the thousands: writers, journalists, publicists, radio technicians, broadcasters. Europeans and Americans alike were eager to join the anti-Communist crusade.

A major charge given to the new action agency by the State Department was to channel the energies of the Soviet and East European émigré organizations in Europe into the fight against the Communist regimes in their homelands. In 1949 the National Committee for a Free Europe was founded by émigrés from Eastern Europe, and in the same year a parallel Committee for the Liberation of the Peoples of Russia was established. Their immediate offspring were two radio stations in Munich, Radio Free Europe (RFE) and Radio Liberation (later Radio Liberty). Several other committees were also established for other areas.

The basic concept underlying the two radios was a simple and sensible one at the time: They were staffed with émigrés able to speak to their own countrymen with their own voices. The émigré staffs kept up with developments in their homelands both through direct contacts inside and through newer émigrés coming out, and were in a position to speak intimately and knowledgeably to their listeners. They put on news and feature programs far exceeding the capacity of an official American instrument like the Voice of America. The early themes were designed to intensify the passive resistance of the people, to undermine the Eastern regimes by weakening the control of the Communist parties, and to hold out the hope for ultimate liberation. Secretary of State Dulles expressed the American purpose most succinctly during his

confirmation hearings before the Senate Foreign Relations
Committee:

> ... We shall never have a secure peace or a happy world so
> long as Soviet communism dominates one third of all the
> peoples that there are and is in the process of trying ... to
> extend its rule to many others. ... If our only policy is to
> stay where we are, we will be driven back. It is only by
> keeping alive the hope of liberation ... that we will end
> this terrible peril that dominates the world. ... But all of
> this can be done and must be done in ways which will not
> provoke a general war. ... Those who do not believe that
> results can be accomplished by moral pressures, *by the
> weight of propaganda* [my italics], just do not know what
> they are talking about.

As the mild thaw set in after Stalin's death, Washington
began to recognize that the Soviet Union and Eastern Europe
were more likely to change by a slow evolutionary process and
not by a dramatic shift of power. The radios dwelt less on
"liberation" and more on themes inviting social and political
change.

The Soviet response to the two radios was expensive jam-
ming, propaganda against reactionary émigré groups, diplomatic pressure to stop the imperialists from broadcasting on
foreign soil, and KGB efforts to penetrate the radio staffs and
disrupt the émigré groups. Although the Soviet response, as
well as a growing number of "letters from listeners," can be
cited as evidence for the success of these anti-Soviet propaganda actions, no judgment is possible on their practical
effect. Many persons inside the orbit were no doubt encouraged by contact with the outside world, and some sections of
the population, especially in Eastern Europe, were rein-
forced in their opposition to their regimes, but no tangible
long-term effect of these propaganda operations on the political or social evolution of these societies can be measured.

The basic ambivalence underlying these propaganda operations was highlighted by the Hungarian revolution in 1956.

To cover its military intervention the Soviet Union followed a familiar line: the Hungarian uprising was a bourgeois counterrevolution fomented by capitalist agents aimed at destroying the achievements of the new socialist state. It charged that RFE, the tool of the Western imperialists, had helped incite the mobs by advocating "liberation" and anti-Soviet attitudes. At the same time in Europe and the United States, many people criticized American policy for inciting the "captive peoples" of Eastern Europe to revolt and then failing to back them up with arms.

A postmortem examination of RFE broadcasts in the period preceding the revolution uncovered no evidence of direct incitement to revolt, but it was clear that the steady barrage of assurances that the West was firmly opposed to the continuing Communist exploitation of subject peoples could not fail to give RFE's listeners the hope that the United States would come to their aid if they did revolt. This ambivalence in American policy toward Eastern Europe has survived to this day: official acceptance of the status quo in Eastern Europe paired with an annual congressional resolution on Captive Nations Day.

Anti-Soviet émigré organizations in Western Europe were also given support to produce a broad variety of publications—from flyers and leaflets to magazines and journals, some of them of high intellectual caliber addressed to a sophisticated audience. Most of this material reached a largely Western audience, but some publications were smuggled behind the Iron Curtain by legal travelers or sent into the East by balloon.

A more systematic program was carried out by CIA within Western Europe itself, in effect as a covert annex to the Marshall Plan. The war had devastated the cultural and intellectual life of Europe as much as it had destroyed its industrial establishment. CIA's financial support was devoted to reviving the cultural groups that had survived the war. Subsidies were given to publications, meetings, congresses. Individual authors and artists were given help. Books were underwritten, travel grants supplied, lecture tours arranged. Organizations like the Congress for Cultural Freedom were founded. As Europe revived, these operations declined.

A longer-range covert effort addressed itself in these early days to a more formidable task: to match and counter the "Red fronts," that vast Soviet apparatus of international front organizations devoted to bringing the democratic Left into the Soviet camp of anti-imperialism. Soviet fronts such as the World Peace Council, the World Federation of Democratic Youth, the World Federation of Trade Unions, were working hard among women, journalists, scientific workers, schoolteachers, and intellectuals.

To provide an alternative forum for the non-Communist elements in these professional and social groups, the CIA's "international organizations" program sought to establish counterfronts. Some of these democratic fronts survived to become viable organizations, others did not.

A substantial effort was devoted to students, always a prime target for both Soviet and Communist Party organizing work. In 1946 a group of American students attended the first World Student Congress in Prague, and the following year organized the National Students Association (NSA) to represent American students in the world forum. The NSA was prepared to join the International Union of Students established after the meeting in Prague, but when its pro-Communist bias became clear after it refused to condemn the 1948 Communist coup in Czechoslovakia, the NSA joined with other non-Communist student groups to form a second international, the International Student Conference. This counterfront soon developed a fairly rigid Cold War program against the Soviet-sponsored International Union.

NSA's international operations were funded by a number of foundations that enabled it to sponsor annual international relations seminars, to provide scholarships for foreign students, and to send its international representatives on foreign tours. Other related projects provided funds for American student delegations to attend the Communist-sponsored world youth festivals and counter their strictly Soviet and anti-American line on the scene. American participation ranged from challenging speakers and debating on the floor to running a fleet of buses from a festival site in Vienna to the Hungarian border to show fellow students from the third world the barbed wire and watchdogs that kept the happy Hungarians inside their socialist paradise.

Most of these operations abroad required the cooperation of American citizens and private organizations at home. In the late forties and the fifties thousands of Americans volunteered their services. Prominent men formed the committees that sponsored the radios and supported the activities of émigrés and cultural and political organizations in Europe, the Middle East, and Asia. Many volunteered to staff the fronts. Labor and student organizations accepted funds in order to increase their capacity to work on behalf of their fellow students and fellow workers in Europe.

None of these "recruits" were "agents" in the usual sense. They were willing collaborators in the anti-Communist crusade of the time. Only a few were aware of the CIA connection, and of these only a handful were on the CIA payroll.

The principal challenge to the covert operators in concealing official sponsorship of all these actions lay in keeping secret the source of the funds involved. Again, hundreds of Americans cooperated, both by making established foundations available as a conduit for "private" grants and subsidies and by establishing dummy foundations for the same purpose. This proved to be the weakest link in the chain of security. To keep the ultimate source of funds secret, many of these foundations became linked together by the grants they made. When one became suspect, an inspection of the Internal Revenue Service records quickly exposed the mysterious source.

In 1966 a series of articles in *Ramparts* magazine exposed these connections to public view. It charged that CIA had infiltrated private American organizations with some vaguely sinister purpose. Its "agents" were using American citizens to carry out its secret programs, thus operating on the domestic front against its charter.

The most serious soul-searching came among the unwitting recipients of CIA money. Had they been "agents" of the U.S. government? Had the unwitting members of the National Student Association or the Congress of Cultural Freedom been independent spokesmen for the West—or just "tools"? What did "independent" mean, when secret funds were coming to their treasury? How should men of principle react to having been "hoodwinked"? Would they have written and acted as they did if they had known CIA was behind their organization?

The furor here and in Europe forced President Johnson to set up a committee headed by Undersecretary of State Nicholas Katzenbach that recommended a new policy for official support of private American voluntary organizations: the establishment of a "public-private mechanism to provide public funds openly for overseas activities of organizations which are adjudged deserving, in the national interest, of public support." Many of the CIA-supported or CIA-sponsored organizations, including the freedom radios, thereafter became the open recipients of U.S. government funds.

Why were these propaganda activities not supported openly from the start? Why were they assigned to a secret agency in order to hide the hand of the U.S. government? Why compel a secret agency to build up this enormous paraphernalia of secret funding channels and confidential intermediaries?

These are questions difficult to answer. Certainly it was not out of diplomatic concern for Soviet sensibilities. Today, in the easier climate of détente, the U.S. Congress openly subsidizes Radio Free Europe and Radio Liberty. It could not have been out of concern for American public opinion at the time, which supported the Cold War crusade with uncritical enthusiasm. Perhaps it was simply that "private" instruments could say things the Voice of America or other openly sponsored propaganda operations could not, or would not, say.

During the fifties these covertly sponsored activities sounded many of the themes that permeated American official and unofficial propaganda. Politics was reduced to a simple black-and-white formula of East or West, slavery or freedom. Liberalism was attacked as an ally of communism, with ex-Communists playing a leading role as the only men who really knew what communism was all about. "Neutralism" was a dirty word, for no one could be detached from the great battle for men's minds. Intellectuals, writers, and artists raised the angel-devil issue to a sophisticated level of international polemics.

In the late fifties, and during the sixties, as the American propaganda effort shifted to the third world, this simple general line had to be tempered for the new noncapitalist audiences. Anti-Communist propaganda had to address itself in more realistic terms to the concrete issues facing individual regimes and the literate sections of their populations.

Covert propaganda operations in the third world were, in effect, a fight for the media, a fight to counter the rapid progress being made by the Soviet regime in influencing the press, propaganda and education ministries, student and labor union journals, etc. Foreign editors and columnists were recruited, newspapers and magazines subsidized, press services supported. Propagandists ranged from paid "agents" to friendly collaborators, from liberal and socialist anti-Communists to simple right-wingers. Facts, themes, editorial outlines, model essays were sent out to third world stations to be reworked for local consumption. Hot stories were published in friendly outlets and replayed around the globe: from "confessions of a repentant Marxist" to the eviction of Soviet officials after an abortive coup.

There were always side products of value. Many propaganda contacts were useful sources of political intelligence.
Others with an insight into local Soviet or Communist Party
activities made it possible for CIA officers to develop personal
contacts in these circles.

Perhaps the most tangible product of these "psywar" operations was the opening up of American contacts with the
political dissidents within the Soviet Union. The earliest
links with dissident groups in Moscow were forged at the
Moscow Youth Festival in 1957, which was featured by a
largely spontaneous dialogue between Soviet and Western
youth. At the USIA exhibition in Moscow two years later the
first underground literature and "illegal" student magazines
came into Western hands. This marked the beginning of the
publication of Soviet underground documents in the West—
and in many cases their being smuggled back into the Soviet
Union for wider distribution. The collection and publication
of manuscripts produced in the Soviet Union has by now
become a large-scale enterprise with many participants, both
open and secret.

"Gray" operations such as the above involved public propaganda secretly sponsored and do not require a secret agency
to run them. "Black" operations, on the other hand, are
designed to be attributed to the other side and must be carried out by a secret agency in order to hide the actual source
of the propaganda. A black radio purportedly broadcasting
from Central Asia or a forged document purportedly coming
out of the classified files of a Soviet embassy requires expertise, secret funds, and anonymous participants.

The Soviet commitment to black propaganda, or "disinformation activities," has always been far greater than the
American. The KGB and its satellite services have committed
special sections to produce forged documents and evidence
for nonexistent events, mainly to underscore the evil intent
of their Western adversaries. Documentary "proof" of
American plans to overthrow third world governments has
been supplied to dozens of countries, sometimes through

Soviet or Communist Party controlled publications, some-times directly to the governments concerned. The Czech "Operation Thomas Mann" in 1964 was designed to expose a mythical hard-line American policy toward Latin America and CIA preparations for political coups in half a dozen countries. It involved counterfeiting a USIA press release, publishing a number of circulars by a nonexistent committee, and forging letters written by FBI Director J. Edgar Hoover.*

Part of CIA's counterintelligence work during the fifties and sixties was devoted to detecting and exposing these forgeries, tracing their origin, and publishing the results through the Congressional Record.

CIA's own disinformation activities have been far more limited and have generally concentrated on narrower targets: the improper antics of a senior official in the local Soviet Embassy or the sinister purposes of a Cuban agent in a Latin American country.

In the late sixties covert propaganda, both gray and black, played a sharply diminished role in CIA's overseas work. The normal instruments of American propaganda, both official and private, were more than adequate to publish American views, at the same time that American policy, particularly in the Vietnamese war, made American propaganda increasingly unpersuasive.

Again, it is as difficult to assess the net result of this global propaganda campaign as it is to evaluate the effects of the freedom radios. The "fight for men's minds" is an elusive fight not open to statistical measurement, and the degree to which American or Soviet propaganda, as opposed to American or Soviet actions, has swayed those minds can never be distinguished.

As the above account may suggest, I do not favor large-

*For details on this and many other disinformation operations, see a firsthand account by Ladislav Bittman, a former Czech intelligence officer, in *The Deception Game,* The Syracuse University Research Corporation, Syracuse, 1972.

scale propaganda actions by a secret agency. High-powered radios and international front organizations demand a large commitment of money and facilities that can easily be traced to their prime sponsors. However desirable they may be, they can only serve to contaminate the other secret operations with which they are intermingled.

Localized propaganda operations are another matter. The essence of politics is propaganda: speeches, handbills, editorials, demonstrations, polls. An election is one vast propaganda exercise to capture men's minds at least temporarily. Propaganda thus forms an integral part of political action operations. Such national operations, whether in Europe or the third world, are easier to keep secret, and their effects can be measured by the votes cast. The conduct of this propaganda by national political parties or labor unions not only obscures the fact of American support, but in most cases will make it more effective.

There is an ironic footnote to the Soviet-American propaganda confrontation of the past thirty years. For decades the KGB has been touted by American propaganda as the sinister arm of Soviet imperialism abroad, and Moscow has attempted to give CIA the same treatment. The recent exposures of CIA's covert action operations have given the Soviet line its greatest boost. Soviet and Communist media can now quote the American Congress and press to fortify their long-standing theme that the United States is the enemy of the third world.

10

COVERT ACTION: PARAMILITARY

Paramilitary operations are the "noisiest" of all covert actions. When they fail, they become public fiascoes, and no official denials are plausible. The history of American paramilitary operations as an element of America's containment policy is one of almost uniform failure.

Within months of its inception OPC was caught up in the Pentagon's contingency plans for the coming Soviet invasion of Western Europe. It was assigned two related missions: to establish agents in Western Europe who could survive under Soviet occupation and to help retard a Soviet ground advance by supporting resistance groups in Eastern Europe and Russia.

The first mission was the simpler, though costly in man-hours and equipment. In Germany, Austria, and France, in the Lowlands and Scandinavia, thousands of personnel, from OPC and from Allied military and security services, made ready for a Soviet occupation. The mission's main focus, however, was on recruiting native agents who would remain in place after their areas had been overrun by Soviet forces.

These stay-behind agents were trained and briefed to supply intelligence from Soviet-held areas, to develop escape routes for downed Allied fliers, to carry out sabotage and antisabotage work.

Since the war did not come, and the Cold War eased, these stay-behind agents no longer served a purpose. Most of them were released from their missions by the mid-fifties. Some secret caches were still being dug up in the sixties.

The more ambitious, and totally unrealistic, paramilitary mission given OPC by the Pentagon's war planners was to retard a Soviet military advance into Western Europe by building up anti-Soviet resistance groups, mainly within the Ukraine and Poland.

To support and build up this anti-Soviet resistance the Ukrainian and Polish émigré organizations in the West were an indispensable instrument. Among Ukrainian groups were benevolent associations, committees of national liberation, and provisional governments, all competing for political support from the State Department and the CIA. Almost all professed to have substantial support from their countrymen within the Soviet Union.

Various groups of Polish émigrés similarly fought for Allied backing in Germany and in Paris, London, and Washington. They too vied with each other in assessing the support they enjoyed in Poland.

Both groups of émigrés were available as intermediaries to their fellow nationals in the homeland. Those outside were eager to help build up the resistance groups inside, not simply as a paramilitary force to fight the Russians, but as the nucleus of a movement that might eventually return them to power.

It was to the leaders of the outside that OPC turned.

The effort faced multiple built-in hazards: the fragmentary communications with the inside groups, many of them channeled through the outside leaders who had some self-interest in exaggerating their strength; the formidable structure of internal security both within the Ukraine and Poland as the postwar disorganization was repaired; and the existence of Soviet and Polish agents within the outside emigration.

THE UKRAINE

At the end of the war in Europe anti-Soviet or anti-Communist resistance forces were most active in the Baltic states and in the Ukraine. In Lithuania the partisans, amounting at one time to perhaps thirty thousand, remained active from 1944 until 1952, and some CIA contact was maintained with them until they were totally suppressed in a large-scale mopping up in 1952.

The largest anti-Soviet forces, some thirty to forty thousand men, formed the Ukrainian resistance army in the Soviet and Polish Ukraine. Organized into military units, operating out of the forests and mountains, they carried out guerrilla warfare operations against the Soviet reoccupation forces, raiding military and militia posts, collecting intelligence on the "enemy," and distributing antiregime propaganda. The resistance collapsed first within the Polish border: A large-scale assault by security and army forces started in April 1947, and the movement was effectively dead within the year.

On the Ukrainian side of the border—mainly in the Carpathian Mountains—the partisans were less militant and survived longer. Their main problem was to live through the winters. In addition to raiding government posts for arms and ammunition, and spreading nationalist Ukrainian propaganda among the peasantry, they were forced to spend most of the summer and fall collecting forage for the winter. Once snow fell, they lived the entire winter in underground caves and shelters around the clock to avoid leaving telltale footprints for the security patrols. The winter toll was high.

By 1950, when the OPC planners examined the resistance potential in the Ukraine as a behind-the-lines counter to a Soviet military action against Western Europe, it was clear that the Ukrainian guerrillas could play no serious paramilitary role. The CIA had made its first contacts with the Ukrainian resistance, as noted earlier, in the fall of 1949, when two couriers were airdropped into the Carpathians. It continued to maintain contact both by radio and by couriers coming out of the Ukraine at irregular intervals with up-to-date reports on the declining resistance situation. Only a large-scale military supply effort would have been of any use to the resistance fighters, and that the war planners were unprepared to carry out.

The resistance survived as a decreasingly effective but still organized movement in the Ukraine until 1953, when security troops in regimental strength carried out a final pitched battle with air and artillery support. Two CIA-trained radio operators (not under KGB control) remained with these forces until the end, in November 1953.

Neither in the Baltic states nor in the Ukraine did American support have any measurable military effect in helping these undergrounds to survive. It served them in only two respects: by giving them a line to their fellow countrymen in the outside world, and by keeping up their morale—a human, if not a political, plus.

POLAND

The most substantial and disastrous paramilitary effort inside the Soviet orbit was carried out in Poland.

The Polish situation in the summer of 1950 appeared much more hopeful to the war planners, though hard information on internal developments was sparse. Poland lay directly across the line of advance for Soviet troops moving from the east into Western Europe, and there, if anywhere, the Soviet advance could be retarded. Further, the Polish emigration in the West was strong and influential.

Two organized instruments were available: the recently established coalition of émigré Poles, the Polish Political Council in London, and the Freedom and Independence movement (WIN, from its Polish initials). WIN claimed the greatest support within Poland itself—some 500 active members, 20,000 partially active, and 100,000 men available for action in the event of war. WIN outside was chosen as the instrument for a retardation program inside. It called for WIN inside to satisfy urgent intelligence requirements, to establish paramilitary units, and to prepare for sabotaging and slowing up any Soviet military advances into Western Europe.

Communications were established in the summer of 1950 and maintained for more than two years. Money, military supplies, and radio equipment were airdropped to assist the leaders inside in organizing and equipping the fighting brigades that the Pentagon hoped would slow up a Soviet advance, an advance that had been made more likely in the minds of the military planners by the outbreak of the Korean war.

Even while the operation was in progress, WIN inside had become a target for counterespionage investigation, but it was not until December 1952 that the extent of government control of WIN inside became clear. The Polish radio announced with great fanfare on December 27–28 that its security forces (UB) had ended an operation whose leaders had confessed that the British and Americans had supported an uprising against the Polish government.

The subsequent investigation showed that, in actual fact, the Polish UB had been in control of WIN inside from 1947 and had deliberately provoked the British and American services to supply the "resistance organization" with support.

The UB succeeded by building up a careful scenario:

After cleaning up the legitimate WIN groups during 1946–47, the UB captured a WIN leader by the name of Sienko who agreed to cooperate with the UB as a double agent. Some time later the first courier in three years from WIN outside arrived in Poland, met Sienko in a UB safe house, and accepted him as a legitimate WIN representative. WIN inside (now totally under UB control) maintained contact with WIN outside mainly by letters from "family" to "friends outside," by occasional meetings between the two sides, and by a WIN inside courier to the West who did *not* know WIN was controlled by the UB.

The UB, through its controlled channel, prodded WIN outside to get in touch with the Americans, and followed every phase of the negotiations. It was able to keep track of WIN American personnel, plans, and operations. Every agent, dollar, and radio dispatched into Poland ended up in UB hands.

The reason for timing the exposure in December 1952 is not clear. Stalin may have ordered it to implicate the CIA in anti-Soviet plots and later to charge the Americans with a hand in several plots he was concocting in Moscow. It is also possible that the Russians were concerned that President Eisenhower might overestimate the armed potential of the satellite countries in his professed policy of "liberation."

In any event the WIN fiasco brought despair to the anti-Soviet emigration, rich fodder to the Communist propaganda machine, and a sharp jolt to the paramilitary planners in the CIA and the National Security Council.

ALBANIA

Nineteen fifty-two marked the end of another abortive paramilitary operation into Eastern Europe, an effort not simply to support existing resistance elements, but a "positive intervention" designed to unseat a Communist regime.

By 1949 Albania had become an attractive target for the military planners in Washington. The rebels in Greece were on their last legs, Tito had isolated himself from Moscow, and the Russians were working hard to stabilize the shaky Hoxha regime in Tirana. The tide in the Balkans appeared to be running against Moscow. Albania looked soft, and a breakthrough there might unsettle the other satellites.

The beginnings of the Albanian operation go back to early British intelligence contacts with Albanian émigré groups in 1946. Its aim was to support a royalist anti-Communist group in Central Albania and organize a guerrilla movement that would gain enough popular support to start a civil war against the Hoxha government. A few trained men were dropped into Albania in 1947, but the main action did not start until 1949 as a joint British-American effort.

For two years from the spring of 1950 on team after team of "free" Albanians was infiltrated by air, sea, and land. They were recruited in Italy, Greece, and Egypt under the umbrella of the "Committee of Free Albanians," organized under the auspices of King Zog's royal guards.

Almost every mission misfired. Teams sent across the border from Greece ran into police ambushes. Teams landing from rubber craft were met at the beach by police. Drop zones were surrounded by Albanian troops. A few radio operators who came up on the air transmitted under Albanian control.

The armed "liberation" of Albania was a disaster, but unlike the WIN operation it was not foiled only from within, but by a Soviet agent in London. Although the British side of the project was run by a former wartime expert in Special Operations, it was under the desk control of Kim Philby in the London headquarters of the British service. There is little question that Philby not only informed Moscow of overall British-American planning, but provided details on the individual dispatch of agent teams before they arrived in Albania. No one in London or Washington, of course, knew at the time why the disaster was so total.

The Albanian operation was the first and only attempt by Washington to unseat a Communist regime within the Soviet orbit by paramilitary means. It taught a clear lesson to the war planners: Even a weak regime could not be overthrown by covert paramilitary actions alone.

ASIA

American support of anti-Communist resistance groups played a far smaller role in Asia.

In the summer of 1950, with the Korean war in full swing, OPC was instructed to initiate psychological warfare and paramilitary operations against the Chinese Communist regime. In the following three years more than a hundred Chinese agents were recruited and trained for resistance operations in China, and several teams were dispatched by air and small boat. They found no signs of the "extensive resistance elements" reported by Chinese Nationalist sources, and after several failures the project was canceled in 1953.

Similar efforts to organize anti-Communist elements of the North Korean population both before and after the outbreak of the Korean war were generally unsuccessful. Some minor air and maritime operations were launched into the North, and a few downed American flyers were recovered and passed through escape and evasion routes to the South, but no resistance groups were found or developed.

The last American effort to support a resistance group within the Sino-Soviet orbit was carried out in Tibet. As the Korean war was winding down, the CIA began sending intelligence agents into Tibet to assess the situation and see what could be done to forestall the Chinese takeover that was in the offing. Tibetan agents equipped with radios were dispatched by air and made contact with the Dalai Lama in Lhasa, giving him a channel of communication with the West.

When the Dalai Lama chose to flee from Lhasa to avoid

capture by the Chinese forces in 1959, he was accompanied on his flight by a CIA-trained radio operator who was able to keep Washington posted on his often hazardous progress. The Dalai Lama's route carried him through the territory of the Khambas, and it was the martial Khambas' rearguard action that prevented the pursuing Chinese troops from catching up with the Dalai Lama's party.

Fighting broke out in many sections of the country with the Dalai's flight, but the Khambas held out the longest. As the Chinese built more roads into Khamba territory, they set up garrisons, installed their own administration and controls, and gradually wiped out the last armed resistance.

In Asia, as in Europe, the Communist regimes remained intact and unshaken. Saving Western Europe from communism had proved easier than destabilizing a Communist government already in power. By the mid-fifties internal dissidence in the Sino-Soviet orbit had become a purely domestic problem of law and order. The brave rhetoric of "liberation" and "rollback" died down, and the words were finally emasculated by American failure to act during the Hungarian revolution in 1956.

GUATEMALA

On two occasions the Eisenhower administration authorized paramilitary operations to subvert leftist regimes in Latin America, the first against Guatemala, the second against Cuba.

In 1944 a domestic coup in Guatemala brought into power a leftist leader, Juan Jose Arévalo, who was not a Communist, but packed his government with Communist Party members and Communist sympathizers. He was succeeded in 1951 by his minister of defense, Jacobo Árbenz, who continued to pursue a hard leftist policy both domestically and in foreign affairs. Official U.S. policy, rigidly anti-Communist, was against the Árbenz regime on both the public level (cutting off military aid and putting political and economic pressures on the regime) and the covert level (attempts to make senior Guatemalan military officers defect and a program of anti-Árbenz radio and leaflet propaganda). The main CIA effort was to support a military plot already in progress.

Colonel Carlos Castillo Armas had begun plotting a coup against the Árbenz regime in 1952 with support from the chiefs of state of two neighbors, Honduras and Nicaragua, and the encouragement of the United Fruit Co. The main covert action was directed at separating the Guatemalan Army from Árbenz, and on May 1, 1954, the CIA-created Radio Liberacíon began broadcasting into Guatemala in an effort to incite the Guatemalan Army leaders to overthrow Árbenz. The propaganda campaign highlighted the semipublic military preparations going on in Honduras, actual and fictional arms drops and border intrusions into Guatemala, and direct appeals to the Guatemalan military officers.

On June 1, Árbenz's security forces rounded up Colonel Castillo's intelligence and action supporters inside Guatemala and arrested and tortured anti-Árbenz suspects throughout the country.

Castillo's paramilitary action took place on June 17–18, when his forces, about 450 men, organized in "shock teams," crossed into Guatemala from Honduras. Assisted by radio broadcasts and air strafing, they forced Árbenz to ask for asylum in the Mexican Embassy on June 25. Two days later he resigned.

The Guatemalan operation was as much a propaganda success as a paramilitary action. The failure of will in Guatemala City kept military casualties to a handful.

CUBA

The watershed in CIA's paramilitary operations was the abortive invasion of Cuba in 1961. As early as 1959 it was clear that Castro the nationalist had become Castro the

Communist. In the climate of the day a Communist state sixty miles off the U.S. coast was, to put it mildly, politically and militarily unacceptable.

Shortly after the failure of the State Department's last effort to work out an understanding with Castro in March 1960, President Eisenhower approved a recommendation by his Special Group, a subcommittee of the National Security Council, that CIA train a brigade of Cuban émigrés for action against the Castro regime. The initial plan called for the dispatch of a small band of trained guerrillas into each of Cuba's six provinces by September—well before the presidential election. In August, however, the Special Group changed plans: The brigade would instead make an amphibious landing on Cuban soil with air support supplied by émigré pilots in unmarked American military planes. The target date was postponed, and the plan was inherited by the new administration.

President Kennedy first heard of the plan from the CIA director soon after the November election, and a week after his inauguration he called a White House meeting to discuss it. His top advisers—the secretaries of State and Defense, the Joint Chiefs of Staff, and the CIA director— recommended he carry it out. After seeking the advice of other experts, he finally gave the go-ahead.

The Cuban brigade moved out of its Guatemalan camp on April 10, 1961. On April 15 an air strike by Cuban-manned B-26's knocked out part of Castro's air force. On the evening of April 16, a Sunday, the boats of the Cuban task force arrived in the Bay of Pigs. By Monday night the émigré- soldiers were pinned down on the beach and their boats dispersed. After fighting bravely for two days against superior arms and forces, the survivors dispersed on Wednesday and were captured one by one.

This, in barest outline, was the operation. Its repercussions were enormous: at the United Nations, within the White House, in State and Defense, in CIA, and around the world. It was a tragedy for the Cuban émigrés, for the anti-Castro elements still in Cuba, and for the new President. It was a handsome gift for Castro, for Khrushchev, and for the anti-American forces in Latin America. It cannot be recalled without anguish by those who were close to it.

Why did it happen?

The public literature on the Bay of Pigs is enormous and continues to grow. It covers the political and military preparations for the invasion, the events on the beachhead, the diplomatic and propaganda aftermath. In much of it CIA is the fall guy, but there have also been serious efforts to understand how and why the project was undertaken in the first place, and a few dispassionate efforts to assign the blame for its failure.

There is enough blame to go around for everyone: for the planners who designed it, for the policy makers who approved it, and for the operators who executed it. Two Presidents were behind it, the Joint Chiefs gave it their military blessing, the secretaries of State and Defense were for it, the director of CIA stood behind it. No other covert operation ever received such careful high-level attention before or since.

Many failures contributed to the disaster. The failure of intelligence to gauge the strength of the Castro regime, the weakness of internal dissidence, the capabilities of the Cuban armed forces; the failure of the military planners in preparing an amphibious assault bound to fail on purely military grounds; the failure of diplomatic judgment in weighing the risks against the probability of success; and the failure of the operators to bridle their enthusiasm with the prescribed dose of professional skepticism.

From a purely operational point of view its weaknesses were obvious before it was launched. It was neither covert nor secret. The American hand was public knowledge weeks before it took place—any denial of official support would have been outrageously implausible. Nor could the invasion itself be kept a surprise—it was too large an operation. The Cuban émigrés involved were too insecure to stay silent. As in all émigré groups, loose talk, bickering, internal politics were the order of the day. Above all, Castro was forewarned—by his agents in the Cuban emigration, by the American and Latin American press, and by the two-day warning from the bombing raids.

The basic question remains unanswered to this day: If the Castro regime was considered by the White House a serious threat to the security of the United States, why a chancy paramilitary effort and not a straightforward conventional military operation?

The project did not involve covert support to an existing resistance group, nor was it an essentially political operation designed to create small resistance groups inside Cuba. It was a straightforward military operation—and in this fact lay the essential stupidity of assigning it to a civilian agency. Whatever role the "successful" Guatemalan operation played in the minds of the planners, Cuba was simply not another Guatemala—in geography, domestic security, or internal leadership.

The fig leaf for official armed intervention was available: to use Cuban threats to our Guantanamo naval base, just as President Johnson later used the safety of American civilians as an excuse for his invasion of the Dominican Republic.

If the Pentagon had carried out the operation, it would have been a guaranteed success. President Kennedy would have avoided disaster. There would have been no Cuban missile crisis. The ifs of history are easy and tempting to work out.

The failure of the invasion did not bring an end to American paramilitary actions against Cuba. A special review committee was established by President Kennedy after the Cuban fiasco to reevaluate our paramilitary programs. The committee labeled Castro "a real menace capable of eventually overthrowing the elected governments in any one or more of weak Latin American republics" and urged that the situation be reappraised and new anti-Castro actions be embarked on.

A major result of this reappraisal was Operation Mongoose, a broad program of covert action designed to overthrow Castro. It was placed under the direction of an Army general (the famous counterinsurgency expert, General Edward Lansdale) and closely controlled by an enlarged Special Group. The new Mongoose program envisaged an open revolt and the overthrow of the regime by the Cubans themselves rather than through an "outside" effort. Thirty-two planning tasks were assigned to State, Defense, and CIA that included the collection of intelligence, the defection of Cuban leaders, propaganda operations, attacks on regime leaders, and sabotage, and involved the use of professional anti-Castro émigrés, labor leaders, youth and church groups, and "gangster elements." The Special Group failed to approve most of the specific action plans brought before it, and the program concentrated mainly on the collection of intelligence. Operation Mongoose was abandoned following the Cuban missile crisis that fall.

A new top policy group then took over the task of working out an American program toward Cuba, and among other actions, in June 1963, it approved a sabotage program by trained Cuban agents against industrial and transportation targets. The new program had a more modest objective than Operation Mongoose. It was designed "to nourish a spirit of resistance and disaffection which could lead to significant defections and other by-products of unrest."* Agents and weapons were infiltrated into Cuba, commando raids were carried out, and small-scale sabotage missions were executed on Cuban terrain.

---

*Alleged Assassination Plots Involving Foreign Leaders, an interim report of the Select Senate Committee on Intelligence, November 1975, p. 173. On the assassination attempts against Castro, see below pp. 196–201.

The Cuban failure spelled an end to the use of CIA for any large-scale paramilitary operations in the sixties—except in Indochina, where for the next ten years the White House and the National Security Council had one overriding purpose: not to "lose" Southeast Asia. CIA joined Defense and State in this latest and most expensive venture in military containment.

INDOCHINA

No facet of CIA's intelligence or operations functions was ignored in the fight for Indochina. Intelligence agents were dispatched by sea, air, and land into Communist-held areas. Operators worked on the Chinese target, the North Vietnamese target, the Pathet Lao target, the Vietcong target. Counterintelligence assumed a high priority: to build up a competent South Vietnamese security service, to help train the police, to infiltrate the North Vietnamese and Vietcong intelligence and security units. CIA—alone or in collaboration with South Vietnamese or other American agencies—carried out psychological warfare programs and played a serious role in the political action operations designed to advance the cause to which Washington had committed itself.

Many of these activities were open or semicovert. In Saigon CIA was a large-scale enterprise, and CIA station chiefs became semipublic figures. Key CIA operators were cited by name and deed in news reporting. Playing its role in a theater of war, the CIA became an all-purpose instrument of action like the Office of Strategic Services during the war with Germany and Japan.

CIA's paramilitary programs were directed both at North Vietnam and at countering the Vietcong guerrillas in the South. In the mid-fifties CIA infiltrated sabotage teams into North Vietnam, helped build up the Vietnamese Special Forces, and trained South Vietnamese soldiers and hill tribesmen in unconventional warfare. As the war escalated, the American military command played a steadily greater role in directing covert action operations, from commando raids to secret air strikes.

In Laos the CIA carried the main burden of creating a secret army designed to evade the Geneva Agreement of 1954 officially neutralizing the country. To counter the expanding power of the Communist Pathet Lao troops backed by Hanoi, CIA was directed to recruit, arm, and supply the Meo tribesmen both for guerrilla operations in Communist-dominated areas and for conventional warfare against the Pathet Lao. This demanding assignment was carried out by a handful of CIA case officers in the field with a high degree of efficiency and courage. Their successful performance is not lessened by the eventual failure of our overall policy in Indochina.

ANGOLA

One of the most recent public debates on our paramilitary ventures has centered around a simple but large-scale guerrilla-supply operation in Africa in 1975.

By the early sixties Africa had become a contested battleground. Various countries—the Soviet Union, China, East Germany, and the United States—supplied moral support, training, money, and arms, particularly to the anti-Portuguese rebel groups. With the departure of the Portuguese from their African colonies, the transition to native rule went relatively smoothly except in Angola, where three tribal factions fought with each other to take over the administration. The Soviet-supported MPLA, after a slow start, threatened to become the victor. After establishing a de facto government in the Angolan capital, Luanda, the MPLA began receiving large-scale military aid from the Soviet Union and at least ten thousand Cuban troops from Havana.

To counter the MPLA, the White House again resorted to

its covert arm. Starting in January 1975, President Ford instructed the CIA to supply secretly some $25 million worth of
military equipment to two anti-MPLA factions via the
neighboring country of Zaire. When this supply operation
was exposed the following winter, Congress prohibited any
further covert support.

Disregarding the wisdom of our intervention—its belated
timing and the complex diplomatic and political factors
involved—the Angolan affair again raised the broader policy
question: Was the use of the covert arm essential or desirable?

The personnel and equipment that flowed into Luanda to
support the MPLA were ferried in not under the auspices of
the KGB, but by Soviet and Cuban ships and airplanes.
Moscow openly supplied military aid to support a "national
liberation movement" that became a government recognized
by many African states. The Soviet-Cuban action was a
straightforward military intervention by official invitation of
a government in power—like the American interventions in
Lebanon, South Vietnam, and Laos.

With a friendly Zaire always available as a convenient intermediary, why did we not respond in kind by the open
delivery of arms to "our side"?

It must have been perfectly clear to the President and his
advisers, particularly in the post-Watergate, post-Vietnam
atmosphere of the day, that the large-scale delivery of equipment to Zaire-Angola would not be kept secret.

Why then use CIA to "cover" an effort that was bound to
become public? Why make plausible denial so ridiculous?

There appears to be only one explanation. The President
and Secretary of State Henry Kissinger were concerned that
the Congress would not agree with their Angolan policy and
would not vote the required funds. Secret funds and secret
delivery provided the easy way out. The use of covert action,
not to achieve a foreign purpose in secret, but to evade congressional scrutiny, degrades the covert instrument into a
domestic political tool.

Angola underlines the lesson that should have been learned from the Bay of Pigs and the "secret army" in Laos: Large-scale paramilitary operations do not belong in a secret agency.

Do they belong anywhere?

That the United States must keep a paramilitary capability in being for wartime use is not questioned by most observers. It is also arguable that unconventional warfare may be essential in any regional conflicts that the United States may participate in short of all-out war with a major power. And one can foresee possible situations that might demand a small-scale paramilitary action such as the Israelis carried out on the Entebbe airport in Uganda to free hijacked hostages.

An inescapable requirement for a civilian agency to carry out paramilitary operations in peacetime is an enormous infrastructure to support them year-in, year-out. Just as the covert propaganda operations in the fifties compelled the CIA to establish scores of front organizations, cover companies, and dummy foundations, the paramilitary program of the sixties demanded an extensive network of CIA-owned companies to provide essential cover. CIA's air companies were an integral part of these actions, whether supplying guerrilla forces in Laos or moving Cuban émigrés to their training bases or ferrying arms to Angola; and they in turn required holding companies, ground maintenance facilities, and fronts for secret recruiting.

Another facet of this infrastructure is the secret procurement of arms, the maintenance of large secret dumps of non-U.S. military equipment, outdoor bases for parachute and sabotage training, and a staff of specialized personnel not qualified by experience for secret intelligence operations and therefore unsuitable for transfer to CIA's major and continuing mission.

The proper place for maintaining these men and facilities is the Department of Defense. All three of our armed services already have appropriate personnel, equipment, and training facilities in being. All that is needed to make Defense effective in covert paramilitary operations is to convert a small section of its command structure into a special operating unit that can be given authority to move funds, personnel, and equipment outside the system of bureaucratic command. At the same time, Congress would be placed directly within the decision-making process for paramilitary as well as military operations abroad, and the burden of proof that covert military action is required would rest with the President.

Years ago some attempt was made to split the paramilitary functions: small-scale operations (involving up to six, ten, twenty men) assigned to the CIA, larger-scale operations to Defense. The division of labor, even if it could be worked out in practical terms, makes no sense. All that CIA requires for espionage operations into a "denied area" is a few specialists and a limited amount of equipment to dispatch by air or sea a small number of intelligence agents equipped with radios. A small staff of CIA paramilitary experts can stay in touch with the Department of Defense and participate in such war planning as may be required by the Joint Chiefs of Staff.

With the reduction over the last decade of CIA's large-scale propaganda operations and the removal of the paramilitary function, CIA's secret operations might again become secret, more effective, and less controversial.

11

COVERT ACTION: POLITICAL

In the field of overseas political action the Soviet regime has the greatest advantage over the U.S. government, for it has been dedicated to global political action since its inception. It enjoys an enormously varied set of instruments to support its national purposes abroad: not only the Communist parties, both legal and underground, but also its international fronts, especially in labor, friendship societies, subsidized periodicals and newspapers, solidarity groups, etc. These instruments permit Moscow to carry out most of its political action programs without using its covert arm, the First Chief Directorate of the KGB. Without such instruments at its command, Washington has been forced to use the CIA for its covert actions abroad—a slender instrument at best.

Covert political action in its broadest sense involves the use of secret contacts and secret funds to affect the power and policies of another nation. It is uniquely different from espionage and counterespionage operations in that it is designed to advance the "agent's" own interests: the increase of his political influence or that of his organization. It is naturally easier to give money to a politician or labor leader to help him achieve *his* purposes than to convince a man to be a spy or to double him against his KGB case officer.

Political action contacts can range from the chief of state to the leader of a political party, from a cabinet minister to the secretary of a labor union, from the chief of a security service to an influential cleric. The funds involved can range from a token payment or service to large-scale funding for an election campaign. In its most dramatic form covert political action can culminate in a coup or countercoup. In its most sensational form it can involve the assassination of a foreign political leader.

Like paramilitary operations, covert political actions can be carried out in support of a friendly government or against its domestic opposition. Covert support of a regime or party in power I will label "benign": It ordinarily has the blessing of the government. Covert support of a domestic opposition against an unfriendly government is clearly "subversive": It is, in the short and long run, designed to replace a regime in power.

WESTERN EUROPE

The earliest political action operations after the founding of OPC were strictly benign.

CIA's political action under President Truman was designed to strengthen the European political structure. Substantial funds were secretly delivered to various political leaders both to assist them in strengthening their party organizations and to increase their election funds. Labor operations, first started under the influence of the Economic Cooperation Administration, helped consolidate and strengthen non-Communist unions. American unions were encouraged to assist their fellow workers in Europe and to support anti-Communist labor federations.

The threat of a possible Communist takeover in Italy in 1948 led President Truman to consider the use of American power to prevent it. Among the recommendations made to him by the National Security Council were to counter Communist propaganda in Italy, to detach the left-wing Socialists from the Communists, and to assist the pro-Western Christian Democratic Party. This program, authorized in February 1948, some six months before the establishment of OPC, helped at least in some part in defeating the Communists in the April 1948 elections.

From that day to this the Communist Party of Italy has been viewed by Washington as the major political threat to the democratic regimes in Europe. For the next twenty years several million dollars were passed annually to democratic party and labor leaders to support their organizing and election efforts. It was a modest counter to the Soviet effort. In the mid- and late sixties the annual Soviet subsidy to the Italian party ranged between eight and twelve million dollars, most of it passed through a complex of commercial and banking facilities.

In countering the Communist insurgencies in Greece and the Philippines the CIA played only a secondary role. Counterinsurgency has always been a total U.S. government effort. It has involved the State Department's diplomacy, its official propaganda, economic aid and technical assistance, military aid, and the commitment of the armed forces.

CIA's role in these early ventures in counterinsurgency focused on the training and logistic support of the internal security services, on providing advice for domestic propaganda programs, and on supplying experts on land reform, economic policy, or electioneering. In these benign interventions the CIA worked with the host government in close coordination with the other U.S. agencies involved.

IRAN

President Eisenhower and his secretary of state, John Foster Dulles, were no less interested than President Truman in using the covert arm, particularly in the newly emerging third world. The first political action operation authorized by the Eisenhower administration was designed to preempt what appeared to be a major Soviet enterprise to extend its influence, if not control, over the oil-rich state of Iran.

Premier Mossadeq had come to power in May 1951 and promptly nationalized the British-owned Anglo-Iranian Oil Company. Washington continued to supply a small amount of aid to Iran until the Eisenhower administration decided that Mossadeq had to go. After Mossadeq refused a conciliatory offer from Washington, the decision was made to get rid of him.

The August 1953 coup, directed by a small group of CIA operators working out of a basement in Teheran, was preceded by a propaganda campaign with a simple theme: If Mossadeq's antishah regime remains in power, the Soviet Union and the Iranian Communists (the then powerful Tudeh Party) will take over the country. The fight was won in the streets. The demonstrations by supporters of Mossadeq and the Tudeh Party against the impending coup were countered by hiring Iranians to lead the anti-Mossadeq mobs, and the U.S. Military Mission in Teheran supplied the anti-Mossadeq army with American equipment that helped turn the tide of street fighting. Mossadeq was forced from office and was replaced by a General Zahedi. A new oil agreement followed.

The rationale for this first U.S.-sponsored subversion of a government outside the Soviet orbit illustrates the readiness with which Washington confused "nationalism" with "communism." Mossadeq organized his National Front mainly on the oil issue, and refused to legalize the Tudeh Party or to accept its cooperation. A strange man, Mossadeq was nonetheless no Communist.

During the years that followed the CIA was called upon, mainly by the Department of State, to use its influence on countless occasions. Modest financial support, the encouragement of talented young politicians and labor leaders, the introduction of American "protégés" to Western sources of open support and fellowships, the persuasion of government officials to adopt a pro-American stand on specific issues, private conversations on the pros and cons (mainly cons) of recognizing the Soviet Union—in these, and many other ways, the CIA stations abroad acted as a confidential extension of American diplomacy.

As counterinsurgency became an increasingly active sector of American foreign policy, CIA's routine liaison with the domestic security services of friendly countries assumed a greater political action role. Part of the basic CIA mission was to strengthen the capacity of these services to deal more effectively with their own local Communist parties, guerrilla groups, Soviet Communist Party connections, etc.

LATIN AMERICA

Up to the mid-fifties most Latin American countries, with the conspicuous exception of Guatemala, were looked upon by Washington as good neighbors. In 1955 Latin America began to emerge as an arena of the Cold War, and CIA became involved in a broad front of covert action: building news services and local outlets for distributing propaganda, supporting non-Communist student congresses, sponsoring or subsidizing anti-Communist publications, extending the activities of its international front organizations into the youth, student, and labor groups from Mexico to Brazil.

As in postwar Europe, the CIA had a twofold task: on the one hand, to promote an understanding of American policy and support pro-U.S. governments and groups; on the other, to weaken pro-Soviet or anti-American regimes and social groups. In simplified terms these were the practical purposes of the Alliance for Progress, and covert operations became an extension of this program.

The entry of Fidel Castro into Havana on January 1, 1959, and the Cuban shift from an economic satellite to a militant Communist foe of the United States intensified Washington's call for effective political action. Increasing Soviet and East European interest across the South American continent, the founding of "Chinese parties," the increasing anti-Americanism, especially in the oil-producing regions, the mounting tide of terrorism—all conspired to produce a greater demand for covert action.

Most of CIA's political action operations were benign—in support of a friendly regime against domestic threats to its stability, the main thrust of Washington's counterinsurgency program. Combined State-Defense-CIA efforts helped defeat the Cuban- and Soviet-supported rural and urban terrorism in Venezuela, the internal guerrilla movement in Colombia, and the embryonic war of national liberation under Che Guevara in Bolivia. In a few cases, as in Brazil under João Goulart and Guatemala under Árbenz, CIA operations were strictly subversive—to unseat the regime in power. In all cases the White House made the decisions on the covert actions to be taken.

CIA's operations in Ecuador and Chile were typical in their scope and purpose.

The CIA task in Ecuador in the early sixties was to counter growing Communist and anti-American influence, to foster a diplomatic break with Cuba, and to strengthen non-Communist parties and organizations. Washington's official policy worked toward these same ends: the diplomatic efforts of the American Embassy, the routine propaganda of the U.S. Information Agency, the various projects of the Agency for International Development, including the training and equipment of the police, loans from the Inter-American Development Bank, the supply of military equipment and training to the Ecuadoran armed forces through the military aid program.

The principal effort, to isolate Cuba, was composed of

hundreds of small operations whose cumulative purpose was to cut down the travel of Ecuadorans to Cuba, to intercept Ecuadorans trained as guerrillas in Cuba, to harass the Communists and other leftist parties, to depict Castro as the major threat to Ecuadoran independence, and to lobby, directly and indirectly, at the highest levels of government for a diplomatic break with Cuba.

The covert effort in Ecuador was supported by a wide range of intelligence operations, for hard intelligence is essential to successful political action. Agents within the Ecuadoran Communist Party and various left-wing anti-American organizations permitted the CIA station to keep track of behind-the-scenes events in the capital and the provinces, to assess the attitudes and personalities of the main political players, and to forecast upcoming plans and policy changes. Some intelligence reports led directly to action by the local police: the cleanup of a planned guerrilla base, the arrest of Ecuadorans returning from a training course in Cuba. Well-publicized, these events added fact to the anti-Communist campaign in the media.

The political propaganda effort covered a wide spectrum. Campaigns in the press and street demonstrations against the bogey of communism attempted to counter local anti-American propaganda based on Castro's speeches and to limit the hostile reaction to the Bay of Pigs invasion. The CIA station supported many small actions as opportunities arose—breaking up a Cuban photographic exhibit, producing a forged and incriminating Communist document, planting a microfilm on a returning traveler from Cuba.

Longer-range political operations focused on building up anti-Communist organizations: a left-of-center political party to draw moderate leftists away from rightist parties, a national labor federation willing to affiliate with non-Communist fronts. The station also supported existing anti-Communist groups—the convention of a Catholic youth organization, anti-Cuban parties of the Center and the

Right—and encouraged visits of liberal politicians from other countries.

The combined pressures of American diplomacy and the covert anti-Communist crusade fortified the anti-Left forces that held mass demonstrations in the spring of 1962 protesting both Ecuador's relations with Cuba and Communists in the government. Ecuador's military forces added their weight to the campaign by the revolt of a provincial garrison and by their refusal to act against the demonstrators. A newly constituted cabinet finally voted unanimously to break off diplomatic relations with Cuba. But President Arosemena's failure to clean out the Communists in his government and the growing threat of domestic Communist insurgency kept opposition to the regime alive both in Ecuador and in Washington. The president was thrown out by the military in July 1963, and as in so many other cases Washington's anti-Communist policy led to the establishment of a military oligarchy.

In Chile U.S. action was, to start with, more affirmative: to bring a democratic party of the Left to power. That effort succeeded, then led to the party's electoral ouster by a radical Left coalition, and ultimately—to *its* ouster by a military coup.*

In Chile the covert arm was used by three Presidents over a period of fifteen years to prevent the election of a radical Left government in the oldest democracy south of the border. From the beginning of the Alliance for Progress up to 1973, the CIA was authorized to spend more than twelve million dollars to support the moderate Left (and elements of the Right), mainly the Christian Democrats, against a leftist coalition of parties under the leadership of Salvador Allende. Allende, a self-professed Marxist, fought in three elections on the same platform: socialize the economy, nationalize

*American actions in Chile are reviewed in a separate publication of the Senate Select Committee on Intelligence Activities, *Covert Action in Chile 1963–1973*.

major industries (especially the U.S.-owned copper companies), expand agrarian reform, and promote friendly relations with the Soviet bloc and Cuba.

American support of the successful Christian Democratic candidate, Eduardo Frei Montalva, in the 1964 elections was coordinated and directed by a special committee in Washington composed of men from the White House, the State Department, and the CIA. CIA's role was twofold: to channel funds to Frei's Christian Democrats for their election campaign and to carry out a massive anti-Allende anti-Communist propaganda campaign that played a significant part in winning Frei a majority in the election. The CIA effort to strengthen the Christian Democrats continued during the Frei administration: supporting moderate candidates in congressional elections, training and organizing "anti-Communist" peasants and labor groups, subsidizing a right-wing newspaper, planting editorials, etc.

With the 1970 election coming up, and Frei ineligible to succeed himself, Washington decided not to support any single candidate in the three-way race, but to make every effort to prevent Allende's election. The result was another high-pitched propaganda campaign, accompanied by efforts to split some of the pro-Allende forces. Again, CIA projects produced countless leaflets and cartoons, radio and press releases, editorials, newsletters, street posters and wall signs, all designed to show, through citing Soviet and Cuban events, that an Allende victory would bring violence and repression to Chilean society.

Allende's failure to win a majority in the September election put the final choice between the two front runners, Allende and a conservative candidate, into the hands of the Congress. During the next six weeks Washington directed a campaign to block Allende's election, but neither economic pressures, propaganda, nor pressures on individual congressmen were able to prevent it.

With Allende in power the full resources of the U.S. government were dedicated to making his regime fail. The White House wanted to "make the economy scream," and Washington stopped any new bilateral or multilateral economic assistance, reduced commercial credits and guarantees to U.S. private investment, dropped Chile's credit rating by the Export-Import Bank, and refused to renegotiate Chile's foreign debt. Military assistance and the training of Chilean officers, on the other hand, rose sharply.

CIA's covert actions under Allende supplemented this public effort. It was authorized to spend more than five million dollars to keep the opposition alive; and it did so by funding the Christian Democratic and other anti-Allende parties in the hope of forming a united opposition. It also provided support to various independent media, among them the prominent *El Mercurio* chain, other opposition newspapers, and various radio and television stations. An economic research service was established and funded, and small amounts of money were given to private groups of businessmen.

The precise role of CIA's covert funding during the tense months preceding the military coup of September 11, 1973, eluded the Senate Select Committee on Intelligence Activities, set up in January of 1975. Among the disorders that led to the coup was a strike of truckers that severely dislocated the Chilean economy and helped bring popular discontent to a head. Did CIA money finance the strike? The Senate report makes two points: No funds were authorized by Washington for direct passage to the strikers, though it was unlikely that their lengthy strike could have been maintained out of union funds. On the other hand, it was impossible to determine how much, if any, of the funds passed to political parties or private groups found its way into the pockets of the strikers.

There is no evidence that the CIA, the American Embassy in Santiago, or the military attaché played any direct role in the military coup that ousted Allende—and led to his death (see below on assassination). The coup leader, General Pinochet, planned his coup in the greatest secrecy, and carried it out under cover of an independence day parade. Not only did no American assist or encourage his plans, but CIA was not able to forecast the exact timing of the coup because only a few Chileans knew about it.

It is an open question whether Allende's regime would have fallen from its own failures without *any* American intervention. In the event, the American effort at containing "communism" in Chile succeeded, at least in the short run, but at the price of its replacement by a repressive and murderous military junta enjoying American support. A benign effort to support moderate political groups in a democratic society thus evolved into a program of open and covert subversion against a government in power.

COUPS AND ASSASSINATIONS

The political scene of the postwar world has been highlighted by hundreds of coups, or changes in government by force, mainly in the Near East, Africa, and Latin America. In most cases these have been the outcome of strictly domestic political, social, or racial rivalries. In some cases outside governments have played a role, directly by supporting the coup plotters or the regime in power, indirectly by pursuing policies favoring one or the other side. In only a few cases has the Soviet regime or the American government intervened directly to unseat a government in power.

Placing the responsibility for a coup attempt on an outside power is among the cloudiest questions the historian faces. Moscow clearly engineered the Communist Party coup in Czechoslovakia in 1948. Washington clearly engineered the anti-Mossadeq coup in Iran in 1953. In almost every other case the fact or the degree of foreign complicity in internal political coups cannot be firmly fixed on the basis of the available evidence. The plotting and execution of any coup is normally carried out in secret, and the exact affiliations of the coup plotters, their sources of inspiration or support, often remain buried even after a coup has succeeded. When it fails, the execution of the leaders most often precludes their interrogation by dispassionate investigators.

The fact that dozens of coups in the fifties and sixties have been ascribed to the Russians or the Chinese does not confirm their complicity; similarly, in the past decade literally scores of coups have been automatically charged to the hand of the CIA. The conspiratorial atmosphere of the Cold War has left few nations or propagandists free of paranoid fantasies.

Many coups are bloodless and evoke only minor global interest. Others involve or end in the assassination of political leaders, and it is this most dramatic form of covert political action that poses the deepest moral and pragmatic issues.

In the history of American covert political operations no acts have been condemned more emotionally than assassination attempts against foreign political leaders.

Two fundamentally different questions are involved: the deliberate attempt by a President to kill a foreign leader by hired hands, and American support of a foreign coup that results in the murder of a chief of state. In the latter case, the responsibility for the murder, often the identity of the assassin, is not clear and must be judged in each instance.

For the first fifteen years of the Cold War there was no talk of assassination in Washington. Even in those sometimes hysterical times I knew of no one at any level who seriously proposed that X or Y be wiped out to advance the national interest.

Then, between 1959 and 1962, the White House, the National Security Council and its Special Group, and members of the cabinet talked seriously about killing foreign leaders and, in two cases, authorized the CIA to arrange their murder. Both the Congolese leader Patrice Lumumba and Cuban Premier Fidel Castro were seen at the highest levels in Washington as grave enough threats to the nation's security to justify their elimination.

The plan to kill Lumumba evolved in the fall of 1960, but did not go beyond the preparatory stage. Some vials of poison were brought by courier to the Leopoldville station, and several agents were brought on the scene who might be successful in administering it. Domestic events quickly forestalled any attempt. Ousted by his Congolese rivals, Lumumba placed himself under United Nations control. He was kidnapped and killed by his Congolese enemies in February 1961.

The determination of the Eisenhower administration early in 1960 to work covertly against the Castro regime in Cuba led not only to the Bay of Pigs invasion, but also to high-level (National Security Council) and low-level (CIA) discussions of assassinating Castro. Plans to kill Castro continued into President Kennedy's administration. It is a historical irony, for which we can be grateful, that this most sensitive action project was executed by CIA with the greatest ineptitude.

Most of these plans to kill Castro ranged from the vague to the weird. The first, in July 1960, authorized the CIA station in Havana to employ one of its intelligence agents to "arrange an accident" to Castro's brother Raoul. The order was quickly rescinded. Others, bright ideas rather than worked out plans, involved the preparation of a box of cigars impregnated with poison (never delivered), the rigging of an "exotic" seashell with an explosive device to be placed in Castro's favorite skin-diving area (never placed), the gift of a diving suit dusted on the inside with a skin contaminant (never given).

A more persistent effort was made to enlist the services of several American underworld figures connected with a Cuban gambling syndicate in a scheme to poison Castro.

The plot, which evolved during 1960 and 1961, was as loose an operation as any secret operator could construct—a string of six contacts: case officer to an American intermediary to gangster one to gangsters two and three to a Cuban émigré leader to a Cuban courier to the assassin. Poison pills were delivered to gangster one in early 1961; he passed them eventually to a Cuban who claimed to have "a contact inside a restaurant frequented by Castro." The pills and some money were reportedly passed to the Cuban leader in March 1961—and later returned. Under no circumstances could the case officer determine exactly what happened to the pills when he was at least five steps removed from the Cuban "agent" who agreed to carry out the operation.

The next effort contracted the loose chain of command by eliminating the three surplus cutouts: the American intermediary and gangsters two and three. The operation then stood: CIA case officer to gangster one to the Cuban émigré leader. The Cuban now wanted to assassinate Che Guevara and Raoul Castro as well as Fidel, and he was given arms and equipment to assist him in his task. Poison pills were delivered to him in April 1962. In May gangster one reported that the pills and guns had reached Cuba. In June he told the case officer that the Cuban had reported the dispatch of a three-man assassination team to Cuba, but it apparently never left Florida. Nothing further was heard from the Cuban leader. The "operation," such as it was, was terminated in February 1963.

The main issue, of course, is not the clumsiness of the operation, but the fact that it was authorized at the highest levels.

How can we explain this resort to assassination as a tool of foreign diplomacy? Although it can be written off as a temporary aberration, it was the aberration of at least one President and a broad array of our top civilian and military leaders at the time.

In 1959 the "Communist threat" was still very much alive in the minds of President Eisenhower, the Congress, the press, and the citizenry. In a mere five years the Soviet thrust into the back alleys of the third world appeared to be making great strides, notably in Indochina and Africa. When the rich Belgian Congo in the heartland of Africa achieved its independence in 1960, and the "pro-Soviet" Lumumba became its first premier, this "man in Soviet pay" promised to communize the Congo as a prelude to communizing Africa, with Nigeria next on the list. The vision of a Soviet-controlled black Africa lay in the back of Washington's thinking.

The greatest threat, however, was closer to home. A Soviet base in Cuba, a center for sparking Communist revolutions in Latin America, a Lumumba-like spellbinder thumbing his nose at the President and the nation—these challenged in the most intense fashion the capacity and the determination of America's leaders. Anger combined with fear and frustration to create what Secretary of Defense Robert McNamara called a mood of hysteria. The two assassination plots were the result.

In the calmer climate of 1975, when the Senate Intelligence Committee issued its interim report on "Alleged Assassination Plots Involving Foreign Leaders," both congressional and public reactions were couched in terms of moral outrage. President Ford expressed himself as "totally opposed to political assassination." Attorney-General Edward Levi stated that no President had the legal authority "to go around ordering assassinations" (as though it might become an everyday affair). For most Americans assassination was morally inexcusable—"an ugly business," sordid, reprehensible, wrong "in terms of the morality of our country, our way of life, and the things we believe in."

The moral issue is a crucial one, but it has sometimes been confused in public discussion. Tyrannicide has been blessed by Greek writers and medieval Catholic theologians as the only means of ridding a people of an oppressive dictator, a proposition that should have some appeal even in a modern democratic nation. That the German Jews or the German generals were justified in plotting Hitler's murder, that Dominicans were justified in killing their tyrant, Trujillo, or the Haitians their tyrant Duvalier—these are at least open moral questions even by professed American standards of morality. To kill a man who kills is the final resort of men who do not want to be killed.

Tyrannicide, however, involves the murder of a dictator *by his own people*. When a foreign nation makes that decision for another society, it is unequivocally wrong by any moral standard. The determination to kill a foreign leader *in its own interest* is not only a sign of moral and political impotence, but an arrogant assertion of one nation's right to control the destinies of all humanity.

Even pragmatically, assassination is an expensive gamble with another man's life: What guarantee is there that his murder will actually serve the nation's interest? If Hitler had been killed by the British or French in the mid-thirties, would Goering or Goebbels have prevented World War II? If Castro had been eliminated in the early sixties, would his brother Raoul have moderated the Cuban "threat" to American security?

The citizens of each nation have the right to take this gamble by killing their own tyrant—for better or worse. Foreign intervention by murder is a crime against them.

The *indirect* involvement of the U.S. government in the assassination of foreign leaders poses a much murkier question—and mainly a pragmatic one: To what extent was Washington responsible for the murders of such men as Diem, Trujillo, Allende, all of them killed by their own fellow citizens?

Several grades of complicity can be operationally distinguished. The most direct complicity is involved in cases where Washington actively supports an individual or dissident group that intends to kill a political leader. Three questions arise: Is Washington clear about the intention to assassinate? Does it encourage the killing? Does it help with guns or explosives?

On May 30, 1961, the Dominican dictator, General Rafael Trujillo Molina, was ambushed and murdered on a country road. Official American policy was hostile to Trujillo, diplomatic relations had been broken off, and official interest had been expressed in getting Trujillo out of office. CIA had developed contacts with anti-Trujillo groups both inside and outside the Dominican Republic and supplied an inside group with money and arms. The group killed Trujillo with the arms supplied by CIA.

Was Washington responsible for Trujillo's death? Yes and no. It encouraged the group's activities, knew its intentions, and supplied it with arms. Yet it did not control the group (they were not agents in any sense) and therefore could not dictate its actions. Nor did Washington officially or unofficially encourage the murder itself. What it did do was to establish an unrealistic "yes and no" policy: to encourage the removal of the Trujillo regime but to "dissociate" itself from any political assassination that might occur. Events did not permit such a simple separation of purposes.

The case of Amlash, a senior Cuban official recruited by CIA in another abortive assassination attempt, illustrates the same level of complicity. An intelligence agent to start with, Amlash's high rank made him a potential leader in an anti-Castro coup. He himself determined that the "execution" of Castro was an essential first step in bringing off a coup. He was promised a cache of arms inside Cuba and was offered a ball-point pen rigged with a hypodermic needle as a poisoning device—in short, he was assisted in his attempt. After President Kennedy's assassination in November 1963, it was decided that he would be given no further help. Nonetheless, in early 1965 Amlash was placed in contact with a Cuban émigré leader, and the two worked out a joint plan for a coup that would start with killing Castro.

Had Castro been killed by Amlash, American complicity would have been even more direct than in the case of Trujillo.

A lesser degree of complicity is involved in the support of a dissident or opposition group that plans a political coup with no clear or apparent intent to kill the leader in power. Whatever the actual plan of the coup leaders may be, the essential question is: Did Washington know, or should it have known (the murkiest question of all), that the coup would involve an assassination?

The deaths of South Vietnamese Premier Diem and Chilean President Allende are cases in point.

In 1963 the administration determined that Diem must be replaced, and its actions led to a situation in which a group of anti-Diem generals began actively plotting against him. U.S. policy toward the plotters might be described as "active acquiescence": No attempt was made to stop the coup and in effect American officials gave the generals a green light. The coup occurred on November 1, and in its course Diem was killed—whether or not on the orders of the generals is not known.

No American official, in Washington or Saigon, ordered Diem killed or knew that he would be killed. The killing was a Vietnamese act.

The American connection with the death of President Allende is even more remote. The military coup that unseated him was not promoted by Washington, nor were the Chilean generals given any official or unofficial go-ahead. However Allende died, and the circumstances of his death are not clear, his suicide or murder was a Chilean act.

A third level of complicity is more tenuous: inaction in Washington when it learns of a planned coup or assassination attempt through its intelligence channels. What responsibility does the U.S. government have to warn foreign leaders of planned attempts against their regimes or lives?

Hundreds of coup attempts and dozens of assassination plans have been reported by CIA agents over the years. These reports have all been passed to the Department of State or the White House, among others, for such action as they might wish to take. In dozens of cases, when the reports appeared reliable, they were passed to friendly governments as a warning of hostile action. Similar reports about actions planned against "unfriendly" governments are not normally passed to them. The judgment in each case is a pragmatic one: What serves the U.S. interest? A policy of selective inaction is difficult to place on the moral spectrum.

A fourth level of complicity is based upon a simple thesis, popular among some revisionist historians, that the U.S. government is responsible for the acts of regimes it actively supports, be they allies, clients, or puppets. Washington can accordingly be saddled with the responsibility for the repressive acts of the Greek colonels, the practice of torture by the Brazilian military regime, or the iron cages of South Vietnam.

The thesis is pure nonsense. Applied across the board, it would make the United States responsible not only for the bad acts of bad regimes, and the good acts of good regimes, but for their constitutions, laws, economics, press, and social habits. Once generalized, this notion takes away from the nation-state in the modern world *any* responsibility for its own actions.

INTERVENTION

The post-Watergate and post-Vietnam debate on American intervention in the internal affairs of other countries has proceeded on both the pragmatic and the moral level, mainly the latter. To take the pragmatic issue first: Do these interventions achieve their purpose?

Interference in the domestic affairs of another country involves certain pitfalls whether it is carried out openly or covertly.

The first hazard is shortsightedness. Since the impulse to carry out a political or military operation is usually a tactical response to an immediate "threatening" situation, the act is only a short-term remedy that may in the long run prove "counterproductive." The coup against Mossadeq in 1953 kept the shah of Iran in power. Is his present power in the American interest? The 1954 invasion of Guatemala unseated a "Communist" regime. Did it contribute to the stability of Guatemalan politics or the satisfactions of its people? Was the Dominican intervention and American opposition to the political forces of the Left in the Dominican or American interest?

These are all questions fitfully argued by political historians. They cannot be resolved even with the passage of time. Even a "successful" intervention achieves only a momentary purpose.

A second hazard underlies the choice of "the good guys" on whose behalf the Americans intervene. The effect of many of our interventions has been the establishment of dictatorial regimes whose policies have not advanced the interests of their people. These must be weighed against their contributions to the American national interest—and there is no scale to weigh them on.

Here the moral issue intrudes, and it is the moral question that became the staple of public debate both in and outside Congress during the Year of Intelligence. The question is one of broad principle: Is it right for the United States to interfere in the domestic affairs of another country?

Intervention is one of the vaguer terms in the international political vocabulary. Each major industrial nation, Communist or capitalist, interferes in the affairs of dozens of other states—with its diplomacy, military and economic aid, propaganda instruments, etc. These are normal and acceptable international practices between governments, for they are, for the most part, open to public view.

The line between open and covert political action, however, cannot be drawn with precision in all cases. Many "open" American interventions in the past twenty years have been carried out under the cover of an official fig leaf. The president of Lebanon is asked to request American troops in 1958 to put down opposition to his pro-Western policies. The president of South Vietnam is asked to request U.S. advisers, then troops—American intervention is (more or less) open and official. The President of the United States invades the Dominican Republic "to protect American citizens" and then proceeds to shape its domestic politics. A fig leaf was involved in the invasion of Cuba: Its purpose was to establish, for however short a time, a provisional government on Cuban soil that could then request official U.S. intervention.

Perhaps the issue should be rephrased: Is it right to interfere *secretly?*

Secret talks and pressures are a part of diplomacy. The American ambassador or his labor attaché have private talks with political or labor leaders. Native journalists are briefed off-the-record to take a U.S. line. Persuasion and cajolery enter into "unofficial" talks with government officials—to break off diplomatic relations with Havana, or to refuse a Soviet "friendship" pact, or to line up with an American position in the United Nations. Secrecy in itself cannot be the main index to immoral behavior.

Perhaps the issue is narrower: Is it right to interfere with money? We have bribed civilian governments to give us military bases with outright grants and loans. We have bribed military governments with military equipment and subsidies to "fight the Communists." We use much of our foreign aid to achieve political, not humanitarian, purposes. Money, in the form of cash or matériel, led not only to the European and Japanese revival, but to the shaping of foreign governments that would support *American* foreign policy goals. The use of money for pragmatic purposes is not in itself either good or bad.

The morality of covert political action operations must focus on an ever narrower question: Is it right to interfere by passing money secretly?

Here the line between covert action and diplomacy becomes very fine indeed. Is it right to give a confidential subsidy to a chief of state for establishing a presidential bodyguard; to give money and equipment for strengthening the internal security service of a (then) friendly state; to pay for the services of a constitutional adviser? Is it right to give a foreign head of government money he will use for his party in an electoral campaign; to give money to a politician who does not happen to be president; to subsidize the career of a promising political leader? When is a travel grant or a fellowship abroad proper or improper? What kind of help to foreign journalists, labor leaders, or students is proper—what improper?

There are no simple answers to these questions. It can be argued that "benign" interventions are good, "subversive" interventions bad, but that is no longer a moral, but a pragmatic, judgment. It can be argued that all interventions not open to public observation are bad—but that is nonsense. It can be argued that all covert operations are illegal, unconstitutional, un-American, immoral, and improper, but that is an assertion of principle that can itself be argued.

In this standing argument of morality vs. pragmatism I have sometimes thought that Americans often profess a virtue they do not possess. Do our county and state governments operate on moral principles? Does business thrive on honesty and openness? Is there no industrial espionage? No confidential deals and agreements? No bribery of foreign officials to sell airplanes? No deception in advertising or political rhetoric? Perhaps we demand more of our foreign policy makers than we do of ourselves.

The world we live in is not a moral world. It is a world of more power and less power, of more goods and less goods, of greater security and lesser security, a world in which war is the final immorality. Nations are inevitably committed to the motto: Better bad than dead. In this world American foreign policy has been and will continue to be pragmatic—to contain Soviet power. The pragmatic test is success or failure, and up to now that policy has been a failure in both our open and covert political action. The fault lies not in the instruments, but in the ways they have been employed and the ends to which they have been directed.

Coups, assassination attempts, political subsidies, election operations have been sufficiently publicized in the past several years to equate covert political action in the public mind with dramatic, large-scale enterprises. Yet at the heart of political action, Soviet or American, are the thousands of confidential "friendships" with indigenous leaders who are in a position to affect decisions in their own societies.

During the past ten years the KGB has been making "friends" of this sort among the power elites of the West: politicians of the Center and the Right, non-Communist labor leaders, bankers and industrialists, journalists and legislators. These contacts range from secret to confidential. Some are on the Soviet payroll—the personal assistant to former West German Chancellor Willy Brandt, or the key European negotiator on a Soviet truck-assembly plant project. Some have been bribed with promises of business opportunities in East-West trade. These agents give Moscow a useful instrument for affecting the attitudes and decisions of other governments on matters of Soviet concern: to lobby for a European Security Conference, or to press for favorable terms in trade or loan negotiations. These "friends" do not spy nor otherwise break the law.

CIA's agents of influence serve the same purpose: to affect the decisions of foreign governments or private institutions in the American interest. They are an extension into the secret arena of the confidential contacts of ambassadors, attachés, and proper diplomats, a quiet companion to American diplomacy. They serve many purposes: to dissuade a government from buying Soviet arms, to stimulate a chief of state to all-out support of an antinarcotics program, to ease out a fanatically anti-American cabinet minister. They can serve as intermediaries for channeling to the right recipient in the government intelligence reports that will be more effective if the American hand does not show. They have been helpful in

straightening out a border conflict short of war and in bringing to a regime's notice the seeds of insurrection in a remote
area.

These confidential collaborators around the globe are the
main day-in-day-out instruments of covert political action.
They can produce no spectacular successes or failures. They
can be employed as instruments for an affirmative American
foreign policy as they have been for containment. Up to now
Washington has bungled the job of covert political action by
relying far too much on great enterprises. A more modest
employment of his third arm can help the President execute
our purposes abroad with greater efficiency and maximum
secrecy.

12

THE CIA AT HOME

The open activities of CIA at home cover a wide range.

Among the "services of common concern" that CIA performs for the intelligence community is the open collection of information on foreign countries from cooperative American citizens and companies. Through some forty field offices scattered throughout the country, CIA officers openly keep in touch with local business firms, academic institutions, and prominent individuals active in the foreign field, and secure information that comes to their attention in the normal course of their business: reports from overseas branch officers, international conferences, tourist observations, etc. These field offices (listed in local telephone directories) have standing information requirements from all government agencies and often receive specific intelligence requests that can be serviced by putting questions to their American contacts. When they receive "tips" from established contacts on Americans allegedly involved in espionage or drug trafficking, these are routinely reported to the FBI.

There is nothing clandestine about these contacts, and no

payment is involved. These CIA officers are not trained to spy, and the Americans who volunteer their information are not spies by any definition.

Contacts with American citizens or organizations in support of the agent work of the Operations Directorate, on the other hand, are uniformly secret, and their substance kept highly confidential.

Both the open and secret directorates of the CIA are, unfortunately, housed together in the overlarge structure of the CIA headquarters in Langley, Virginia. When the building was planned in the late fifties, many senior operators objected strongly to being housed in such a public place together with "the open side of the house," but they were encouraged to believe that the open directorates would supply a cover for their presence. Ironically, while CIA has come to stand in the minds of most people for secret operations, the daily trek of thousands of cars and dozens of buses in and out of the headquarters compound provides a public display of a secret agency that is unique in the Western world. It is a simple task for an unfriendly embassy in Washington to collect all the license plate numbers of CIA employees and, with somewhat more effort, to identify their owners. Newspaper photographs, journalists' visits, and large conferences do not enhance the secrecy of a secret service.

Most of the operations housed in this complex are carried out by open directorates.

CIA's Intelligence and Scientific-Technical directorates maintain extensive relations in the academic and scientific communities. Their purpose is to keep the government researchers and analysts up-to-date on private research, make use of top men in their fields as consultants, and stimulate interest within the private sector in matters of concern to the intelligence community in Washington.

The Support Directorate supports both the open and secret operations parts of the agency.

The Personnel Division maintains contact with academic

personnel on many campuses and often sends its representatives to the campus to interview prospective candidates for CIA employment. Its academic contacts recommend students at undergraduate or graduate level who appear to be qualified for any branch of CIA work: scientific research, political or economic analysis, photoanalysis, administration—and potential case officers for the Operations Directorate.

The Office of Security not only investigates candidates for CIA employment and rechecks many of its current employees, but is responsible for following up any case in which a CIA employee is suspected of misusing the classified information he or she possesses. The office is also committed to maintaining the physical security of all CIA installations in this country. Its closest approach to the work of the Operations Directorate comes in the clearance of American citizens for use in secret operations. Countless private citizens have been "cleared" to assure their political and personal reliability before being asked to participate in secret or covert operations. In each such case the FBI and other federal files are checked, and in some cases a security investigation is carried out as well, before an American citizen is cleared for an operational contact.

OPERATIONAL SUPPORT

Domestic support of CIA's secret operations is extensive. It is essential to our foreign mission. It is carried out in secret with cleared individuals, and often involves the secret handling of money and contracts. It ranges from confidential contacts with individual citizens to complex arrangements with large corporations. The most crucial element in the domestic support of CIA's secret operations is the provision of cover for overseas case officers.

CIA operators overseas do not normally advertise themselves as "CIA" even in friendly countries where their main

business is to work with the local security intelligence services. The latter prefer that the affiliation of their American
colleagues not be made public.

In the vast majority of overseas assignments CIA officers
operate under official American cover—as employees of the
Department of State or Defense or the Agency for International Development, usually depending upon the nature of
their assignments and the area involved. During the American occupation of Germany, for example, virtually all CIA
officers were DACs: Department of Army civilians. In Indochina during the sixties, Army and AID cover was most
appropriate. Today most CIA officers operate from our embassies abroad.

Operating out of an embassy has many advantages for any
service, not least of which is diplomatic immunity for its
offices, files, and personnel. "Diplomats" are not arrested
and tried for espionage, but simply expelled. The main disad-
vantage, both for the CIA and the KGB, is the ease with
which official cover operators can be identified, surveyed,
and sometimes provoked. If diplomatic relations are broken
off, of course, the operators are forced to leave with their
legitimate colleagues.

Nonofficial cover—operators acting as ordinary American
citizens on business abroad—makes a less obvious target for
suspicion and often permits access to circles not open to the
local embassy. It also permits CIA case officers to remain in
place in a country that has broken off diplomatic relations
with the United States. It poses one rather drastic disadvan-
tage. If a man under unofficial cover is caught spying, he can
be arrested and jailed.

Several types of "commercial cover" have been employed
over the years. In most cases CIA officers have been sent out
as employees of a company created and owned by the CIA,
so-called proprietary companies like Air America or front organizations like Radio Free Europe. In other cases small
firms have been established by CIA with the express purpose

of supplying a notional cover for a few men operating in one or more countries. These covers require the cooperation of many non-CIA Americans in setting up the companies and acting as officers.

Sometimes a CIA officer is provided cover by an established American company with offices abroad. In these cases a training period at company headquarters is often a preliminary to a foreign assignment, for the CIA officer must be qualified to carry out the firm's business. The main handicap in this type of assignment is that the CIA officer often must spend most of his time on his cover work, sometimes to the detriment of his operational assignments.

Since an officer under unofficial cover is subject to arrest for espionage acts, his assignments are normally confined to handling an already recruited agent whose value and reliability have been proved. He is normally in touch with the local CIA station and can recommend potential recruits for follow up by a "diplomat."

American manufacturers are also a vital element in CIA operations involving advanced technical equipment. In the late fifties CIA contracted with Lockheed to build the U-2 supersonic aircraft for overflights across Soviet territory. A decade later plans were made to raise a sunken Soviet submarine in the Pacific, and contracts were let to the Summa Corporation to build a highly sophisticated salvage ship, the *Glomar Explorer*. These are only two of the most conspicuous examples of the contributions made by American science and technology to CIA's collection of foreign intelligence.

Other CIA activities in the United States in support of its overseas intelligence operations have very little to do with American citizens. Foreign agents who cannot be trained at overseas sites are handled at home—for example, the high-altitude training of Tibetans in Colorado, or the selection and training of Cuban émigrés for intelligence operations against Cuba. CIA agents working abroad sometimes visit the United States or are assigned here on official or unofficial business.

Contact is maintained with them while they are here and often provides an opportunity for more intense training and debriefing than is practical overseas. Most high-level Soviet and other intelligence defectors are brought to the United States for interrogation by interested Washington intelligence agencies. In these cases private American citizens or companies often play a part in resettling them by helping to cover their real identities, getting them a job or credit status, etc.

CIA AND THE FBI

The principal focus of CIA espionage work in this country, however, is the recruitment of visiting foreigners for eventual use as intelligence agents when they return to their own countries—the main task of the Foreign Resources Division. Every foreign intelligence service has found that it can approach a high-level foreigner on its own soil more easily and more securely than it can in his native capital. He is not only psychologically more susceptible to a recruitment approach away from home, but the case officer who wants to assess and possibly recruit him is working in a friendly environment.

In carrying out these recruitment operations close contact is maintained with the Federal Bureau of Investigation. It is, however, in the field of domestic counterintelligence and counterespionage that the CIA and the FBI cooperate most closely.

The internal security mission belongs to the FBI alone, and a precise limit to the authority of the CIA within the United States was clearly set in the National Security Act of 1947: ". . . the Agency shall have no police, subpoena, law-enforcement powers, or internal-security functions." Nonetheless, since counterintelligence knows no national boundaries, the CIA has been able to contribute substantially to the Bureau's internal security mission.

It is a practical truism in any country that the internal

security service must have the cooperation of its foreign intelligence service to carry out its task effectively. This cooperation is not always an easy one, but it is indispensable for the United States in a period of history when a large proportion of the threats to internal security originate abroad—in the corridors of the KGB's First Chief Directorate in Moscow, in the planning section of the Cuban Intelligence Service in Havana, in the International Section of the French or Italian Communist parties, in the heads of Argentinian terrorists or fedayeen action groups.

The pattern of CIA-FBI cooperation is clearest in the most specific form of counterintelligence: counterespionage. Here the targets are persistent and easily identified: the actions of any hostile intelligence service directed against the American interest.

For thirty years the CIA and the FBI have worked closely together against the Soviet and East European intelligence services, especially the KGB, exchanging information about Soviet intelligence officers and providing each other with leads to suspect agents. In the last fifteen years the volume of hostile espionage operations against the American target has climbed perceptibly. During the sixties KGB officers were making more than two hundred approaches a year to Americans stationed abroad. In the late sixties more than three hundred KGB officers were stationed in New York City.

The line of demarcation between the two agencies in counterintelligence work is by statute quite clear. The investigation of suspect Americans or foreigners is the exclusive province of the FBI within the physical confines of the U.S. The CIA has the exclusive responsibility for counterintelligence and counterespionage work abroad. The only confusion that may arise is when a CIA agent, say a KGB agent doubled by the CIA, comes to the United States. In such cases his handling must be worked out between the two agencies, for in most cases an agent cannot simply be turned over from one case officer to another without a loss of trust.

CIA-FBI cooperation in counterespionage matters is

mostly a one-way street—from the CIA to the FBI. Since the great majority of Soviet, East European, and Cuban espionage operations against the United States are mounted overseas, the CIA has naturally been able to supply more leads for the FBI to follow up in the United States than conversely.

When the CIA station in Vienna reports from an agent source the dispatch of a Soviet illegal, or staff officer under private cover, to the United States, the FBI takes over his surveillance at the point of entry.

When an American technician in Italy is recruited by the KGB for the purpose of getting computer data from his home office, the follow-up in Italy is CIA's job; on his return to his headquarters, that of the FBI.

When an embassy file clerk in Tokyo is approached by a young KGB officer and agrees to accept his proposition under the direction of the CIA station, the FBI is informed of the case when she is about to return to Washington. The FBI can then request that the operation be terminated overseas or it can elect to take over the handling of the double agent in Washington.

Cooperation between the two agencies on counterespionage is even closer when the CIA is able to provide a means of access to a Soviet or East European intelligence officer stationed in the United States. In one such case, a naturalized American citizen whom the CIA was preparing for an assignment in Latin America had at one time in his life abroad come to know a secret KGB courier who was about to make a three-day stop in New York City en route to Mexico. The CIA agent was quickly brought from Pittsburgh to New York, and elaborate arrangements were made to create a "chance" meeting at the airline terminal. With both FBI and CIA officers watching closely, the agent ran into his old acquaintance at the airline counter and exchanged hasty but warm greetings. The two agreed to meet again at the courier's next stop, and another possible counterintelligence source was established.

This and similar counterespionage operations against foreigners offer a simple model for counterintelligence operations against American citizens who are FBI targets. The basic operating rule is the same: investigating American Communists, dissidents, or terrorists within the United States is the FBI's job. Supporting these FBI operations abroad is the job of the CIA.

Here again FBI-CIA liaison is mostly a one-way street, but since the targets are Americans on the domestic scene, the main flow of leads is from the FBI to the CIA for action overseas.

Since World War II the FBI has made countless requests for action on American Communist leaders traveling abroad to determine whom they visited, what instructions they received, what funds they might bring back. Other FBI targets have been reported on by CIA during their attendance at peace congresses and other Soviet front meetings in Europe and Cuba.

In the sixties these requests mounted and broadened in scope as the militant activities of the New Left, the intensifying civil rights movement, and antiwar demonstrations created widespread turmoil on the American scene both on and off campus. In 1968 the White House put direct pressure on CIA to increase its coverage of "dissident" groups abroad, and in mid-1968 CIA established a special group within the Counterintelligence Staff for recording and coordinating all information on the foreign connections of American dissidents. During the next five years this effort, labeled "Operation Chaos," became the central repository of all information on American dissidents—from the FBI, the National Security Agency, Army intelligence, and from CIA agents and liaison services abroad. Some 300,000 names were computer-indexed, and some 7,000 personality files set up on Americans active in or connected with the dissident movement. Regular reports were sent to the FBI and, on priority matters, to the White House and Secretary of State.

The Chaos unit also worked closely with CIA's Office of Current Intelligence in responding to the continuing White

House requests for overall assessments of the international connections of American dissidents. These studies, focused on the peace movement, student dissent, and "revolutionary protest movements," came up with an unequivocal message: Domestic dissidence was a strictly American affair. There was simply no evidence for overseas direction or guidance of these movements, no "Communist" control or financial support, although, of course, Communist propaganda highlighted and encouraged the American radical movements. These reports, however, apparently did not weaken President Nixon's conviction that foreigners must somehow be involved.

More than half of the extensive Chaos files consisted of memoranda from the FBI listing individuals of interest to them, some with specific indications of their planned foreign travel, and requests for CIA reports on their activities abroad.

A leading antiwar militant makes a trip to Paris, apparently to visit the North Vietnamese delegation. The FBI wants to know: Whom does he meet? What do they talk about? Does he make any other contacts?

A Black Panther on the run flees to Algiers. Does he plan to return? With whom is he in touch? Does he make any contacts with African revolutionaries?

These requests ran into the hundreds. They were often easy to satisfy with the help of friendly foreign security services who had as great an interest as the FBI in running down the international connections of *their* militant and revolutionary groups. Sometimes the answers were obtained from CIA agents whom the local station had inserted in the wide-ranging Soviet and other Communist establishments, mainly in Europe, to monitor their nondiplomatic activities.

CIA sources within the New Left groups in Europe were relatively thin, since the profusion of such non-Communist groups as the "proletarian socialist" parties and the Trotskyites, Maoists, and Castroites that grew up in the sixties had not yet become a priority for CIA agent operations—after all, those most directly concerned were the

German, French, and British internal security services. The continuing White House pressure for overseas coverage led Operation Chaos to recruit American students and some nonstudents for the purpose of penetrating these European groups.

In April 1970, Operation Chaos was authorized to recruit and train its own agents. Between 1970 and 1973 twenty-three agents were recruited to penetrate radical student groups in Europe. About half the candidates were recommended by the FBI.

To prepare for their mission these student recruits were instructed to join radical student groups on American campuses for building up their cover. They were expected to acquire a familiarity with the jargon, techniques, and personalities of American student activists so that they would be acceptable to the foreign student organizations they planned to join. During their training in the United States they reported their contacts and observations, and some of their reports were given to the FBI. Some of them took on full-fledged assignments abroad. Others made short trips to cover specific targets.

Operation Chaos was terminated in March 1974. In responding to the pressures of two Presidents to record and define "foreign links" with the American dissident movements, it carried out an efficient and objective counterintelligence task. Its activities and files bordered so closely on domestic security, however, that it became a controversial issue with many CIA operators at its inception and, later, a target of public attack. Chaos reflected a White House effort to contain "communism" when there was nothing to contain.

CIA AND WATERGATE

Although in the normal course of its operational work the CIA has always been in closest touch with the FBI, it has also cooperated closely with other federal agencies. It has provided special equipment such as lie detectors to the Department of State and given it assistance in communications. It has run operations and counterespionage courses for the Department of Defense. It has worked closely with the Secret Service in preparing for presidential trips abroad. It has performed innumerable odd chores for all federal agencies.

Some of the oddest, and most publicized, chores included the CIA's cooperation with President Nixon's White House in the early seventies. The CIA involvement in the Ellsberg and Watergate affairs came out of the White House effort to plug leaks and collect political intelligence by setting up a Special Investigative Unit (the Plumbers). It was a unique episode in the history of intelligence services outside the Soviet Union and, for a time, did CIA grievous harm.

The scene was set with the recruitment in July 1971 of E. Howard Hunt as a White House consultant and, later, of James McCord as security officer for the Committee to Re-elect the President. Both men had long experience in the CIA, and Hunt particularly was familiar with CIA facilities for supporting secret operations abroad.

There were three more or less separate episodes.

On July 7, 1971, the deputy director of CIA, Marine General Robert E. Cushman, Jr., received a call from John Ehrlichman asking him to help Hunt. Hunt visited Cushman two weeks later and stated that he had been charged with "a highly sensitive mission by the White House to visit and elicit information" from an individual whose ideology he was not entirely sure of. He needed identification documents in alias and material for physical disguise for this one-time operation.

Placed in touch with Technical Services Division personnel in a Washington safe house, Hunt first received a set of alias documents, a wig, glasses, and speech alteration device, and later a tape recorder in a typewriter case and a Tessina camera in a tobacco pouch. Almost all this material, of course, is commercially available, and its purchase is not incriminating. False identity documents, on the other hand, require a degree of technical competence, specialized equipment, and available blanks normally not found outside security and intelligence services or well-organized crime syndicates.

Once Hunt got what he wanted for his quick in-and-out, he went on to get his operational boss, G. Gordon Liddy, fitted out with a false identity and, later, asked the CIA technicians to develop and deliver the film he had used in casing the office of Ellsberg's psychiatrist. When he made further demands for support, the technicians sensed Hunt was up to something more than a one-time interview and passed the word up the chain of command. On August 27, General Cushman called off any further support of Hunt and so informed the White House.

How culpable or indiscreet was Cushman in acceding to Hunt's original requests?

On the face of it, Hunt's initial demands were modest, though unusual, and implied nothing more than a taped, incognito interview in a sensitive White House matter supervised by Ehrlichman, the man in charge of stopping high-level government leaks. Even if Cushman had been an experienced professional operator or had felt no obligation to respond automatically to a White House request, it is hard to fault him for being "insufficiently cautious." He could not know what the plumbers were up to nor had he any suspicion of their targeting on Dr. Ellsberg. He simply complied with a direct White House request dealing with "national security"—however much that term has been abused since.

The second episode of CIA involvement was more serious: Director Helms's acquiescence in giving the White House a psychological profile on Daniel Ellsberg.

Hunt was aware of CIA's work in "indirect assessment," the evaluation of a man's personality or state of mind without direct interview by a psychologist. This technique has been used not only to produce profiles on key political figures in the tradition of Professor William Langer's published OSS profile on Hitler, but also to help in assessing the reliability of a foreign agent—say, an official behind the Iron Curtain— who is seen only infrequently by his CIA handler. Data on his physical appearance, dress, manner, speech, habits, social and political attitudes, etc., carefully analyzed, can provide the material for an indirect assessment helpful in determining his reliability.

Apparently prodded by Hunt, White House aide David Young requested such a profile on Ellsberg. He rejected the first version (somewhat flattering to the subject) and provided further classified materials from the FBI and the State Department for a second version, which CIA delivered on November 12.

The use to which the White House wished to put the profile material on Ellsberg is irrelevant. The overriding fact is that Ellsberg was an American citizen, resident in the United States and uninvolved in any CIA or other intelligence agency operation abroad.

The delivery of the profile was the least creditable action of the CIA in its bizarre liaison with the White House. The request, by a junior member of the White House staff, was on its face improper, if not illegal, for it asked the agency both to violate its charter and to disregard the professional ethics involved in producing a medical judgment on an American citizen.

The plot thickens and the roles of the players become murky in the third episode—the immediate aftermath of the Watergate break-in. The scenario is confused by mushy memories and direct contradictions about who said what to whom in the dozen or so meetings that involved the CIA.

A major mystery lies behind President Nixon's assertion that a few days after the Watergate burglary he was "advised that there was a possibility of CIA involvement in some way." If this means anything, it means that CIA directly or indirectly participated in the break-in.

Who so advised the President? His own staff? Was suspicion aroused because of Hunt's and McCord's involvement? Yet the key White House staffers knew Hunt was a White House employee, knew what McCord's job was, and knew within hours of the break-in that Liddy had played a managerial role. Why, above all, would the CIA want to break into the Democratic National Committee headquarters? And, more practically, why did the President not call Director Helms at once and ask him?

One can only conclude that CIA was being set up as a scapegoat for the Watergate break-in—and it did not stop at the mere arousal of public suspicion. There apparently was a serious proposal in the initial cover-up discussions to give CIA the credit for the break-in, but according to President Nixon's special counsel John Dean it was rejected. Dean nonetheless made several panicky efforts to involve CIA, sounding out Deputy Director Lt. General Vernon Walters, who succeeded Cushman in May 1972, on CIA's willingness to put up the bail and pay the salaries and family expenses of the Watergate defendants. To this ludicrous proposal the answer was an explicit no, and the White House was forced to find and disburse its own funds. McCord himself was convinced before his trial that the White House was trying to lay the Watergate operation "at the CIA's feet."

A second, and still puzzling, concern of the President was "to insure that the investigations of the break-in did not expose either an unrelated covert operation of the CIA or the activities of the White House investigative unit."

His concern was translated into action on June 23, when presidential advisers Ehrlichman and Haldeman met with Helms and Walters at the White House. Here, after Director Helms clearly disavowed any CIA participation, Deputy Director Walters was instructed to talk with Acting FBI Director Gray about the likelihood of the FBI investigation uncovering unrelated covert CIA operations.

Although Haldeman's remarks at the White House meeting were not clear about just what CIA operations were threatened (there apparently was even a reference to the Bay of Pigs!), the talks with Acting Director Gray made the White House focus clear: The sensitive area was Mexico City where some of the Republican campaign funds used in the Watergate operation had been laundered. After some confusion lasting until July 6, Gray was explicitly informed by CIA that his investigation in Mexico held no threat to CIA operations.

The President's solicitude for CIA's operational security is puzzling. Was he thinking only of its Mexican operations when he instructed Haldeman to call in Helms? Why Mexico? Did he know then that the Watergate dollars had passed through a Mexican bank? Did he have some source outside the FBI and CIA for this specific anxiety?

Operationally it would, of course, be most unlikely that the investigation of certain bank accounts in Mexico City would run into any CIA espionage or counterespionage operations—which, the White House might be aware, or could assume, were mainly directed at Cuban and Soviet targets. If, by any odd chance, an FBI investigator had stumbled on a CIA agent, did not the White House know that the FBI would immediately inform the CIA and not broadcast the news?

It is now clear that CIA was being used in a diversionary tactic to limit or at least slow up the FBI investigation of Watergate.

An ironic aspect of CIA involvement in the Ellsberg and Watergate affairs is that none of these episodes directly involved the Operations Directorate, the only CIA component capable of carrying out espionage or counterespionage operations of any sort. The CIA-White House connection was on the highest bureaucratic level and involved, within CIA, only its support staffs: the Technical Services Division (for equipment), the Medical Division (for the profile), and the Office of Security. The Operations Directorate made only one small, but signal contribution: It assured the director that an FBI investigation in Mexico City would not endanger any CIA operations.

I cannot forbear a comment on another irony in this bizarre episode: the ambivalent appeal of "dirty tricks" to the layman. The mystique about secret operations, apparently shared by Attorney General John Mitchell and the top White House aides, gave the "operators" Liddy and Hunt a psychological advantage in selling their amateur espionage proposal to their lay superiors. A professionally couched plan, a certain amount of trade jargon, the use of special technical equipment, the availability of some "good men" to do the job—all these combined with assurances of total security can lull even hardnosed bureaucrats into a false sense of confidence in the darker arts. Secret affairs, fortunately in this case, are as liable to bungling as public affairs.

In retrospect, and on balance, the Ellsberg and Watergate episodes reflect a self-serving misuse by the White House of both the domestic and foreign American intelligence services. CIA was used to assist the plumbers in carrying out illegal actions, to delay proper FBI investigations, to help in the cover-up, and in a futile attempt to become the scapegoat for the Watergate break-ins.

The abuse of his two secret agencies is in some ways President Nixon's most discreditable action in the whole affair, for it involved the integrity and good name of both the CIA and the FBI. The White House role, inept in its execution, was destructive in its effects. It did not, and could not, work and served only to discredit both intelligence agencies and to raise public and congressional suspicion about the role of secret operations within the United States.

That suspicion reached unparalleled heights within a few months of President Nixon's resignation, when CIA was accused of large-scale domestic spying.

13

THE CIA AT BAY

In May 1973, spurred by the agency's involvement in Watergate, the new director, James R. Schlesinger, compiled a list of present or past CIA activities that "might be construed to be outside the legislative charter of this Agency." This long document of actual or possible "abuses," based on the reports of CIA's own employees, was properly passed to one of the House oversight committees on intelligence.

On December 22, 1974, the *New York Times* Sunday edition came out with a four-column headline on its front page:

HUGE C.I.A. OPERATION REPORTED IN U.S. AGAINST ANTI-
WAR FORCES, OTHER DISSIDENTS IN NIXON YEARS

The first three paragraphs of the following article by Seymour M. Hersh read:

> The Central Intelligence Agency, directly violating its charter, conducted *a massive illegal domestic intelligence operation during the Nixon Administration against the antiwar movement and other dissident groups in the United States* [my italics] according to well-placed Government sources.

>An extensive investigation by the New York Times has established that intelligence files on at least 10,000 American citizens were maintained by a special unit of the C.I.A. that was reporting directly to Richard Helms, then the Director of Central Intelligence and now the Ambassador to Iran.
>
>In addition, the sources said, a check of the C.I.A.'s domestic files ordered last year by Mr. Helms's successor, produced evidence of dozens of other illegal activities by members of the C.I.A. inside the United States, beginning in the nineteen-fifties, including break-ins, wiretapping, and the surreptitious inspection of mail.

The lengthy article continued with various charges of "domestic spying" made by unnamed sources, comments by government officials and congressmen, a section on the Counterintelligence Staff, rumors about mysterious burglaries after Watergate, etc. The extent of CIA's domestic spying was not specified, and the only actual figures included were those of 10,000 files on American citizens and "dozens" of other illegal activities.

The reaction to the *Times* article was intense and extensive, and events began moving rapidly. Two days after its appearance Schlesinger's successor, CIA Director William Colby, made a report on CIA's domestic activities to President Ford, and on January 5, 1975, the President appointed a commission under Vice President Rockefeller to investigate the charges.

A single sensational news report started the Year of Intelligence in Washington. Its substance is worth a second look in the light of the facts brought out in the later investigations.

The gist of the report was that "huge" or "massive" domestic intelligence operations had been conducted by CIA against American dissidents. The charge of illegality could, of course, be sustained only in court.

The charge of "massive" spying was almost immediately challenged by both official and unofficial commentators, and

Mr. Hersh felt constrained to state in another lengthy article
on January 15 that:

> The Times did not quote its sources as saying, either in its
> initial dispatch on the C.I.A. or in later dispatches, that
> the agency had maintained domestic surveillance on
> 10,000 citizens.

True. The *Times* had made no such assertion, but the Hersh
story had followed its lead "massive illegal" paragraph with
the item on the 10,000 files. The reader could hardly fail to
interpret the second paragraph as evidence for the first, since
no other facts or purported facts were included in the story to
sustain the "massive" spying charge. The "10,000" was
clearly the figure that created the headline and the intense
public response.

Actually, the figure of 10,000 files was both too low and
too high. As noted in the previous chapter, more than
300,000 names and organizations were indexed in the computerized files of Operation Chaos, and personal dossiers
existed on 7,200 American citizens.

The number of files, however, had no connection with the
number of Americans on whom the CIA was "spying" in this
country or abroad.

A counterintelligence file is simply a record on a person or
organization of actual or potential counterintelligence interest. It does not imply an investigation or an agent operation.

More than half of the 7,200 personal files consisted of a
single piece of paper, a memorandum from the FBI giving the
name and identifying data of an American "dissident" or
"militant" on whom the FBI wanted information from CIA's
overseas sources. In some cases the FBI request spelled out
as well the travel plans of the citizen and asked for information on the contacts he made abroad. When CIA was able to
come up with such information, it was forwarded to the FBI
and a copy placed in that person's file. Other files were set up
on the basis of CIA's independent reporting from abroad—
from its agents, from foreign press reports, and from friendly

security services. CIA sources abroad would, for example, supply the names of all Americans who attended a Stockholm Peace Congress, visited the premises of the North Vietnamese delegation in Paris, joined a demonstration at the Sorbonne, etc. These were also supplied to the FBI.

Since the number of files is not the index to the extent of CIA's domestic spying, the key question is: How many CIA case officers or agents were devoted to spying on American dissidents in the United States?

The Rockefeller Report properly distinguished the activities of the Operations Directorate, which handles agents, and the Office of Security, which guards the CIA's premises and classified information. Its answers were precise.

How many agents were recruited by Operation Chaos to spy on American dissidents in this country? None.

How many CIA-recruited agents did nonetheless spy on domestic dissidents and report the results to CIA and the FBI? Three.

Of the thirty-odd agents recruited by Operation Chaos for assignment overseas, most developed their cover on American campuses and routinely reported on their associations and activities. Their reports were carefully examined and assessed for clarity and precision as part of their training. Any reports of serious intelligence value were disseminated to the FBI.

In three cases Chaos agents were employed on a purely domestic assignment: one to participate in demonstrations in late 1969; one to report on the activities of the leadership of a dissident group; the third to penetrate the organizers of the May Day demonstrations in Washington, D.C., in 1971.

These three were violations of the CIA charter against purely domestic operations.

The Office of Security also went beyond its proper authority in a number of cases directed against dissident Americans. The agents it recruited had no foreign intelligence function, but were used to infiltrate dissident groups in the Washington, D.C., area in order to warn CIA of any threats to its employees and installations. Beginning in February 1967, the Office of Security hired some local Washington residents, most of them manual laborers, to work as part-time informants. They attended various local meetings and demonstrations, provided information on the size, income (when they could), leaders, and plans of local organizations, took photographs, and reported the gist of speeches. There were never more than a dozen of these untrained informants on the payroll at any one time. The project was discontinued in December of the following year since the Washington Metropolitan Police Department had by then developed the capacity to monitor these groups on its own.

These actions, though minor in scope, violated the agency's charter against domestic investigation of American citizens, and should have been performed only by the FBI or the local police, who are responsible for protecting all federal installations.

How "massive" were these domestic operations? "Three," "twelve," or "thirty," no matter how one adds them up, are neither huge nor massive. Taken together, they produced a thin sheaf of observer reports on public meetings. The first two paragraphs of the *Times* report were blatantly exaggerated. The "at least 10,000" files was the red herring that misled both the writer, the headline writer, and the managing editor.

Apparently the *Times* had access to the report of "abuses" supplied to the House oversight committee by CIA. What the *Times* reporter unfortunately did not get was the actual number of cases cited in the CIA report.

A second report by Mr. Hersh a week later in the Sunday edition of December 29 illustrates another hazard an investigative reporter faces in exploring a field in which he has no firsthand knowledge. He can be duped by a walk-in.

In this article Mr. Hersh printed a long confession by a purported CIA "ex-agent" detailing his four years of work in the late sixties and early seventies spying on radical groups in New York City. It was an important story, for it was the one and only statement by an actual participant in "domestic spying" to appear in the extensive *Times* coverage of the issue.

The ex-agent charged that he and his fellow agents had not only infiltrated student activist groups, but had participated in telephone wiretaps and break-ins. He included such James Bond romance as the employment of "boom-microphones" to overhear distant conversations. The *Times* apparently made every effort to check both the source's CIA affiliation and the facts he alleged, but whoever the source was, most of the alleged facts were fabricated.

The Rockefeller Commission "found no evidence that any of the agents or CIA officers involved with any of the dissident operations employed or directed the domestic use of any personal or electronic surveillance, wiretaps or unauthorized entries against any dissident group or individual." The *Times* did not feel it appropriate to have their ex-agent source appear before the Commission. In fact, the *Times* article quoted the source as stating that if he were exposed, he would deny any link to CIA.

The hazard the investigative reporter faces in dealing with volunteer informants of this sort is the same hazard we face in counterintelligence work abroad. When an unidentified man walks into an embassy with a sensational report, say about a Soviet intelligence operation, either the man or his story must be checked out. Normally, the story cannot be checked without compromising the source or exposing a secret operation. Often the only recourse is to subject the source to close questioning, determine his address, jobs, friends, etc., and check *him* out. The acceptance of his story often rests upon the judgment of the case officer questioning him. The counterintelligence operator has one advantage over the reporter: He feels no compulsion to rush into print before he is sure one way or the other.

OTHER DOMESTIC ABUSES

This is not, of course, to dismiss CIA's actual abuses.

Although the initial publicity on CIA's domestic operations focused on its work against dissidents, the subsequent investigations covered operational abuses against other American citizens. Some involved the use of agents, as in the work of CIA's Office of Security, others did not, as in the mail intercept program. All were included in the May 1973 CIA report listing "potential flap items." All were stopped before they were "exposed."

Most of the special investigations carried out by the Office of Security over the years have been directed against current or former CIA employees who were suspected of security breaches: leaks, improper behavior, association with known or suspected foreign intelligence personnel. It conducted almost a hundred personal surveillances, some thirty wiretaps (the last in 1965), thirty microphone installations (the last in 1968), and a dozen surreptitious entries (the last in 1971).

In five cases it investigated non-CIA personnel. On three occasions between 1967 and 1972, Security personnel surveyed newspaper reporters to help determine the source of classified intelligence leaks, and on two occasions, in 1959 and 1962, it tapped the telephones of three reporters. These CIA actions against non-CIA persons were clearly improper.

The CIA's mail intercept program was far more extensive and lasted more than twenty years—from 1952 to 1973. It involved both mail cover (photographing the outside of the envelope) and mail opening (carefully unflapping the envelopes, examining or photographing the contents, and resealing the flaps).

The mail intercepted was mainly correspondence from the Soviet Union and other Communist countries to addressees in the United States, mostly to American citizens, written by various correspondents, both American and foreign. The mail openings had three purposes:

(1) To glean from these letters intelligence information on internal Soviet matters. In the early fifties our knowledge of what was going on within the Soviet Union was enormously limited, and *any* information, even on a local scene, helped fill the gaps. These items of intelligence were turned over to the Soviet analysts in CIA and elsewhere.

(2) To detect Americans or non-Americans in this country who were being developed by Soviet intelligence services as possible sources of information. These counterintelligence leads were of principal interest to the FBI—the main consumer of the mail-cover and mail-opening information.

(3) To examine correspondence for Soviet censorship techniques, particularly those employed to uncover secret writing. This information was pertinent to the technicians developing secret writing methods for use by our own intelligence agents in Russia who were writing to mail drops in the West.

There can be little question that, however essential it was considered at its inception, the intercept program lasted far beyond its real usefulness to CIA, though the FBI continued to be interested in its product for internal security purposes. Whatever its purposes, and despite the varying degrees of coordination with the postmaster general and attorney general, the intercept program was clearly illegal.

Perhaps the greatest single abuse of an American's civil rights occurred in the course of the extensive CIA-Defense Department program, started in the early fifties, of testing the effects of new drugs on the human organism. CIA's main operational interest was to develop the most efficient possible "truth drugs" for use in interrogation as well as drugs to counter the effect of those employed by hostile services in interrogation or brainwashing. As part of this program, the CIA administered LSD and similar drugs to volunteer participants, some without their knowledge. In the course of the experiment, one participant committed suicide shortly after he had taken LSD. The failure of the agency to inform his family of this fact I consider its most irresponsible act. The overall merits of the program itself may be questioned, but technically it fell within the boundaries of ethical as well as legal scientific research.

Much of the congressional investigation was concerned, not with specific charges of "crimes" or "abuses," but with CIA work within the United States essential to its operations abroad: its cover mechanisms, its large network of proprietary companies, its arrangements with individual American citizens. Another large sector of congressional interest was CIA's covert operations abroad, which, however unpalatable to the Congress or the public, were fully authorized by the President or the National Security Council. Nonetheless, many of these proper and legal activities, as they came to light from congressional leaks and investigative reporting, were portrayed as further examples of CIA's improper if not illegal behavior.

PUBLIC REACTION

As the Year of Intelligence proceeded, the constant stream of revelations about this hitherto most secret agency created a heightened climate of public concern. Each new exposure was labeled "shocking," "sordid," "unsavory." The CIA was a "monster," a "cancer" requiring radical surgery, "a world of grotesque shapes and shadows," "a many-chambered house of deceit, fear, power, and intrigue." CIA operations officers were "killers and fanatics," "a free-wheeling assemblage of dangerous romantics," "bribers, subverters, and burglars," a set of "adventurers, screwballs, and intriguers" who "will do anything for each other—lie, cheat, steal, kidnap, suborn perjury, bribe, corrupt, subvert, kill and kill again." These phrases came from the pens of otherwise sensible men, not screwballs.

The charges made against CIA by Americans at home

reached spectacular limits of absurdity. The CIA penetrated the White House. The CIA used police departments to spy on American citizens. The CIA was responsible for a whole series of mysterious burglaries and break-ins in the Washington area after Watergate. The saddest charge: CIA must have had something to do with the assassination of President Kennedy.

They were more than matched by the anti-CIA barrage overseas. A revue of German blondes in black leather boots entertaining in a Lisbon nightclub was "another CIA plot" according to the Portuguese Communist Party. An outgoing prime minister of Australia charged the opposition that ousted him with CIA links. In Brazil an innocent missionary was arrested as "a CIA agent." In Peru the president and the Cuban ambassador jointly determined that the United States was planning to overthrow the regime. In Great Britain, of all places, some Labour members of Parliament demanded that CIA officers in the London station be thrown out although their leader conceded he knew of no CIA "wrongdoing" in England.

THE EFFECT ON OPERATIONS

No federal agency can be attacked with such vigor and heat without suffering ill effects. The most obvious is the morale of its employees, who see their careers dismissed as an evil occupation, who see their embattled leaders vainly trying to defend the good name of the agency. A good self-image is a key ingredient in efficient performance.

The ill effects are much more tangible with a secret agency, above all a foreign intelligence service. The anti-CIA campaign drastically reduced CIA's capacity to do its job: to recruit and retain the best agents that can be found in the key target areas around the world.

The campaign and the exposure to public view of secret

acts and facts, the persistent efforts of the congressional committees to wrest more and more of its secrets from the executive branch, and the constant flood of leaks from congressional staffs, former CIA staff officers and contract personnel, and other members of the national security establishment—all of these together might make any sophisticated foreign CIA agent wary. Some agents simply broke off contact with their case officers to lie low until the storm blew over. Other agent prospects, developed through close personal cultivation for months or years, understandably refused to accept a proposal for recruitment.

Any intelligence agent must have complete confidence in the service he is working for. He must be assured that his identity will be kept secret and that his reports will not be exposed to unauthorized persons. In agreeing to accept tasks that might affect his career and, in some cases, his life, what counts most is his feeling of security. With "CIA" in the headlines of his own local newspaper, he can be forgiven for entertaining a few qualms.

The adverse reaction of friendly foreign intelligence services, particularly the European services, was equally understandable. For years they have supplied the CIA with *their* secret intelligence reports on targets of common interest, and these have often been of unique value to the departments of State and Defense. Watching the exposure of "American secrets" in Washington, they were bound to worry. When would a British or French or Italian report from a highly sensitive source be exposed to congressional scrutiny? When would an agent of theirs be sacrificed on the altar of American openness? The cooperation among the CIA and the NATO-country intelligence services has been a close and valuable one for twenty-five years. If the notion that "the Yanks can't keep a secret" becomes embedded in the minds of the European service chiefs, American security will suffer a needless loss.

In Moscow, of course, the KGB was laughing. The constant effort of Soviet propaganda to depict the CIA as the main repressive instrument of American imperialism was now strengthened by quotable items from the American press. Not only was America, the much-vaunted free democracy, a police state, but its nefarious efforts to unseat progressive regimes abroad underlined its stand against progress for humanity in the third world. KGB officers were now in a position to warn off potential recruits for American intelligence by underlining the suicidal nature of such work and proffering the more secure alternative of working for the Russians. In the secret world the American connection became suspect.

Another loss cannot be gauged. Over the years some of the most valuable sources on Soviet espionage have been disaffected members of the KGB and GRU who have walked in to cast their lot with the West. They have been assured, until recently, that the CIA would handle them with the utmost discretion, arrange conditions for safe interrogation, and resettle them securely with a new identity and a new start in life. What confidence can a potential defector now have that his identity will be safeguarded and his life protected? Perhaps his only recourse is to place himself in the hands of a more reliable service like the British SIS.

It is this atmosphere of unreliability that will plague the CIA for some years to come in its work abroad. The American public's confidence in CIA is desirable, but not essential to its performance. The morale of CIA headquarters personnel is an element in its efficiency, but not crucial. The price we pay abroad, however, is the same price we pay for Watergate and Vietnam—the loss of confidence in America's capacity to act effectively.

CIA AND THE PRESIDENT

In an unguarded moment Senator Church, the chairman of the Senate Select Committee on Intelligence Activities, labeled CIA "a rogue elephant rampaging out of control."

If there is one clear fact that emerges from the reports of his own committee, as well as the Rockefeller Commission, it is that the CIA has operated since 1947 under the direct control of the President and his National Security adviser. CIA is an instrument of the White House, and it would be odd indeed if any President let his director of Central Intelligence go off on his own to engage in secret actions deeply affecting the nation's diplomacy and security, any more than he would give the secretaries of state or defense license to do whatever they wanted to.

The facts that emerged from these numerous committee reports are clear. Operation Chaos was established at the direct request of the White House. Plans for assassinating foreign leaders were carried out at the express direction of the President or his appointed representative. Every major covert action project from Radio Free Europe to the 1975 intervention in Angola was the result of a presidential instruction.

The report of the House Select Committee on Intelligence, completed in January, 1976, but never officially released, simply states:

> All evidence in hand suggests that the CIA, far from being out of control, has been utterly responsive to the instructions of the President and the Assistant to the President for National Security Affairs.

And, as Secretary of State Kissinger assured the Congress in November 1975, "Every operation is personally approved by the President."

Nonetheless, the CIA has been uniformly blamed for America's covert operations. How much of the blame should be assigned to the President and his policy makers, how much to the CIA?

The CIA should be blamed only for faulty execution, not for the efficient carrying out of bad policies. In one of its most .efficient operations, the "secret army" in Laos, the fault lay in the policy behind it. In the worst covert disaster, the Bay of Pigs, the CIA must share the blame with the White House, the Secretary of State, and the Joint Chiefs of Staff.

Yet the CIA is bound to be the fall guy for every covert operation that misfires or is exposed. The reasons are not hard to find. Since covert operations are mounted to avoid official responsibility, it is the normal practice for governments in Moscow, Paris, or Washington to disregard or disavow them when they are exposed. In only two cases has an American President personally and publicly accepted the responsibility for covert ventures: President Eisenhower for the U-2 incident, President Kennedy for the Bay of Pigs. It is part of the CIA director's job to be the fall guy for the President.

There is another specifically American reason. In our society the prejudice against secrecy runs deep, and it was deepened by Watergate. As *the* secret agency of government, the CIA has always been a natural target for both Congress and the press, and even its legitimate activities exposed as somehow evil and un-American.

The CIA is also a fall guy within the Washington bureaucracy. Many diplomats in the Department of State resent the activities of an agency that might embarrass them and give the United States a bad name abroad. The FBI opposed the creation of another intelligence agency in the first place and bitterly resented having to relinquish its wartime responsibility for operations in South America. Sniping at the CIA within other elements of the intelligence community is a common luncheon sport in Washington. CIA operators will never win a popularity contest among their intelligence colleagues.

The CIA is often left out in the cold even at the highest levels. A senior White House official once exhorted the CIA to get more deeply into student and labor organizations in Area X. Query: "Will you stand behind us?" Reply: "You're on your own if anything blows."

In the case of Chile the CIA got it both ways from the

policy level. "Why didn't the CIA forecast Allende's election victory?" The analysts did, but the top men apparently did not read their reports carefully enough. "Why didn't the CIA do more to forestall Allende's election?" It did what the policy makers had instructed it to do.

One red herring that the Senate Committee's final report has introduced into the issue of presidential control is a gross misreading of the doctrine of plausible denial. It suggests that the President might be purposefully kept in ignorance of a covert operation in order that he might honestly deny it. This is nonsense. No President can willfully choose ignorance in order to absolve himself from being responsible for the acts of his subordinates.

As the Year of Intelligence wore on, the calls increased for more "control" of the intelligence community. Dozens of formulas were thrown into the hopper by the Rockefeller Commission, the press, and the public: the strengthening of the inspectors-general in the various intelligence agencies, a "review committee" of highly placed private Americans, a new unit for "federal corruption" in the Department of Justice, the strengthening of the President's Foreign Intelligence Board, etc.

In February 1976, before the congressional committees had completed their report, President Ford introduced his own reforms. He made some modest changes in his top intelligence hierarchy, mainly to raise the level of decision on covert action projects and broaden the supervision of both programs and possible abuses. He has, on paper, enhanced the role of the CIA director as the overall head of the intelligence community.

The CIA directors have always worn two hats: as head of the community and head of their own agency. Up to now no directors have been able to carry out their first role with any clout. Presidents Kennedy and Nixon formally instructed them to do so, but they faced an impossible task: to tell the Secretary of Defense what to do with *his* intelligence agencies. Military intelligence, including the Defense Intelligence Agency, the National Security Agency, and the intelligence arms of the three services, has more than five times as many people and more than ten times the budget of CIA and State Department intelligence combined. The CIA director could coordinate and cajole. He could not give orders.

It remains to be seen what effect the new arrangement will have. One test will come up in the next budget: Can a CIA director do what most needs to be done—cut down the overgrown intelligence bureaucracy to a more economical and efficient size? Will he examine the recommendation of Congressman Otis Pike's report that the Defense Intelligence Agency be eliminated? Will he review and possibly curtail the enormous scope of electronic interception carried out by the National Security Agency? These are among the larger issues a director with clout should deal with.

The President must have effective control of his secret agencies, yet that control in itself poses several hazards, each in its own way the danger of politicization.

Presidential control implies the possibility of presidential abuse. The extreme example, of course, is the use of the CIA and the FBI for President Nixon's partisan purposes in the Watergate episode and the monitoring of the White House "enemies list." It can happen again if the wrong man becomes President. There is no legislation the Congress can write, nor any mechanism of oversight that can prevent a President from using any of his federal agencies in his own personal or political interest. That is a simple fact that we now alertly live with.

A more insidious hazard is the danger of politicizing the intelligence function by appointing a political figure as director of Central Intelligence. A partisan director who works on behalf of the President who appointed him rather than for the presidency he serves runs the danger of wanting to satisfy his boss—by shaping intelligence estimates to suit the policy requirements of the White House or to support a specific policy, as the Vietnam war.

The politicization of the intelligence function is the end of its usefulness. When there is pressure on intelligence collectors and analysts to "give the Man what he wants," their reading of events in active policy areas will be subtly skewed, or they will avoid distasteful projections of "alternative courses of action," or they will fail to send directly to the White House disconcerting or unpalatable agent reports.

Independence is crucial in the field of foreign intelligence judgments—that is the main reason we have a *central* intelligence agency without its own diplomatic or military policy commitments to protect. A docile director can only distort the very reality he is supposed to clarify.

There have been four CIA directors in the three years from January 1973 to January 1976. Choosing a director for a six- or eight-year term without regard for his party affiliation would help keep him independent. A man of strong will, private means, and hard experience outside government is the least likely to be used or abused.

There is a final issue on the President's use of his foreign intelligence agencies that no one can do anything about: No President need regard what his intelligence estimators tell him. His policy judgments are often as much the product of his domestic concerns, of previous presidential policies, or of the climate of American public opinion as of the objective situation he confronts abroad. The Vietnam war is a tragic case in point. If President Johnson had accepted CIA estimates on the capabilities of the North Vietnamese, the war might have ended earlier. Good intelligence is only an aid to a good foreign policy, not a substitute for a bad one.

CIA AND THE CONGRESS

For the past twenty years the exposure of secret CIA operations has automatically elicited public outcries for "a thorough investigation" and "more congressional oversight."

During the Year of Intelligence the Congress conducted

the most thorough and broad-ranging investigation of the intelligence community in its history. It has done so at a price.

The Rockefeller Commission's inquiry into CIA's domestic activities was conducted in closed hearings, leaks were minimal, and its final report was a precise and balanced record of the facts and a concrete list of recommended actions. The widely voiced suspicion at the time that a presidential commission would attempt to cover up abuses within the executive branch proved unfounded.

The Senate Intelligence Committee, on the other hand, found it desirable to hold many of its hearings in public session. The committee initially planned first to hold a series of three or four open sessions devoted to acquainting the press and the public with the basic facts about the intelligence agencies they were investigating, and only then taking up the abuses. These educational sessions would have served the public well by clarifying the organization, the essential jargon, and the normal activities of such mysterious agencies as the CIA, the DIA, and the NSA.

The exposure of abuses, however, took precedence over education in the open hearings. Whatever the political or publicity concerns involved in drawing up the agenda for these open hearings, their effect was to create a distorted picture of the normal activities of the intelligence agencies involved. They exaggerated the sinister and immoral aspects of these agencies in a public mind already made wary by the entire post-Watergate atmosphere. They failed to balance the good and the bad, to place past acts in their historical context, to give some right of reply to government officials who sat at the witness table like criminals in the dock.

The open hearings, and the committee's final reports, also exposed countless details of highly, and properly, classified secret information that were not essential to the purposes of the inquiry. The texts of internal memoranda, excerpts from coded cable communications, thinly veiled agent identities, staff and program cryptonyms, the mechanics of specified operations in named foreign countries—much of this could have been avoided without affecting the committee's findings or recommendations.

There is no good reason to hold open hearings on intelligence agencies. No other democracy indulges in this expensive practice. The systematic pursuit of an investigation, the cool balancing of judgments can best be pursued in private without violating either government secrets or personal dignity. Drama, sensationalism, political posturing, half-facts, nonfacts can all be avoided. The final report can give the public the deliberate unvarnished exposure of the facts it deserves. The rest is expensive theater.

For many Americans our sustained self-criticism and self-laceration are more than justified in spite of the damage done; others find the price too high. We can be smug about the capacity of our democracy to survive self-inflicted blows, but we cannot be smug about the price the nation pays in reducing American capacity to be effective in the world. The final judgment must be a practical one: What future profit will come from the Year of Intelligence? Will the Congress finally play its proper role as overseer of the President's secret agencies? How far can a congressional committee, or two committees, or six committees, go in guiding, controlling, or second-guessing the White House in running its secret business?

The ideal congressional instrument for oversight is a joint Senate-House committee with exclusive jurisdiction over both the civilian and military intelligence agencies. Given the congressional facts of life—the jealousy of committee and subcommittee chairmen for their present prerogatives, the reluctance of congressmen to join permanent committees that provide no forum for personal exposure to the public—the ideal solution is impractical. The Senate has already established a single oversight committee for the CIA, but it shares responsibility for the FBI and the military intelligence agencies with other Senate committees. If the House follows suit, the CIA's secret operations will be overseen by two committees—a solid step forward.

How effective can these committees be?

The answer is different for each category of secret operations, for espionage, counterespionage, and covert action operations vary in the degree of secrecy with which they are carried out and therefore the degree to which they can or should be subject to congressional oversight. They are also generated within the executive branch in sharply different ways.

Covert action operations like the anti-Allende program in Chile or the supply of arms to the Angolan rebels are the most accessible to congressional scrutiny. Action projects are generated at the White House or National Security Council level and are part of the bureaucratic record. A legislative requirement that action operations be cleared with the Congress is unlikely to be disregarded by any President. Since these action operations are a part of American foreign policy, and should be evaluated in that light, it is my personal view that they should be cleared with the Senate Foreign Relations Committee rather than a less qualified overall oversight committee, but the latter is unlikely to agree.

Ordinary political action on a small scale—minor support of individuals or running agents of influence—is bound to remain within the discretion of the Executive. It is this ground-level of political action that cannot, and should not, be open to name-by-name scrutiny by the committees. It makes no sense for an oversight committee to second-guess the State Department or CIA on who should or should not be on the list of America's secret political contacts, for it has nothing to contribute in the way of expertise or political judgment, and its knowledge can only jeopardize their security.

Congress faces similar, even greater limitations, in overseeing espionage operations overseas. The requirements for foreign intelligence, both open and secret, are generated within the intelligence community as a whole. The main priorities are set by the White House and the departments of State and Defense directly or through the analysts within the various intelligence staffs throughout the government. These information objectives come out of the strategic and tactical concerns of the diplomatic and military policy makers, and reflect *their* needs. The only function of intelligence is to serve those needs.

Congress is not only incapable of overseeing secret intelligence operations, but it can be argued that they are none of its business. This is an axiom in the European democracies. Congress can determine how much money is to be spent on intelligence collection, and it can be *informed* of the requirements and the results by the Executive. Yet such briefings will naturally reflect the Executive's estimates of its own performance, and the Congress is bound to accept this self-evaluation, for it will have no basis for questioning these judgments.

Nor can it ride herd on individual intelligence operations, however politically sensitive. It is up to the Executive to decide whether the recruitment of a high-level agent in Moscow will affect détente adversely, or whether the possible embarrassment involved in the penetration of a friendly foreign office is justified by the information to be gathered.

Only in such large-scale technical intelligence operations as the U-2 and the *Glomar Explorer* can the Congress justifiably demand some degree of prior consent. It is conceivable that a standing committee might send a handful of investigators into the halls of the CIA and the DIA to ferret out less expensive intelligence operations to which they or their bosses might take exception, but the loss in security would hardly be compensated for by any improvements in the quality of intelligence collection.

Foreign counterintelligence operations are even more impenetrable to oversight or control. They are, to start with, almost completely self-generated, for they normally arise out of the actions of other intelligence services—a KGB officer cultivates the society of an American embassy clerk, or a native walks in to announce that he is a Soviet agent and wants to work for the Americans. In short, a CIA station reacts to events. Only in the rarer cases of shaping a recruitment attempt directed at a presumably susceptible Soviet or East European intelligence officer does a station take the initiative.

There is no policy level in Washington at which a congressional committee can grapple with these operations. Nor can the maximum security required to conduct them against a vigilant hostile service be compromised without degrading or destroying them. Once the need to know is extended to Congress, and counterintelligence files are scanned for the names of targets and agents, the countereffort becomes a farce.

Even within these limits the Congress can be far more effective than it has been in the past. It can legislate clearer authorities and charters, it can define precise limits to domestic surveillance by any agency, and—above all—it can determine the size and shape of the intelligence community.

The heart of the "intelligence problem" in Washington is the enormous size of the intelligence bureaucracy.

It is no secret that the entire federal government is too large, too confused, and too inefficient, but these vices are especially telling in the intelligence function. There is a paper glut—millions of items a week come in from overseas. There is a personnel glut—thousands of people pore over the same reports, write duplicating research papers, read each other's handiwork. There is a glut of "dailies" and "weeklies" keeping everyone informed about everything. In some respects intelligence analysts form an incestuous bureaucracy catering to each other's requirements and avid urge to know. Yet the only function of intelligence is to help the policy makers in State and Defense make correct decisions, and the policy makers are often too busy to read most of the finished reports produced by the intelligence community.

The estimators are the backbone of the intelligence system, the men who read, evaluate, and interpret the information at hand and provide the President with the most objective possible estimates on matters of top-level concern. Most of the reports coming in to Washington today are irrelevant to their work: minor facts on important nations, important facts on inconsequential nations. If the paper glut were cut in half or more, the estimates would not suffer. Secret agents produce less than one-tenth of one percent of the raw information they use, information that is good, bad, or indifferent, but even here there is more than is needed.

What neither the Congress nor the President has yet done is to reexamine the entire intelligence structure in Washington, and come up with formulas for reducing the glut. If the intelligence committees can come up with sensible and reasoned cuts in the budgets of the Central Intelligence Agency, the National Security Agency, the Defense Intelligence Agency, and the intelligence units of the three services, they will have partly justified the Year of Intelligence.

Waste is one thing, abuses another. What can the Congress do to prevent future misdeeds by intelligence agencies? The problem is not one of law or agency directives, but of the conduct of persons or units in the federal government who willfully or ignorantly violate the law or exceed the limits of their bureaucratic charters. Can a committee reach into the more secret recesses of the White House or the federal security bureaucracy to detect in advance and forestall illegal actions against American citizens?

The Congress is a frail instrument to rely upon for this task. The operations of the White House plumbers, the Pentagon's wholesale compilation of dossiers on American civilians, the FBI's extensive program of investigation and harassment of American dissidents, the CIA's participation in several incidents of domestic surveillance all eluded the attention of Congress while they were going on. An oversight committee can review gross expenditures, scan policy instructions, and put searching questions to senior officials. It cannot detect infractions of policy or law by errant federal officials in Los Angeles, New York, or Washington.

There is a practical solution, one that is coming into vogue in other sectors of our society. It is to approach the problem from the bottom up rather than from the top down.

A counterintelligence ombudsman in Washington could well serve as the overseer of our guardians. He should be a man of character and experience, a well-known figure with an established reputation—someone like Professor Samuel Dash of Watergate fame. He would require only a small staff of investigators and a well-publicized address and telephone number.

The ombudsman, or his staff, would be available to any federal employee in the White House or in any intelligence or investigative agency who has reason to suppose that he, his boss, or his agency is carrying out an action that is improper or illegal.

This system would permit a lowly clerk or a presidential appointee, discreetly and without threat of retribution, to blow the whistle on what offends *his* sense of legality. He can make his complaint in the full confidence that he will be taken seriously and his charges investigated.

The ombudsman offers the same opportunity to any American citizen whose rights are violated by a federal intelligence agency. The improper targets of domestic investigation or harassment have a right to be heard, and at no cost to them. Crank complaints are inevitable, but a bright investigator can winnow these out without wasting time.

An ombudsman of this sort could work under the authority of the Senate Judiciary Committee or of a Joint Committee on Intelligence—if one were to be set up.

Why an ombudsman, and not the committee itself?

Both the man in a classified job and the put-upon citizen are much more likely to trust a known individual than any anonymous committee of part-time members. Leaks to the press are not addressed to the management of a newspaper, but to a known journalist of proven discretion. They will also know their complaints will not be caught up in the maelstrom of politics and publicity-prone legislators, for only an apolitical ombudsman can act without regard for what party occupies the White House or runs the committee.

If internal security matters are to be kept out of politics, a neutral ombudsman might help. An overburdened Congress could try the experiment at little expense.

A FOOTNOTE

The Year of Intelligence in Washington ended with the murder of the CIA station chief in Athens, gunned down on his doorstep. The killers have not been identified and the motivation for the killing is unknown, but it is hard to isolate Richard Welch's murder from the climate of public opinion abroad engendered by the CIA spectacular in Washington and fortified by the Soviet and Communist propaganda apparatus, the vituperative journalism of local extremist groups on the left, and the systematic publication of CIA officers' names and addresses by both foreign and American anti-CIA professionals.

As a former station chief, now safely retired on my farm in Virginia, I may be forgiven for a few personal thoughts about my own country inspired by the pointless death of a colleague.

There is a passage in the Senate Committee's interim report on "Alleged Assassination Plots Involving Foreign Leaders" (p. 2) that justifies the minutely detailed exposure of these plots:

> Despite the temporary injury to our national reputation, the Committee believes that foreign peoples will, upon sober reflection, respect the United States more for keeping faith with its democratic ideal than they will condemn us for the misconduct revealed. We doubt that any other country would have the courage to make such disclosures.

I find this statement incredibly naïve, if not childlike.

Who are these "foreign peoples" whose respect America has won? The Cubans, Russians, or Chinese? The Germans and Italians? The Koreans and Congolese? The Indians and the Arabs?

Who abroad, or here, is given to "sober reflection" on such matters as assassination and intervention? The British, perhaps? Certainly not heads of state, European politicians, Japanese civil servants, Latin American journalists, German Social Democrats. Has there been much sober reflection on publicizing our misdeeds in our own Congress, our press, our universities?

Has the Senate Committee shown "courage" or does it pretend to a moral virtue none of us possesses? How far does public contrition absolve a nation from its past sins?

Self-criticism is at the core of Soviet and more especially Chinese party indoctrination, with self-improvement as its goal. Most Communist self-criticism is carried out in closed party meetings. Keeping faith with the American democratic ideal appears to require not only sober self-criticism, but sustained self-flagellation—and in public. For some Americans this practice reflects our courage and underlying strength. For my own part I see it as an unrealistic surface piety that covers an underlying insecurity about ourselves and our real place in the world.

Without dignity, a mature assurance, and a firm grasp of the real world around us, American democracy cannot remain great even in its own eyes.

14

THE FUTURE OF SECRET OPERATIONS

Secret operations, however well executed, like diplomacy and military action, are no better or worse than the foreign policy they are designed to support. For thirty years CIA operations have played a role, often major, in our policy of containing the extension of Soviet power and influence. A fundamentally defensive strategy, containment leaves the initiative to the other side. For a generation Soviet national aims have dictated the shape of American purposes in the world. They still do.

Since the end of the Korean war, containment has been a losing exercise. It may have frustrated Castro's campaign for revolution in Latin America. It may have slowed up the growth of the Italian Communist Party. It helped prevent the secession of a Moscow-oriented Katanga from the Congo. It forced the withdrawal of Soviet missiles from Cuba. It destroyed the Marxist coalition in Chile.

There is little else on the record but failure. Even at the zenith of its military and economic power in the fifties and early sixties, America proved to be an inferior adversary to the Soviet Union in their competition for global influence.

The historical record speaks for itself, but in examining that record it may be useful to view it in the long-term perspective of the men in Moscow. What is important to a Marxist-Leninist is the general trend of events, the direction in which they are moving. In the Soviet vocabulary, such phrases as the "balance of forces," the "crisis of capitalism," the United States as the "Main Enemy," are not propaganda blurbs, but tools of political analysis.

Three broad trends stand out for the Marxist in the twentieth century.

The enormous increase in Soviet national power since World War II has brought an end to the "capitalist encirclement" of the Soviet Union. It has made the Soviet Union the second-ranking industrial power in the world, provided it with a nuclear deterrent, and appreciably raised its standard of living.

The final breakdown of the European colonial system has brought the end of easy profits for the capitalist nations and increasing competition among the American, German, and Japanese capitalists for commodities and world markets. At the same time the former colonial nations have become natural Soviet allies against the capitalist camp.

The Communist movement has advanced steadily since 1917. Thirteen countries have become Communist in the last thirty years. The global trend in politics is toward the Left, toward "progressive" regimes and left-of-center parties. The global trend in economic production among the new nations is socialist, not capitalist.

Against this perspective the Soviet leadership can afford to be optimistic about the eventual outcome of the global issue of our time: whether society will follow the capitalist or the socialist/Communist path. Their optimism is supported by the events of the past twenty years.

The greatest Soviet advances have been made in the third world in the bare twenty years since the Twentieth Party Congress of 1956 decided to "fight the imperialists" for control of their former colonies. Starting from scratch, Moscow employed the conventional Western instruments of diplomacy (military and economic aid, friendship treaties, propaganda, cultural exchange) and the support of "progressive" forces (Communist parties, revolutionary movements, wars of national liberation) to extend Soviet power into areas far beyond the reach of Imperial Russia.

The Soviet Union has made its most significant advances in three key arenas of Eurasia.

In the Middle East it has become a force in the Arab world by providing military and economic aid to Egypt and Syria and political support to the Palestine Liberation Organization. No Middle East settlement is now possible without Soviet participation.

In South Asia it has replaced the British and the Americans as the dominant outside power on the Indian subcontinent. It has supplied large-scale military and economic assistance to India, the key strategic counterbalance to China in Asia. Its Indian ally has become immune to American influence, and Pakistan, America's protégé, has become a weak rump state.

In Southeast Asia the American failure in Vietnam has left the Indochinese peninsula in the hands of "progressive" forces and diminished American influence from Thailand to the Philippines.

Soviet progress in other parts of the third world has been modest but tangible.

In Africa, an area of primitive, unstable states, Soviet influence is substantial in Somalia, Guinea, Nigeria, and Angola. The support of black independence movements against the Rhodesian and South African governments may extend that influence in the future. The training of five thousand African students each year in Soviet and East European universities is a direct investment in the future leadership of a largely illiterate continent.

In Latin America, the "back yard" of U.S. imperialism, the Soviet Union has supported socialist Cuba by forcing the

Americans to guarantee its independence in 1962, by modernizing its armed forces, and by building up its economy. Cuba is a socialist fixture in the Western Hemisphere that is now developing friendly relations with most Latin American nations and is playing a revolutionary role in Africa. "Progressive" military regimes devoted to social reform have emerged in Peru and Bolivia. Panama is finally asserting its rights against the American imperialists.

Meanwhile, in a Europe whose frontiers have been stabilized on the pattern of Soviet demands, the solidarity of the NATO alliance is weakening, with its southern tier politically unstable from Spain and Portugal to Greece and Turkey. The Communist parties of Italy and France have excellent prospects of entering coalition governments that are bound to develop closer relations with the Soviet Union.

How does the Main Enemy look from Moscow? The Russians have become much more knowledgeable and realistic about the United States in the years since Khrushchev, and they are now aware that Wall Street does not run Washington and that capitalism will be around for a long time to come. Yet they note with some satisfaction that the influence of the United States in the world has declined steadily since the early fifties. Its threatening ring of military bases and anti-Soviet pacts has proved an empty shell, and the bases are now being dismantled. Its dependence on the threat of nuclear missiles has been made sterile by Soviet deterrent power. Its once extensive foreign aid program has had no tangible results. Its war in Vietnam has not only cost it dear in lives and money, but has won the anger and distrust of countless nations and people. Its power to control the United Nations has evaporated, and its influence over its allies in Europe and Japan has weakened. Its economy will continue to pass through stages of inflation and unemployment and will be even less capable of competing with the German and Japanese capitalists. It is now joining with them in the export of capital and technology to the socialist countries, thereby strengthening Soviet industry—the final irony of monopoly capitalism.

This view of the world, however simplistic or unrealistic to a non-Communist, is rooted in history and cannot be shrugged off as mythical.

There are various ways in which we can gull ourselves into painting a brighter picture. We can decry the totalitarian nature of the Soviet state, highlight the dissent of Soviet intellectuals against their own system, or legislate against Soviet emigration controls. We can recall the brutal Soviet suppressions in Hungary and Czechoslovakia. We can harp on its current problems: its faltering agriculture and backward technology, its relations with China, its failure to impose "proletarian internationalism" on other Communist parties. Yet none of these have hampered the steady expansion of Soviet influence.

We can also reassure ourselves by listing Soviet setbacks: in Indonesia, Zaire, the Sudan, Ghana, Chile, Portugal. We can stress the shaky Soviet position in Sadat's Egypt or in Syria, and note the Chinese competition the Soviets face in Cambodia, Tanzania, and the South African liberation movements.

Yet the strategic issue is not how much of the Soviet effort has been wasted. It will take dozens of Soviet losses to match the American waste in Indochina. The basic issue is how much the Soviet investment has advanced its national interests. Soviet losses are not automatically American gains, and conversely, but the globe is finite, and "influence," though an intangible element of national power, forms an aggregate that can be measured against a nation's overall investment. The Soviet overseas investment, in rubles and men, has been far smaller than the American in the past twenty years. Its return has been far greater.

Nor can we assume that the Soviet setbacks are permanent. After being ousted from Indonesia by an abortive Communist revolution, Moscow returned to the scene in

1976 with a technical and financial aid program. After fighting for years to save Guyana from Marxism, Washington recently heard its former protégé, Prime Minister Burnham, announce on the tenth anniversary of its independence a policy of total nationalization led by his Marxist-Leninist party. Will Egypt's pro-Western policy outlive Sadat? Will the military dictatorship in Chile survive?

One overriding fact emerges from this overview of the Soviet-American confrontation: The world is fundamentally an arena of economic and political forces. The Russians, as good Marxists, have known this all along and have harnessed these forces to their own national interests: the drives of nationalism, tribalism, and religion, the wars of national liberation against European occupiers, the crucial significance of raw materials, the powerful drives for economic development and against starvation and poverty. If interdependence means anything, it means economic interdependence—both in the production of goods and of industrial pollution.

Only today are Americans beginning to realize that we live in an economic rather than a military world. For thirty years we have been committed to a policy of military strength, military alliances, and military bases. Even today our principal commitment is to a high defense budget—and not much else. Yet the Soviet Union has achieved its successes without directly confronting American military power. Given the mutual deterrence of nuclear capabilities on both sides, the day-to-day Soviet-American competition plays itself out in countless diplomatic, political, and economic small-scale actions.

It is in this kind of world that America's secret operations will play a useful or a marginal role in the next twenty years. With or without a policy of American containment, it will be a confused and confusing world for American policy makers, and they will need the best intelligence about it they can get. One simple confrontation will remain unchanged: CIA's counterespionage effort against the persistent Soviet intelligence effort. The usefulness of covert action operations will be determined by an enlightened or unenlightened American foreign policy.

Our foreign purposes, poorly or clearly articulated, will dictate the role of secret operations in the years ahead. There are three fundamental questions:

Can our secret intelligence service adapt to the political-economic complexion of the world ahead?

Do we need a foreign counterespionage service?

Should we conduct covert political action operations abroad?

ESPIONAGE

How good are our present espionage operations?

The CIA Operations Directorate does not lack for money, and its communications network is the best in the world. It has attracted, even in its public doldrums, some of the best and brightest young Americans—sharp, highly motivated, patriotic, eager to become professionals. Many of them are proficient at handling foreign agents who are turned over to them. Some are natural headhunters: aggressive in their pursuit of a new agent to recruit. Some are mainly concerned to move up the bureaucratic ladder. Some, naturally, are lazy, others inept. Yet they have been, as a group, the most competent, hard-working, and zestful men in the federal bureaucracy.

Its greatest weakness, as I have noted, is its size. I am firmly convinced that the American service is too big, too bureaucratized, and too tactical in its intelligence targets to give American policy makers what they need.

I recall a discussion in the early fifties held in Washington with several of our British colleagues. How can a professional secret service avoid becoming just another government bureaucracy? The main conclusion: Keep it small. In that we have, in good American fashion, failed.

Relatively modest and independent in its beginnings as the Office of Special Operations, the service doubled, then tripled in size. It went the way of the entire intelligence community: a large bureaucracy with large staffs, interminable coordination, and countless echelons of decision making.

The lethargy and timidity normal to a civil service bureaucracy exact a particularly heavy cost in an intelligence service, whose main business is taking chances based on personal judgment. A service is as good as its agents, and its agents are as good as the competence and initiative of the case officer on the spot. Faced with a hypercautious, if not anxious, headquarters, the case officer soon learns not to take chances. He plays it safe by keeping the bread-and-butter agents he has and not invading dangerous new ground—like the local foreign office or security service. The service suffers.

As it grew, the service also became more and more closely integrated into the civil service bureaucracy that is the Central Intelligence Agency. Relatively independent at its inception, with its own administrative support structure, it gradually became dependent on the CIA for its logistics, staff recruitment and training, personnel and accounting procedures, etc. Its integration into the agency was capped by the move of all CIA components into a single headquarters building in Langley, Virginia.

These, and other, considerations led some operations officers over the years to raise the notion of a separate, truly secret intelligence service, a small professional elite devoted exclusively to recruiting high-level agents against carefully selected long-term strategic targets. There would be no pressures for current production, no wholesale reporting requirements, no leaks to analysts, journalists, or Soviet officials, no bureaucracy to hold up recruitment, no vast intelligence community to service. Its foreign operatives would live under private, mainly commercial, cover reporting by unofficial communications to a small head office in, say, New York, whose anonymous chief would be directly responsible to the director of Central Intelligence in his capacity as the President's head of the intelligence community.

The present Operations Directorate of the CIA would remain the integral part of the intelligence community it has become. It cannot be extracted from its present structure—as, for example, it would be administratively simple to extract the Federal Bureau of Investigation from the Department of Justice. Nor should it be. Although the Operations Directorate would no longer be depended upon to provide agent coverage of strategic intelligence targets, it would continue to function abroad on a reduced scale and with a more innocuous mission: to maintain liaison with local security and intelligence services, to protect our embassies from hostile penetration, to handle agent or defector walk-ins. It would also serve as a channel for confidential communications between our ambassadors and the President or between host governments and the State Department, and supply local support for other elements of the intelligence community, including the National Security Agency, and military services, and the FBI. Wherever feasible, and with deference to the sensitivities of the local situation, the CIA station chief might be overtly accredited as the CIA representative. He would, in any event, act as the ambassador's overall assistant for intelligence matters.

However quixotic on the surface, a small American secret service separate from the federal bureaucracy is not at all impractical—given the will in high places. The concept of such a service is not too far removed from the Soviet system of illegals: carefully selected personnel, hand-tailored communications, small-scale operations, select priority targets. It would remain professional and secret.

What would be its mission?

It would concentrate exclusively on strategic intelligence targets, information of key importance to American policy makers. It would focus on filling the gaps in priority areas of military, but especially political-economic knowledge.

A few of the hard military targets will remain indefinitely: Soviet and Chinese research and development, for example. Our satellites can monitor Soviet compliance with the SALT pacts, but agents will be needed on the ground to test compliance with any agreements reached on the mutual reduction of armed forces in Europe.

Some old and new political targets will be high on the agenda: the content of Moscow-Peking communications, Tokyo's relations with Moscow and Peking, the Moscow-New Delhi-Peking triangle, the Bonn-Moscow connection, the evolving relations among the Arab countries. A crucial aim in Europe must be to determine the exact nature of the private talks between the Italian and Soviet Communist Party leaders as they consider the complex contingencies that will arise out of Communist participation in a European government.

Secret coverage of strategic economic targets offers problems of another sort, for in the political-economic world we now inhabit some essential operations will involve delicate and diplomatically sensitive contacts. Much of the secret information our government requires exists in the capitals and corporate headquarters of friendly countries. Does Washington need an insight into the secret plans of European bankers and industrialists, of Japanese conglomerates, of Arab petrodollar investment counselors? Of secret commodity deals for Rhodesian chrome or Jamaican bauxite? Of planned cartel actions?

It is precisely in areas like these that the present CIA operations structure is least likely to be successful. In the friendly nations of Europe and in Japan our CIA stations are an adjunct to American official diplomacy, and the Department of State would look with strong distaste on secret efforts to penetrate the host government's secret political or economic plans and intentions. These are clearly unfriendly acts, and must be carried out with the greatest care and on only the most significant targets.

National and multinational economic interests leave little

room for friendship, and if our "friends" will not give us the information we need, they must forgive us for taking it. Only the most careful professional recruitment and handling of a few highly select agents can prevent Washington's curiosity from coming to their attention. It is a job for a tight handful of operators, not a large bureaucracy.

COUNTERESPIONAGE

Counterespionage work is the rock bottom of any secret intelligence service. If it were determined that American policymakers no longer require secret intelligence on foreign targets, and that American covert action would be totally outlawed, there would still be a need for overseas counterespionage operations. If *they* were banned, there would be little hope of protecting the nation's genuine secrets. What is most needed is a strengthening of our overseas counterespionage effort. A damaging fallout from the Year of Intelligence was the weakening of the long tradition of a strong Counterintelligence Staff at CIA headquarters.

The activities of the KGB were almost totally disregarded in the elaborate 1975 investigations (the final Senate report included a five-page appendix on Soviet intelligence). Yet they are a part of the world we live in, and if we take seriously the protection of our own national secrets they require serious attention. The Western world is not at present undermined by Soviet intelligence or action operations, but its military, diplomatic, and business establishments are on the way to being riddled by Soviet spies and agents of influence. Not only does the greater East-West intercourse of our day facilitate the Soviet Union's recruitment of Westerners, but the entrance of any Communist Party in Europe into a coalition government will broaden Soviet capacity to get the intelligence it wants without going through the tedious process of recruiting strangers.

Three steps are essential to improving the American counterespionage effort.

First, within CIA, there must be a greater focus on selecting men temperamentally suited to counterespionage work, giving them a concentrated course of instruction, and assigning them to the right spots abroad.

Second, we must restore the confidence of the European intelligence and security services in the ability of the CIA to keep its operations secret. KGB operations do not observe national frontiers, and effective counterespionage work depends to a great extent on the cooperation of many services, their files, and their investigative capacity. Their confidence can be restored only by a period of quiet in Washington.

Third, and most concretely, we must put the cooperation between the CIA and the FBI on a clear and consistent procedural footing.

The transmission to the FBI of CIA leads on suspect persons planning to enter the country poses no serious problem: The FBI is informed and takes appropriate action.

The confusion comes out of the movement of CIA-recruited Soviet agents to the United States from their overseas location. In some cases these agents are turned over to the FBI. In some cases the FBI will not be equipped with either the language or the area knowledge required to handle the agent effectively. In other cases, agents will refuse to be turned over to a new handler—frequently a traumatic experience.

Each case must be decided on its own merits, and no guidelines can cover them all. It should be the task of the CIA director in his new role as head of the intelligence community to adjudicate any FBI-CIA differences.

The line between foreign and domestic counterespionage is often not simple, since no rigid division is possible in operations that run across frontiers. Even a modicum of common interest in being effective against a joint enemy can guarantee that no Soviet agent profits from American rivalry.

COVERT ACTION

The conspicuous failures of America's past covert actions can be attributed both to their nature and their purpose. Large-scale paramilitary and propaganda operations cannot be kept secret. Covert political actions can. All, however, have been the instruments of a containment policy that has failed across the board. The failures of covert actions, from the Bay of Pigs to the intervention in Angola, are in great part failures of American diplomacy.

If American diplomacy changes to a forward strategy, if America's positive purposes can be articulated, covert political action can play a useful role as *one* alternative for the National Security Council to weigh in responding to any emergency action required overseas. The President has insisted that he retain this option, and after a brief debate in October 1974 on an amendment forbidding the CIA to carry out any covert operations, the Senate supported him by defeating the amendment 68 to 14. Political action, benign or subversive, was for the first time officially sanctioned by the Congress.

It is now only common sense to insist that any specific political action operation be thoroughly worked out by the Executive and assessed on three counts: it will be undertaken only in situations of crucial importance to the American interest; it will be evaluated by intelligence analysts and working-level policy people in the Department of State to assess the likelihood of its success, the dangers involved, and the price for failure or publicity; and, finally, it will not run into severe objections from congressional committees to which it will be referred. Congress should not have a veto on covert action decisions, but its reactions must be taken into account as a measure of popular American support.

The lessons of the past are clear. No President should look upon his third arm as a means of achieving large-scale effects. It cannot be casually or whimsically employed to achieve a convenient short-term purpose. It cannot be a mechanism for evading congressional scrutiny.

The proponents of political action are regularly called upon to cite hypothetical situations that might require secret actions to protect serious American interests. Whatever situations are constructed will be clearly open to challenge: The facts of a future moment are bound to be fuzzy, and the alternatives arguable. Yet I will venture a few scenarios in which covert action might be justified, at least as a preliminary to open military action.

The most persuasive scenario is the imminent threat of a hostile government coming to power on our borders: A radical left coalition threatens a takeover of Mexico in a democratic election. Its program is the expropriation of all American-owned properties without compensation; friendship pacts with Moscow, Peking, and Havana; a people's army equipped with Soviet weaponry.

This rather hairy scenario raises some vital questions for Washington: Do we support the government in power covertly to avoid the reaction open support would elicit? Do we make secret contact with the leftists to make a deal before or after they win? Do we send in troops before the election at the government's request, or intervene militarily after the anti-American regime is installed? Or do we just sit tight and remain vigilant?

A second and more realistic scenario hinges not on our national security, but our vital economic interests: In the Near East, the United States emerges as the sole supporter of Israel, and Arab hostility leads to the threat of another oil embargo.

Shall we try to persuade the Shah of Iran to adopt an anti-Arab position, perhaps to act as our proxy in taking control of the oil fields in the Persian Gulf by playing the political action game with the ruling groups of the Arab sheikdoms?

A less vital threat to our oil supply would emerge from the

coming to power of a radical anti-American regime in Venezuela. Do we try to make a deal with the leftists—covertly, at least to start? Do we take any covert political action to ensure the continued supply of chrome from a black Rhodesia that threatens to boycott its sale to the United States if we do not withdraw our investments in South Africa? However unlikely these scenarios, we cannot forecast what *will* happen in the economic world to threaten our prosperity.

Two political fantasies will serve to round out these futuristic dramas.

As the Peking-Tokyo axis strengthens, a failing Japanese economy and increasing Chinese support of the Japanese Socialists and Communists threatens to bring in a radical anti-American regime. We are faced with the prospect of Japan's becoming an industrial adjunct to the populous People's Republic of China, and a severance of military ties with the United States. Do we exclude covert action?

After Marshal Tito's death Moscow increases its support of "pro-Soviet" factions in Yugoslavia, and supplies them with money and arms to start a civil war. Do we intervene, openly or covertly?

Whatever use the White House may decide to make of its scaled-down third arm, political action is a cheap instrument measured against our more open expenditures. There is, for example, no overhead in maintaining a CIA ability for political action. The same men who run espionage and counterespionage operations can, on instruction, be covert operators. It is their intelligence task to develop agent relationships with well-placed persons in any society of interest. They are continually in touch with leaders of the political opposition, including Communists, and with rebel or radical groups in the third world. If and when the White House decides to embark on a political action operation, the needed contacts will for the most part already exist in the field, and the intelligence officer becomes an action officer.

Discreet political operations normally involve the secret passage of money to support a man or group in carrying on their normal political propaganda programs. Unless the sums are inordinately large, the exchange of money can be kept as secure as the exchange of secret intelligence.

The all-purpose use of the covert arm is somewhat belatedly coming to an end. Covert propaganda operations no longer serve a tangible purpose even vaguely justifying their continuance by CIA or the Department of State. Paramilitary operations are not CIA's business, but that of the Department of Defense. Political action, half-brother to political espionage, can be a useful, if minor, standby for American diplomacy.

THE UNITED STATES AT A CROSSROADS

Can America's foreign policy shift from the automatic reactions of containment to a policy of positive action in the world? Can we shape a clear national purpose that will contribute to our security and prosperity? Can we create, for the first time in our history, an *American* foreign policy and pursue it with the vigor and persistence exhibited by our competitors in Moscow?

The lessons of recent history are clear: The Soviet Union cannot be contained by a large American defense budget or by a single-minded, if not simpleminded, anti-Communist political and military strategy. Yet residues of the Cold War still distort our thinking.

Four Cold War myths are still alive and well.

The simple concept of the Soviet Union as a mainly military threat to the security of the United States has survived détente. It has been encouraged by the more reactionary elements in our society, and fortified by the annual alerts from the Department of Defense as the time for presenting the military budget arrives. It is fortified by columnists, both foreign and American, who have made their careers out of taking an apprehensive look at events in Moscow.

A parallel myth, the bogey of "international communism," has survived thirty years of national communism. The splits between Belgrade and Moscow and between Peking and Moscow are only the most spectacular. Tensions exist between Moscow and other Communist parties in power (Vietnam, Laos, North Korea, Rumania, and Cuba), and are not likely to diminish as "proletarian internationalism" weakens in the face of the parties' national interests. The key Communist Party in the non-Communist world, the Italian, has asserted its right to a national policy, to follow its own road to socialism, and there is no reason to believe that the French party will not follow suit. The Communist monolith has been steadily giving way to the same force of nationalism that Moscow has exploited so effectively in the third world.

A subordinate myth, the domino theory, is still with us. It distorted our thinking about Vietnam. First Cuba, then a Marxist Chile, were seen in Washington as the spearhead of a shift toward socialism in Latin America. The White House saw Angola as the spearhead of revolution in southern Africa. The domino theory reflects only our visceral reflexes, not the reality of unique nation-states.

A final myth is a more subtle product of the black-and-white mentality: that capitalism is an essential part of democracy. It is an updated version of the old equation between communism and socialism: Communists are Socialists, and Socialists are Communists. That social democrats, or democratic socialists, can run a multiparty political system and preserve democratic rights is attested to by the Scandinavian countries, Venezuela, pre-Allende Chile, and (with concessions to private property) the Federal Republic of Germany. If socialist democracies have a better future than capitalist democracies in the rest of the world, it would contribute to the interests of true freedom for America to give them wholehearted support. We are only now barely coming around to that point of view.

The most paralyzing heritage of *military* containment has been the strange and distasteful bedfellows we have accumulated. In the process of reacting to the Soviet threat we have exercised no discrimination whatever: Any man or nation *against* communism became our ally or friend. Being against human rights did not make them ineligible. In Europe we supported the Spanish and Portuguese dictatorships and, for a time, the dictatorship of the colonels in Greece. In Asia we tilted toward the generals in Pakistan and spent our blood and treasure bolstering feudal generals in South Vietnam. We now accept without shame a regime of human repression in South Korea.

Fighting Communist threats in Latin America has created friends of the same ilk: The military regime in Chile is only the most recent and among the worst.

We have allied ourselves with the non-Communist "ins" of the world—military juntas, civilian dictators, one-party and no-party oligarchies, feudal regimes in their terminal stages. We have supported the anti-Communist "outs" of the world—dispossessed monarchs, exiled politicians, party renegades, and, the most tragic and futureless groups of all, anti-Soviet émigrés. Our policy of reacting has become a reactionary policy.

Can we change our goals and our commitments? Can we develop a strategy that will give the Russians some trouble in containing *us*?

That is the leading question facing the American people in this confused time. A national consensus on American aims abroad was fragmented by the war in Vietnam. The generation gap is growing between the old politicians and pundits and the young activists both inside the halls of Congress and in the media. The Republican right stays right on military spending and détente. The Democrats, working to stabilize a domestic consensus, speak with a dozen voices on all overseas issues except Israel.

The question remains—and no one man or group can answer it: What is the role of America in the last quarter of this vibrant century?

It is possible in a sanguine moment, to envisage a select joint congressional committee sitting down with the National Security Council and talking about the fundamental problems America faces in the decades ahead. The President forces them to confer until they come up with a clear statement in simple English of our long-term national objectives and a concrete list of specific areas, countries, commodities, or air and sea lanes vital to our nation's interest. Let their agenda be made the subject of national debate by organizations and individuals from the Left to the Right, from the top to the bottom, from the foreign affairs "specialist" to the average citizen.

The President can raise the level of that debate by being more open with the public on our present commitments, our industrial requirements and security situation—honest facts and figures. He can also, without jeopardizing our security, publish some of the now classified information available within the executive branch—a sampling of our excellent satellite photographs, or select national estimates on strategic situations abroad, or current intelligence reports on significant events as they occur. If the CIA estimates on Vietnam included in the Pentagon Papers had been publicized when they were written, the war in Vietnam might well have been shortened. An effective democracy requires an informed public, and the President can help educate all of us.

If we decide to maintain a policy of global intervention, we can at least apply the broadest lesson of the past: Neither covert nor open actions can show long-term profit if they run against the grain of history. If they are designed simply to slow powerful forces of inevitable change, they will be wasted for a minor short-term advantage.

Hard questions will have to be raised.

Do we gradually shift our political support to the Left throughout Latin America and Asia? Do we become even at this late date prime advocates of revolutionary change, even violent change? Do we support democratic socialism for the developing countries? Do we develop closer relations with the Italian Communists or the French Left to bring their own interests closer into line with ours? Do we take positive action against the oligarchies of the world from Chile to Korea? Do we attempt to detach Albania from the Communist world or to weaken the Soviet economic hold on Poland by long-term trade with the West?

Or do we give up our global strategy and become hard-headed realists in using our power only in specific countries and areas that *are* essential to our prosperity? Do we work in the coming decades to build up strong democratic regimes in Brazil and Argentina—and forget about the rest of Latin America? Do we focus on the Arab oil states and Israel, and pay little attention to Iran? Is Indian democracy relevant to the American interest? Is Japan our ally or our competitor?

In either case a fundamental question of method intrudes. Shall we work abroad mainly through multilateral institutions or by bilateral agreements? Shall we form a trilateral consortium, an industrial board of directors, and take the actions we do only after close coordination with Europe and Japan? Can we work out our fiscal and economic interests effectively *within* this consortium, or must we sacrifice some of our national interests for the benefit of our Atlantic or Pacific partners? Is it feasible to talk about common European-American policies on the Middle East, on the sale of arms and nuclear reactors, on the terms of capital investment in the Soviet Union, Eastern Europe, and eventually China? It is easy to be skeptical, for it is precisely the ad-

vanced postindustrial societies, including our own, that have
the greatest built-in compulsion, and the least flexibility, in
pursuing their individual national interests.

Whatever the outcome of the debate, whatever purposes
we determine, we have a powerful instrument to achieve
them: our economic clout. We have used our foreign aid, our
food, our technology, our trade, and our capital almost aim-
lessly in the past. Using these pragmatically, and not for
some vague purpose of doing good or bolstering Cold War
friends, we can carve out the positions we need in the outside
world.

There are two main handicaps to any drastic shift in our
foreign policy. A President, however enlightened, must deal
with a Congress, however unenlightened, about foreign affairs. Every act in a long-term strategy will have to be argued
and fought for in the Congress and in the press, for no
strategy can be maintained in a democracy without the support of the people. Domestic political concerns can shift that
strategy, however enlightened, at least every four years, and
a continuing American consensus will become harder to
achieve as the problems we face become more urgent and
closer to home.

The greatest handicap in using our economic power to
achieve our foreign purposes lies in the nature of our system.
No President, or Congress, is in a position to employ it directly. Our capitalist economy, from shoe manufacturers to the
multinational corporations, pursues its own economic interests and cannot simply be corraled for national political purposes. Only by working out better government-business relations, however informal, can American society work with a
single purpose abroad. A clear, long-term political-economic
strategy is essential for our security and continuing prosperity.

Whatever policy we adopt, the world will be a lively arena,
and neither the Russians nor the Chinese nor the European
powers nor the Japanese will cease to pursue their own national interests in it—openly and secretly. Whatever we do or

do not do, ignorance of their intentions and their behind-the-scene actions can only handicap the pursuit of our national interests, and secret intelligence can at the least keep us alert to the hidden realities of world affairs. Whatever we decide to do, our diplomacy can only profit from intelligent use of covert actions for our political and economic goals.

Perhaps there is yet time to force the Russians to react to our actions in select countries and areas of our own choosing. Containing the Russians has been a failure. A greater failure would be to be contained by the Russians. Isolationism may be a policy, but isolation in the present world is a terminal disease.

INDEX

ABOUT THE AUTHOR

Harry Rositzke was born in Brooklyn, graduated from Union College in 1931, and received his Ph.D. in Germanic philology from Harvard in 1935. From 1936 to 1942 he taught English at Harvard, the University of Omaha, and the University of Rochester.

After four years in the Army—the last two with the Office of Strategic Services in London, Paris, and Germany—he went to Washington and worked for the Central Intelligence Agency for the next twenty-five years. Perhaps no man is more qualified to write about the CIA than Rositzke, for his experiences covered a wide range of activities and gave him a unique overview of our intelligence operations for a quarter of a century. In Munich in the early fifties, he conducted intelligence operations into the Soviet Union and Eastern Europe. From 1957–62 he was station chief in New Delhi, where his principal responsibility was working against Soviet and Chinese intelligence targets. In Washington, from 1962 until his retirement in 1970, he worked on domestic intelligence operations against Soviet and East European officials in the U.S. and coordinated operations against Communist parties abroad.

He has written articles on secret operations and intelligence for such publications as *Foreign Affairs, The New York Times, The Washington Post,* and *The Los Angeles Times,* and is the author of *The USSR Today* and *Left On!,* a political satire on American society. He has made numerous appearances on national television, and lectures widely on intelligence matters.

He lives on his farm near Middleburg, Virginia, writing and raising beef calves.